Shop by Mail

A FIELD GUIDE
TO SHOPPING BY MAIL

ELYSA LAZAR & EVE MICELI

LMG

Lazar Media Group, Inc
Publishers, New York

Books by the same authors
Museum Shop Treasures
Outlet Shopper's Guide

Published by Lazar Media Group, Inc.
112 East 36th Street, New York, New York 10016

ISBN 1-881642-00-3

First Printing. Printed in the United States of America

Cover design: Anne Cowin
Cover photos: Robin Bowman

Library of Congress Catalog Card Number 92-97141

10 9 8 7 6 5 4 3 2 1
First Edition

ACKNOWLEDGEMENTS

We wish to extend sincere thanks to our dedicated staff who helped research and gather the enormous amount of information necessary to write and publish this book. Special thanks to Ann Rizzo, Debra Schatz, Victoria MacDonald, Gina Ciccone, Robert Skiena, Jonathan Lewis, and Amy Claydon.

Warm appreciation to George Read, who untiringly offered his suggestions and support; to John Miceli, for his patience and understanding; to Tom Raney, for his clever guidance; to Matt Smith, for dedicating many late nights and weekends to this project.

Many thanks to Lauri Flaquer for her artistic wizardry.

Special thanks to the following companies who were supportive in our efforts: Canon, Constructive Playthings, Just Justin, Pottery Barn, The Cracker Box, Vermont Castings, Yaeger Watch Corporation.

CONTENTS

ACKNOWLEDGEMENTS   v
INTRODUCTION   viii
HOW TO USE SHOP BY MAIL   ix
ART   1
AUDIO & VIDEO EQUIPMENT   3
AUTO & MOTORCYCLE   5
BABY PRODUCTS   7
BEAUTY   9
BED, BATH & LINENS   14
BOATING   19
BOOKS   22
CAMERAS & PHOTOGRAPHY EQUIPMENT   27
CARPETS & RUGS   29
CHILDREN'S CLOTHING   32
CHINA, CRYSTAL & SILVER   36
CHINA REPLACEMENT SERVICES   41
CHRISTMAS ITEMS   42
COMPUTERS & ELECTRONICS   43
COOKING & KITCHENWARE   47
CRAFTS & HOBBIES   51
CURTAINS   59
DECORATING   61
DEPARTMENT STORES   63
FABRIC & SEWING   65
FAMILY CLOTHING   69
FLAGS & BANNERS   75
FLOWERS & PLANTS   76
FOOD
    BAKED GOODS & MIXES   83
    CANDY & CONFECTIONS   87

FOOD CON'T.

CHEESES	89
COFFEES & TEAS	90
FRUIT & NUTS	92
GOURMET FINE FOODS	97
JAMS, JELLIES, RELISHES & SYRUPS	100
MEATS & SEAFOOD	102
ORGANIC FOODS	105
WINE ITEMS	106
FURNITURE	107
GAZEBOS	116
GENERAL MERCHANDISE	117
GIFTWARE	118
HEALTH & MEDICAL ITEMS	129
HOME APPLIANCES	131
HOME IMPROVEMENTS	133
HOME PLANS & PREFAB HOMES	138
HOUSEWARES	140
JEWELRY & ACCESSORIES	145
LAWN & GARDEN ITEMS	149
LIGHTING & CEILING FANS	151
LINGERIE & HOISERY	152
LUGGAGE	155
MATERNITY CLOTHING	157
MEN'S CLOTHING	158
MUSIC	160
MUSICAL INSTRUMENTS	162
OFFICE SUPPLIES	165
OPTICAL	168
OUTDOOR FURNITURE	170
PACKAGING	172

PEDESTALS & COLUMNS	174
PET PRODUCTS	175
PICTURE FRAMES	178
SHOES & BOOTS	180
SPORTING GOODS	
APPAREL	184
BICYCLING	185
CAMPING/OUTDOOR	187
EQUESTRIAN	189
EXERCISE EQUIPMENT	190
GOLF	191
POOL/SCUBA	192
TENNIS	193
STAIRS & STAIR KITS	194
STATIONERY	195
SWIMWEAR	200
TABLE PADS	201
THEMED ITEMS	202
TOBACCO & SMOKES	204
TOOLS	205
TOYS & GAMES	209
TRAVEL	214
UNIFORMS	215
UNIQUE & UNUSUAL ITEMS	216
VIDEOTAPES	218
WALLCOVERINGS	221
WATCHES & CLOCKS	224
WINDOW TREATMENTS	226
WOMEN'S CLOTHING	229
COUPON SECTION	235
INDEX	240

CONTENTS

Introduction

We know life in the '90s can be riddled with stress. The job gets more demanding each day. You're rushing to the office, home to make dinner, or away for the weekend. Meanwhile, there's no time whatsoever to shop.

Ninety million Americans have found the solution to these modern problem scenarios. They've become dedicated 'armchair shoppers' who know just how easy it is to shop by mail or phone. We've scoured the pages of thousands of mail order catalogs from around the country and abroad. The result is a comprehensive insider's guide to 850 of the top mail order merchants with a wide range of quality products and services.

Shop By Mail is your guide to everyday and hard-to-find items, at prices you can afford. Whether you're looking for Louis Armstrong Compact Discs or Queen Anne file cabinets, and live in Montauk or Malibu, or anywhere in between, we can help you find what you're looking for. We guarantee it. And rest assured that we've included great discount sources, with savings up to 75% off the retail prices.

We'd like to make life a little easier for you. If you're throwing a last-minute dinner party tomorrow night, don't fret. Pick up the phone and start off with Beluga caviar from *Caviarteria,* then add Maine lobsters from *Graffam Brothers,* Louisiana yams from *Harry and David* and a scrumptious lemon cake from *Miss Grace Lemon Cake Company* to the list. Or if you've been itching to spruce up the garden, try a few miniature roses from *Rosehill Farm,* then frame them in tulips and irises from *Bluestone Perennials* and enjoy the view from your gorgeous Colonial Gazebo, courtesy of *Vixen Hill.*

We've had a terrific time putting this book together and are excited about the mail order treasures we're examining for the next edition. If you have any suggestions or questions, we'd like to hear from you. Please write to us at:

SHOP BY MAIL
Lazar Media Group, Inc.
112 East 36th Street, 4th Floor
New York, New York 10016

How To Use Shop By Mail

Be warned! This is the beginning of a completely different mail order experience. Once you start to take advantage of these interesting and money-saving catalog resources, you might forego the retail circuit altogether! But that's not our aim. Do shop the retail markets at your convenience. Be familiar with products, services and, most importantly, prices out there. Compare them with those offered by mail order merchants we've researched. We're confident you'll draw the obvious conclusions.

Organization

In addition to helping you save loads of time and money, we think you'll find Shop By Mail a breeze to use. The mail order companies are listed alphabetically by product category.

Symbols and Headings

In addition to standard ordering information you'll find important details that eliminate common mail order questions. "Which credit cards do they accept?" "Can I return the merchandise for exchange or can I get a refund?" "Who are the really big discounters?" The answers are all there, by symbol. We also indicate the cost of the catalog, if any, so that you can 'get shopping' right away.

A Few Words About Shipping

Mail order companies now ship faster and more safely than ever before. Shipping times can vary from 2-3 days to 6-8 weeks, with overnight service widely available, particularly on perishable food items. Our research has shown the standard is usually 4-6 weeks. However, when ordering custom items (engraved, monogrammed, altered or specially sized), don't expect them as quickly. Such items usually take more time, but then some companies may surprise you. Our advice is to call the company directly if you're uncertain.

Shipping methods are based on a number of factors, including company policy, purchase amount and where you live.

Flat order shipping fees are dollar amounts charged on purchases, regardless of weight or quantity. A flat fee can prove to be a bargain on large orders, but some firms charge extra for heavy, outsized or fragile items.

Sliding scale fees are based on the dollar amount you order. The cost may be, say, $2.00 on orders totaling $15.00 or less; then $3.00 on orders totaling between $15.01 and $20.00.

Tables give the shipping fee based on weight, and sometimes distance. You compute shipping weights with the item prices individually, find your zone on the chart provided, and then find the shipping charge.

Regardless of how shipping charges are computed, your order will be shipped by *United Parcel Service, United States Postal Service or by truck.* Many businesses prefer UPS, where your package is automatically insured for up to $100. UPS' Common Carrier Service handles packages weighing up to 70 lbs. with a combined girth and length of no more than 108 inches. Based on the final destination, overnight delivery is also available through Next Day Air Service or 2nd Day Air delivery anywhere within the continenttal U.S. and some parts of Hawaii. UPS does not deliver packages to a post office box. You'll need to make arrangements for the package to be sent by Parcel Post.

UPS bases its shipping charges on how far the parcel is being shipped, its weight and size. They've divided the country into 7 zones; "Zone 2" to "Zone 8", based on distance. To compute shipping costs, consulting a current Common Carrier Chart, which lists rates for packages weighing up to 70 pounds; plus surcharges for additional services like C.O.D. delivery and address correction.

Method of Payment

Never send cash by mail. The safest form of payment is with a major credit card. Should there be a problem with the goods you've ordered, you have recourse through the credit card issuer. And today almost every mail order company accepts a major credit card. We strongly recommend you use a credit card, where accepted, whenever you shop by mail. It not only speeds the mail order process, but some cards offer loss, damage and/or theft protection as well.

Returns, Credits & Exchanges

Thanks to sound advice or grave misfortune, we've all been taught the basic rules of shopping, by mail or any other means. Always keep receipts and invoices, as well as original packaging, in case the merchandise must be returned. But there are other factors to consider, such as who pays for return shipping; will you get your money back or just a credit or exchange; and how do you prove damage by some force other than your own. When ordering by mail, always check the company's policy governing returns. When your order arrives, check it thoroughly and notify the company immediately of any damages.

Hidden Costs

When comparing prices on goods from catalogs, consider the costs of shipping, insurance, tax and handling as part of the total.

Price Quotes

Many of the companies listed in this book will gladly give price quotes over the phone, provided you can give them detailed information like the manufacturers' name and model/style number. Be sure to record the name of the customer service representative who handled your call, in case there's a billing discrepancy.

ATLANTIC GALLERY PUBLICATIONS

721 Gibbon Street
Alexandria, VA 22314

Telephone: 800-433-2322
Fax No: 703-549-4256

Catalog $5.00

Return policy: Money-Back Guarantee if returned within 14 days

Atlantic Gallery Publications offers a selection of beautiful reproductions of traditional fine art at a fraction of what you'd pay for the original. They have a classic collection featuring facsimiles of 18th and 19th century botanical, architectural, natural history and sporting prints. Reproductions are available in black & white or they can be colored at an additional charge.

HEIRLOOM EDITIONS

520-B Route 4
Carthage, MO 64836

Telephone: 417-358-4410

Free Catalog

Return policy: Money-Back Guarantee if returned within 10 days

Heirloom Editions offers a potpourri of old fashioned beauty in authentic reproductions of original turn-of-the-century prints and note cards. The catalog displays a massive array of Victorian, Americana and country art designs. The prints are available loose, framed or matte framed with your choice of moulding in oak, walnut or ornate gold finish. The card selection includes charming reproductions by artist Maud Humphreys, plus Christmas cards, gift enclosure cards and post cards.

MOUNT NEBO GALLERY

R.R. Box 243, P.O. Box 94
Eagle Bridge , NY 12057

Telephone: 518-686-4334
800-328-6326
Fax No: 518-686-5381

Free Catalog

Return policy: Money-Back Guarantee

The piquant charm and rich heritage of American folk art lives on in richly painted lithographs, prints and serigraphs by Will Moses. Moses, the renowned New England folk artist, has signed, numbered and personally inspected each piece to insure their value and authenticity. All of the works are available unframed or they can be framed at an additional charge. An ample selection of colorful note and Christmas cards are available as well.

OLD GRANGE GRAPHICS

12-14 Mercer Street, P.O. Box 297
Hopewell, NJ 08525

Telephone: 800-282-7776
Fax No: 609-466-0507

Catalog $4.00, refunded with first order

Return policy: Money-Back Guarantee if returned within 30 days

When you want to add elegance of original period art to your decor, a mere reprint can't match the quality or investment value of a professional canvas reproduction. Old Grange Graphics has employed a special technique which gives you museum-quality reproductions at substantial savings. A variety of classic and contemporary artists are represented; from Mary Cassatt to Norman Rockwell. Old Grange Grange Graphics can even take your own art reprints and immortalize them on canvas!

THE GREATEST SCAPES

1613 Hawthorne Street
Pittsburgh, PA 15201

Telephone: 800-786-3022

Free Catalog

Return policy: 30-Day Satisfaction Guarantee

Who can't use framed art in their home? No matter how much you own, there is always room for more color and beauty on your walls. If you order through The Greatest Scapes, not only will you fill your life with art, you won't empty out

your wallet. Shipped direct from the factory, The Greatest Scapes offers the finest quality framed art reproductions of favorite works and renowned artists throughout history at low discount prices. Contemporary posters and pieces are also available. The 175-page MasterCatalog shows the complete line of 800 available prints. If they don't have it, they will custom order anything.

THE NATIVE HAND

1307 East Colfax
South Bend, IN 46617

Telephone: 219-233-3388

Free Catalog

Return policy: Money-Back Guarantee if returned within 10 days.

Those art lovers with a soft spot for the American Southwest will find this catalog merchant a fantastic resource for authentic, one-of-a-kind Native American works, most signed by the artist. You'll find hand-crafted pottery, hand-tooled rugs and wall hangings, woven baskets and lots of other treasures from the alamo. What's more, due to their high popularity and one-of-a-kind value, each piece is guaranteed to appreciate with time.

AMERISOUND SALES, INC.
Jacksonville, FL 32241

Telephone: 904-262-4000
818-243-1168

DISCOUNT

Free Information

Return policy: Money-Back Guarantee if returned within 30 days

Florida-based Amerisound Sales offers the best prices available on quality audio components by Carver, Nakamichi, Bang & Olufsen, Crown, Tandberg, Halfer, Adcom, Yamaha and many, many others. Professional consultation is available, so call their computerized customer service center 24 hours a day. All products are covered by their own full manufacturer's warranties. Discounts of 20-35%.

CRUTCHFIELD
1 Crutchfield Park
Charlottesville, VA 22906

Telephone: 800-955-3000
Fax No: 800-338-9756

DISCOUNT

Free Catalog

Return policy: Money-Back Guarantee

Discover why over one million people buy from Crutchfield. A toll-free call is your ticket to low, discount prices on the best names in car stereos, telephones, audio/video equipment and a wealth of other items. Their catalog gives you a thorough knowledge on buying the right products for your needs without wasting time or money. Kenwood, Sony, Clarion, Sanyo, Sherwood, JVC, Pioneer and Blaupunkt are the brands of choice. Don't miss the tremendous selection of accessories and parts available to update and expand your existing equipment.

FOTOCELL, INC.
49 West 23rd Street
New York, NY 10010

Telephone: 800-368-6235
In NY 212-924-7474

DISCOUNT

Free Information

Return policy: Money-Back Guarantee

Get in gear with Fotocell - your best resource for car stereos, car alarms and radar detectors. Choose from top brands like Pioneer, Sony, Alpine, Kenwood stereos; as well as radar detectors by Cobra, Bel, Uniden and Whistler. Fotocell is one of the country's largest mail order houses for great prices on photo, video and home office equipment. If all that's not enough, they ship worldwide, too.

J&R MUSIC WORLD
59-50 Queens Midtown Expressway
Maspeth, NY 11378-9896

Telephone: 800-221-8180
Fax No: 718-497-1791

DISCOUNT

Free Catalog

Return policy: Exchanges or store credit only when returned within 30 days.

Sure, the name says music. But that's only the beginning. Their catalog is chock-full of the latest electronic equipment for your home, car and office. All the quality and service you'd find in the J&R Music stores is now available in their exclusive discount catalog. They truly have it all: TVs , stereos for your home or car, VCRs , computers, home appliances, and yes, music! All your favorite tunes are available on top quality cassettes, CDs and laserdiscs at tremendous savings.

SELECTRONICS

1166 Hamburg Turnpike
Wayne , NJ 07470

Free Information

Return policy: Money-Back Guarantee

Telephone: 800-444-6300
Fax No: 201-628-8069

DISCOUNT

Selectronics has the lowest prices on high-quality brands, like JVC, Mitsubishi, Sony, Pioneer and Toshiba. Audio-video receivers, cassette decks, laser disc and CD players (including portables), 2" to 100" TVs and camcorders in all formats - Selectronics has your home entertainment! Professional equipment such as special effects generators, color correctors, mixing boards, universal remotes and more is also available. They ship within 24 hours.

A
U
D
I
O

V
I
D
E
O

4

BELLE TIRE, INC.
3500 Enterprise Drive
Allen Park, MI 48101
Free Catalog
Return policy: No Returns

Telephone: 313-271-9200
Fax No: 313-271-6793
DISCOUNT
COD only

Believe it! Whether your vehicle is standard or commercial, luxury or economy, you can buy tires by mail at fantastic savings. Here's a broad selection of brand name all-season and high performance tires to fit the type of automobile you drive at a price you can afford. Michelin, Delta, Kelly and Pirelli are just some of the dependable brands. There's also a grouping of automotive supplies and special tires for sporting vehicles, such as boat trailers, golf carts and lawn care equipment.

CAR RACKS DIRECT
575 Broad Street
Bridgeport, CT 06897
Free Information
Return policy: Money-Back Guarantee

Telephone: 800-722-5734
Fax No: 203-368-0654

Car-owners know that there are often times when a little extra storage space is needed, no matter how large the vehicle. If you're traveling long distance, moving or transporting locally, Car Racks Direct offers you discount prices on a complete line of multipurpose roof racks, ski racks, bike racks, boxes and rear mount systems. Many models can be coordinated with lock devices for added security. They also have a limited selection of home storage systems by THS.

DENNIS KIRK
955 South Field Avenue
Rush City, MN 55069
Free Catalog
Return policy: Money-Back Guarantee if returned with 15 days

Telephone: 800-328-9280
DISCOUNT

Dennis Kirk offers the best deals on automotive & recreational vehicle parts and accessories available by mail. Free catalogs, free freight & same-day shipping head the list of services. Call toll-free 24 hours a day, 7 days a week for a comprehensive listing of over 25,000 parts and accessories for motorcycles, ATV's, dirt bikes, snow mobiles and personal watercrafts, all at unbeatable savings.

ECKLER'S
P.O. Box 5637
Titusville, FL 32783-5636
Catalog $3.95; supplements $2.95
Return policy: Full refund or exchange if returned within 30 days

Telephone: 800-327-4868
Fax No: 407-383-2059

America's premier sportscar - the legendary Corvette - takes to the open road in this catalog of parts, accessories, tools and personal memorabilia designed to keep the spirit alive. Stereos by Pioneer and Custom Autosound, tire accessories, protective car covers, maintenance supplies, and hard-to-find parts. You won't believe some of the clever merchandise they've dreamed up for 'Vette lovers, including Corvette Wear apparel for those with a fetish too strong to hide. If you're a true 'Vette fan or not, this is a fantastic resource for the auto enthusiast.

A
U
T
O

M
O
T
O
R
C
Y
C
L
E

EXOTO'S COVERUP

1040-F Hamilton Rd.
Duarte , CA 91010

Telephone: 800-872-2088
Fax No: 213-858-8527

Catalog $3.00

Return policy: Money Back Guarantee with authorization; No returns on special orders

Protect your car's lustrous exterior and interior finishes with Exoto's superior line of protective car covers, floor mats and front-end masks. All covers are made of super-durable, weather and stain resistant materials. There are a variety of stylish colors available to complement you car's finish, while protecting it's beauty.

J.C. WHITNEY & CO.

1917-19 Archer Avenue,
P.O. Box 8410, Dept. C071
Chicago, IL 60680

Telephone: 312-431-6102

DISCOUNT

Free Catalog

Return policy: Money-Back Guarantee

Save up to 50% on everything automotive. Auto enthusiasts can save big on all of the latest technology in stereos, car covers, nose protectors, performance parts, hard-to-find items and thousands of other parts and accessories. Special sections in their catalog are devoted to 4-wheel drive vehicles, RVs, motorcycles, "muscle cars", and both domestic and imported cars and trucks. Subscribe now and get a full year of free J.C. Whitney catalogs.

MID-AMERICA DESIGNS, INC.

One Mid-America Place, P.O. Box 1368
Effingham , IL 62401

Telephone: 800-637-5533

Catalog $5 ($3 refunded with order)

Return policy: Money-Back Guarantee

Automotive enthusiasts take heart! This is a superb shop-by-mail resource for car memorablilia and accessories. Fans of the classic Corvette sportscar will enjoy the tremendous selection of apparel and sporting equipment, including sleek leather jackets, duffel bags, jewelry and even golf clubs - all emblazoned with the famous logo. You'll also find all the right parts, tools and optional equipment to keep your investment running smooth and looking great.

VICTORIA BRITISH, LTD.

P.O. Box 14991
Lenexa , KS 66285-4991

Telephone: 800-255-0088
Fax No: 913-599-3299

DISCOUNT

Free Catalog

Return policy: Money-Back Guarantee if returned within 6 months

Victoria British, Ltd. is THE mail order resource for great prices on thousands of reproduction and high performance parts, accessories, original equipment and interior finishes for the imported car. MG, Triumph, Sunbeam, Austin Healy and Datsun Z are some of the targeted models. Discounts up to 40% on parts and accessories.

A
U
T
O

M
O
T
O
R
C
Y
C
L
E

AMERICAN BRONZING COMPANY
P.O. Box 6504
Bexley, OH 43209
Free Information
Return policy: Money-Back Guarantee

Telephone: 614-252-7388

COD

Of all the wonderful memories you cherish of the things your baby has learned to do and say, there's one you can preserve forever. American Bronzing helps you remember the first few steps forever. They'll bronze your baby's first shoes and mount them on a choice of beautiful bases with or without picture frames. An engraved nameplate adds your child's birthstone and zodiac sign, too. Pictures fade and even home movies lose their novelty. This memory will lasts forever.

~~~~~~~~~~~~~~~~~~~~~~~~~~~~~~~

BABY-GO-TO-SLEEP
P.O. Box 550
Colorado Springs, CO 80901
Free Information
Return policy: Money-Back Guarantee

Telephone: 800-537-7748

If your bundle of joy tends to become a big bundle of frustration at the mention of sleepytime, don't fret. Get the Safe Sure Sleep tape. Established in hospital use, it's the only medically proven audio therapy tape designed to stop crying and soothe your child to sleep. Recommended as safe and effective for children up to six years of age. Just play it at bedtime as part of a regular routine. It uses a real human heartbeat as the soothing rhythm of ten traditional lullabies.

~~~~~~~~~~~~~~~~~~~~~~~~~~~~~~~

ONE STEP AHEAD
P.O. Box 517
Lake Bluff, IL 60044
Free Catalog
Return policy: Satisfaction Guaranteed

Telephone: 800-950-5120
Fax No: 708-615-2162

You know how quickly changes in size occur, and how rapidly education needs grow. Like the name implies, here's a way to stay One Step Ahead of your baby's needs. Necessities for diaper changing are listed along side great playthings to inspire curiosity and teach hand-eye coordination. Many items will develop with your child, so you actually save money in the longrun! This is a great catalog for parents with someone on the way, or just arrived.

BABY PRODUCTS

THE LIVONIA CATALOG, INC.
306 Hebron Street
Hendersonville, NC 28739

Telephone: 914-469-2449

Free Catalog

Return policy: Money-Back Guarantee if returned within 30 days

This is a great catalog for hard-to-find items your infant or toddler. From charming name/date baby shoes to the finest skin and hair care products, Livonia is truly a valuable resource. There's Suzy Prudden's Exercise Program for Young Children and the "My Little Footsteps" stickers that take the guesswork and frustration out of learning left from right. Perfect baby shower or newborn gifts They have adorable baskets of cuddly stuffed animals, baby toys and more.

THE RIGHT START CATALOG
5334 Sterling Center Drive
Westlake Village, CA 91361

Telephone: 800-LITTLE-1
Fax No: 818-707-7132

Free Catalog

Return policy: Satisfaction Guaranteed

Get your child's life off on the right start with the great products available from the appropriately named Right Start Catalog. Items for every aspect of your baby's life are available. From games and toys that enrich your child's development to sheets and towels for Baby's tender skin. Turn-a-tot car seats are designed for safety and convenience. They make your life easier by swiveling around to the open door so you don't bump a tiny head when entering the car. Other products make your kitchen a safe place instead of a hazzard. If you're expecting, you should expect to order many things from here.

BABY PRODUCTS

8

ALCINA COSMETIC SPECIAL OF GERMANY   Telephone: 612-934-7068
16752 Creekside Lane
Minnetonka, MN 55345
Free Brochure
Return policy: Money-Back Guarantee

For serious skin and hair care that combines scientific research with the art of beauty, look to Alcina of Germany. Their Cosmetic Special Line offers a full range of total body care products for men and women. There are specially formulated cleansers, toners, day and night moisturizers and anti-aging elixirs - all proven effective in achieving specific results. There is also an artful collection of color cosmetics to accent the visible difference in your skin.

ARIZONA SUN   Telephone: 800-442-4786
P.O. Box 1786   Fax No: 602-998-0388
Scottsdale, AZ 85252-1786
Catalog $1.00
Return policy: Money-Back Guarantee

It's the year-round effects of the hot Arizona sun that provide ideal surroundings for skin care and tanning research. At Arizona Sun, they've found that plants native to the region like aloe, jojoba, sage, wild roses, mistletoe and cacti hold the secrets to how Native Americans and early settlers protected their skin. Perhaps this is why their sun-smart moisturizers, sunburn relievers, tanning products, shampoos and conditioners are all formulated with such botanical extracts. They're non-greasy, sun-protective and perfect for warm-weather skin care.

BEAUTIFUL VISIONS   Telephone: Mail only
810 South Hicksville Road
Hicksville, NY 11855-4001   DISCOUNT
Free Catalog
Return policy: Money-Back Guarantee when returned within 60 days

Once you've taken advantage of a few of these fantastic beauty bargains, you just might skip your local cosmetic counter altogether. Max Factor, L'Oreal, Maybelline, Cover Girl - all names you trust at up to 90% savings. Plus, great beauty helpers and tools to keep the good looks going! Also, check out the incredible bonus value on name-brand 'collection' suprise packages, usually found near the order form in the catalog's center section.

BEAUTY BOUTIQUE   Telephone: 216-826-3008
6836 Engle Road; P.O. Box 94520
Cleveland, OH 44101-4520   DISCOUNT
Free Catalog
Return policy: Money-Back Guarantee

Believe it! Get savings of up to a whopping 90% on many of your favorite names in skin care, hair care, fragrances, cosmetics and grooming tools for men and women. Revlon, Almay, Estee Lauder, Clinique, Max Factor, Maybelline and a wealth of other names can be found in the color catalog. Wide assortment of beauty organizers, helpful household gadgets, costume jewelry & much more.

CASWELL-MASSEY, CO. LTD.
100 Enterprise Place
Dover, DE 19901

Telephone: 302-735-8900
Fax No: 800-676-3299

Free Catalog

Return policy: Money-Back Guarantee

Since 1752, Caswell-Massey has been providing quality personal grooming, beauty and fragrance products for women, men and even babies. The best thing is that they're formulated with only the purest of ingredients. With today's choice of products packed with vague, unpronounceable ingredients that don't work, this is good news. Almond, cucumber, currant, eucalyptus and comfrey are just a few of the extracts that enable their products to do what they're supposed to do; cleanse, treat and beautify the skin.

CRABTREE & EVELYN
1310 Madison Avenue
New York, NY 10128

Telephone: 800-289-1222
212-289-3923

Catalog $2.50

Return policy: Store Credit or Exchange

Renowned throughout the world for a distinctive range of products and single-minded dedication to quality, Crabtree & Evelyn toiletries and groomers reflect the perfecet blending of science and nature. Exquisite fragrances, soothing botanical soaps, effective moisturizers and smart grooming tools are the hallmarks of the line. Don't miss the select group of delicious cookies, teas, preserves, sauces and cookware.

EARTH SCIENCE
P.O. Box 1925
Corona, CA 91718

Telephone: 714-524-9277
800-222-6720
Fax No: 714-524-5705

Free Catalog

Return policy: Money-Back Guarantee

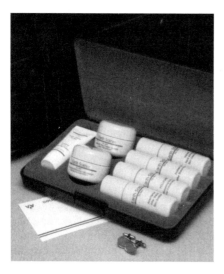

In the ever-popular spirit of earth-conscious consumerism, Earth Science continues its commitment to effective products that are environmentally safe. Their packaging is printed with biodegradable soy bean ink, they do no animal testing and use no animal extracts. However, the wholesome ecological commitment is only the beginning. The products are sensational: all-natural skin and hair care for the whole family made with botanical extracts and other eco-friendly ingredients.

FRAGRANCE INTERNATIONAL
398 East Rayen Avenue
Youngstown, OH 44505

Telephone: 216-747-3341

DISCOUNT

Free Catalog

Return policy: Money-Back Guarantee, less 10% restocking fee

Fragrance International is a wholesale distributor of designer fragrances, health & beauty aids and gift accessories, including handbags and luggage. Their volume of sales allows them to bring you the best merchandise at the lowest possible prices. These are not imitations or miniatures! Designer originals in a wide assortment of sizes satisfy the most discriminating consumer. A world of savings awaits you.

B
E
A
U
T
Y

~~~~~~~~~~~~~~~~~~~~~~~~~~~~~~~~~~~

H2O PLUS, INC.
676 North Michigan Avenue; 39th Floor
Chicago, IL 60611

Telephone: 800-242-BATH
Fax No: 312-642-9201

Free Brochure

Return policy: Money-Back Guarantee

Aside from their innovative chain of beauty stores around the country, H2O Plus has done it again with their mail-order line of Progressive Bath and Skin Care for the entire family. All of the products, which include gentle cleansers, lotions, and sun care products for kids, are blended with water, botanicals and their exclusive H2O Hydrogels. Together, they soothe, invigorate, pamper and protect your body from head to toe.

~~~~~~~~~~~~~~~~~~~~~~~~~~~~~~~~~~~

HOLBROOK WHOLESALERS
1205 Broadway; #204
New York, NY 10001

Telephone: 800-347-3738

DISCOUNT

Free Catalog

Return policy: Money-Back Guarantee

Holbrook Wholesalers can save you up to 35% on over 500 brand name designer fragrances for ladies and gentlemen, like Obsession by Calvin Klein, Jazz by Yves Saint Laurent, Drakkar Noir by Guy Laroche, Fendi, Poison by Christian Dior, and many, many others. Just give them a toll-free call or write them for the catalog. Orders are processed within 24 hours.

~~~~~~~~~~~~~~~~~~~~~~~~~~~~~~~~~~~

KEY WEST ALOE, INC.
524 Front Street; P.O. Box 1079
Key West, FL 33041-1079

Telephone: 305-294-5592
Fax No: 305-294-0138

Catalog $2.00

Return policy: Money-Back Guarantee

For well over 20 years, Key West Aloe has maintained a distinguished position as a leader in the mail-order skin care and cosmetics industry. Their Aloegenetics line of skin-savers and hair care products for men and women is the result of years of laboratory research with aloe vera and other botanical extracts. Look for their exclusive collection of intriguing fragrances for men and women, too. They also have a complete line of sun-smart products to help you get and maintain that golden Key West tan, with or without the sun.

NEW YORK COSMETICS & FRAGRANCES

318 Brannan Street
San Francisco, CA 94107

Telephone: 415-543-3880
Fax No: 415-896-0373

DISCOUNT

Catalog $2.00

Return policy: Satisfaction Guaranteed

New York Cosmetics & Fragrances is the premier discount resource for your favorite perfumes, toiletries, cosmetics, skin care and grooming tools for men and women. Prices are discounted up to 70% off the manufacturer's suggested retail prices. They carry well-known names like Dior, Givenchy, Gucci, Yves St. Laurent, Balenciaga and many more. Save time and money when you shop by mail, phone, or fax. You'll even get a free gift with your first order.

OLE HENRIKSEN OF DENMARK

8601 West Sunset Boulevard
Los Angeles, CA 90069-2301

Telephone: 310-854-7700

Free Information

Return policy: Exchanges Only

Megastars like Madonna, Christy Turlington, Naomi Campbell, Gloria Estefan, Laura Dern and even Sly Stallone have gotten first-hand knowledge of what this man's products can do. You too can enjoy the same scientifically formulated skin care products that keep them looking their celebrated best. Ole Henriksen's salon in West Hollywood now offers its most popular Scandinavian Formula products to you by mail including cleansers, natural soaps, day and night moisturizers, eye cremes, facial masks, sunblocks and medicated blemish lotions. They're all made with pure botanical extracts like aloe vera, apricot, chamomile, lavender and comfrey, as well as Vitamins C and E.

PAULA YOUNG FASHION WIGS

P.O. Box 483
Brockton, MA 02403

Telephone: 800-472-4017
Fax No: 508-238-1965

DISCOUNT

Free Catalog

Return policy: Money-Back Guarantee

Inside the Paula Young Fashion Wigs catalog, you'll see how easy it is to treat yourself to a comfortable, ready-to-wear hairstyle that looks and feels as good as your own. You'll be amazed at the natural look of their wigs, while enjoying the benefit of shopping quickly and easily by mail in the privacy of your own home. A full range of natural looking wigs and hairpieces for women are offered in a variety of flattering styles and shades. Valuable coupons save you up to 50%.

SEARS SHOP-AT-HOME BEAUTY BOUTIQUE

6836 Eagle Rd.; P.O. Box 94892
Cleveland, OH 44101-4892

Telephone: 800-776-0202
800-800-8200

DISCOUNT

Free Catalog

Sears,

Return policy: Money-Back Guarantee

America's oldest catalog retailer now brings you savings of up to 90% on nationally advertised cosmetics, fragrances and toiletries for the entire family. Estee Lauder, Charles of the Ritz, Almay and Elizabeth Arden are some of the famous name brands. You'll also find a complete array of clever household gadgets and beauty tools to make looking good a lot easier.

THE BODY SHOP

45 Horsehill Road
Cedar Knolls, NJ 07927-2014

Telephone: 800-541-2535

Free Catalog

Return policy: Money-Back Guarantee

The Body Shop offers reliable skin and hair care products, along with minimal packaging, respect for the environment, social activism, no animal testing and a healthy dose of fun. They offer unique products, like their Peppermint Foot Lotion, Banana Shampoo, Japanese Washing Grains and many more.

TOVA CORPORATION

188A North Canon Drive
Beverly Hills, CA 90210

Telephone: 800-777-8682

Catalog $3.00

Return policy: Money-Back Guarantee if returned within 30 days, excluding audio/video materials

The TOVA Corporation is commited to bringing you the absolute best in upscale, specialized beauty products straight from their innovative Beverly Hills salon. An effective culmination of creativity, science and nature was the catalyst for their luxe line cleansers, toners, moisturizers, sun care and bath products derived from the botanical essences of four cacti. Additional vitamin E provided in these ancient Aztec formulas result in hydration, emolliency and moisturization needed for younger, healthier looking skin and hair. Accentuate the refined texture of your glowing, 'new' skin with cosmetics from their TOVA Colorine Collection. Pull it all together with their flattering, aromatic fragrances including the new Body, Mind & Spirit. Don't miss their line of products for men, as well as the chance to save 20% on all these products and more by joining The TOVA Club.

APPLE TREE QUILTS

Telephone: 216-345-8802

3363 Oak Hill
Wooster, OH 44691

Catalog $6.00

Return policy: Money-Back Guarantee (less shipping charges)

Documenting the artistic style and taste of different periods in our country's development, quilts were necessities that became art forms. Apple Tree Quilts now makes enjoying them part of our heritage as well. They offer a wide variety of quilts - from the simplistic, yet powerful styles of the Amish to those with bright floral and geometric appliques. In fact, they have a number of talented artisans on hand who'll custom-make quilted items in the patterns and sizes you specify. All products are handmade and exemplify superior craftsmanship.

BEDROOM SECRETS

Telephone: 402-727-4004
Fax No: 402-727-1817

Box 529
Fremont, NE 68025

Catalog $2.00

Return policy: Satisfaction Guaranteed.

Transform your bedroom in one easy step! Get a copy of the Bedroom Secrets catalog and watch it happen. A division of Designer Secrets, this source of quality bedding, window and wall coordinates makes it easy for you to obtain all of your bedroom furnishings from one source. Dozens of photographs of sample rooms make this catalog a cornucopia of design ideas. Fabric and wallpaper samples are available.

CACHET ANTIQUE LINENS & ACCESSORIES

Telephone: 802-867-5725

RR2, Box 1390
Dorset, VT 05251

Free Information

Return policy: Money-Back Guarantee with proper authorization

Take your home back in time with the old-world charm of bedroom and table accessories hand-crafted from antique linens. Cachet offers envelope style pillows in lace, cutwork, eyelet, drawnwork, hand-embroidery, hand-crochet and punchwork. Each crisp, white pillow is one of a kind and shipped to you direct from the sources, starting at $20. You'll also find a selection of elegant table-cloths, teacloths and napkins fashioned from the same luxurious materials.

CHAMBERS

Telephone: 800-334-1254

Mail Order Dept.,P.O. Box 7841
San Francisco, CA 94120-7841

Free Catalog

Return policy: Satsifaction Guaranteed.

Offering high quality furnishings for bed and bath, Chambers features comfortable robes, absorbant towels and blankets, as well as coordinating flat sheets, flanged cases, bedskirts, shams and duvet covers sets. Stainless steel bath carts, brushes, towel bars and waste baskets are only some of the accessories for home and bath presented here.

CUDDLEDOWN OF MAINE
312 Canco Road
Portland, ME 04103

Telephone: 800-323-6793
Fax No: 207-761-1948

DISCOUNT

Catalog $3.00

Return policy: Money-Back Guarantee

Cuddledown of Maine is a family business dedicated to the design and manufacture of beautiful products for home comfort, which are then sold right to you. They make most of their goods themselves, so you can be assured of great service and manufacturer-direct discount prices. Cuddly down-filled comforters, pillows, linens and accessories come in a variety of gorgeous prints and solids. Also, find children's goods and adult sleepwear of the same high-quality.

DIAL-A-MATTRESS
(Phone orders only)

Telephone: 800-MATTRES

DISCOUNT

Free Brochure

Return policy: Exchanges Only Within 30 Days.

DIAL-A-MATTRESS is the national shop-at-home service where you can order a mattress today and have it delivered anywhere in the U.S.! Ask about their 90-day deferred payment plan on all mattresses. Professional bedding consultants will you choose the perfect mattress, including Sealy Posturepedic, Simmons Beautyrest and Serta Perfect Sleeper at or up to 60% savings! Express 2-hour delivery from 6am to midnight, 7 days a week (where available). Somma flotation beds, electric beds, futons, hirisers platform beds, folding beds and more!

DOMESTICATIONS
P.O. Box 40
Hanover, PA 17333-0040

Telephone: 717-633-3313

DISCOUNT

Catalog $2.00

Return policy: Money-Back Guarantee

The Domestications catalog offers an incredible array of linens and accessories for bed, bath and beyond. Virtually every color and pattern mix you can think of is available in comforters, matching sheet sets, window treatments and table linens to complement any decor. You'll also find a great selection of sophisticated furnishings and accent pieces - from handmade Chinese rugs and wicker patio furniture to exquisite table linens and charming dinnerware.

ELDRIDGE HOUSE CORPORATION
549 Middle Neck Road
Great Neck, NY 11023

Telephone: 800-622-0272

DISCOUNT

Free Information

Return policy: Money-Back Guarantee

Eldridge House features an eclectic mix of items for your home. For the bedroom, you'll find major European and American brand linens. Bath and kitchen items include a wide range of towels, placemats & potholders. A large infant selection includes quilts, diaper stackers, dust ruffles. But don't stop there - they carry unique mirrors, baskets, hat boxes, jewelry boxes and home frangrances. Save 20-40% on famous names, like Fieldcrest, Martex, Little Viking & Boynton.

HARRIS LEVY, INC.
278 Grand Street
New York, NY 10002

Telephone: 800-221-7750
In NY 212-226-3102
Fax No: 212-334-9360

DISCOUNT

Free Catalog
Return policy: Money-Back Guarantee

Here's a huge array of over 100 styles and patterns in sheets from every major mill, including Wamsutta, Martex, J.P. Stevens, Fieldcrest, Crown Craft and Croscill. Virtually every major designer is represented, like Laura Ashley, Bill Blass, Mario Buatta, Adrienne Vittadini, Fendi and Katja They have a large selection of imported linens for the kitchen and bath ; plus they specialize in custom monogramming and custom linen sizing. Discounts of 25-50% off retail prices.

HOMESPUN WEAVERS
55 South Seventh Street
Emmaus, PA 18049

Telephone: 215-967-4550

Free Brochure
Return policy: Money-Back Guarantee

Their name reflects an era in which Early American women wove heavy cotton fabrics on their home looms. Today, with a little boost from modern technology, they use much the same methods to give you color-fast, machine washable fabrics that never need ironing and are reversible. Ideal for table linens, drapery, bedspreads, slipcovers, accessories and crafts, this fabric can be purchased by the yard or they'll custom make pieces. Available in 15 colors and 2 original pattern designs.

J. SCHACTER CORP.
85 Ludlow Street
New York, NY 10002

Telephone: 212-533-1150
Fax No: 718-384-7634

DISCOUNT

Free Catalog
Return policy: Store credit on returns; custom-made items non-returnable

The J. Schacter Corporation is New York's oldest quilt manufacturer, with a distinguished reputation for high quality and service at discount prices of up to 60%. A complete line of bed linens from infant to king-size, imported and domestic. Also in stock are down-filled comforters, Hudson Bay Point blankets, and comforters of 100% pure wool or cotton. They can custom-cover your own sofa pillows and cushions or refill down comforters and coverlets at added cost.

LONDON LACE
167 Newbury Street
Boston, MA 02116

Telephone: 800-926-LACE

Free Catalog
Return policy: Money-Back Guarantee if returned within 3 weeks

"Precious bits of history" are Victorian textiles that were the inspiration for the exquisite lace goods this company produces. Hand-strung on the same Victorian looms used centuries ago in the British Isles, curtains, tablecloths and doilies represent the finest quality lace goods. Original 19th- and 20th-century patterns adorn these delicate recreations, unbelievably priced given their quality workmanship.

MAPLELEAF WORKSHOP
Telephone: 800-354-5501
P.O. Box 218
Stanford, IL 61774
Free Catalog

Return policy: Money-Back Guarantee

Thumbing through this catalog is like strolling through a country craft fair! Its filled with charming, handmade decorative crafts like their Country Kitchen accent linens, lovable cloth dolls and rustic wooden furnishings. They also offer Mayhaw Tree jellies and condiments to give your dishes a distinctive down-home flavor. Don't forget to check out their adorable calligraphy magnets to complement gifts and greeting cards.

MOTHER HART'S NATURAL PRODUCTS, INC.
Telephone: 407-738-5866
P.O. Box 4229
Boynton Beach, FL 33424-4229
DISCOUNT
Free Catalog
Return policy: Money-Back Guarantee if returned within 30 days

The Mother Hart Natural Products catalog offers savings of 50-70% on natural-fiber bedding and personal-care products, including flannel sheets, cotton duvet covers, down comforters, untreated sheets, featherbeds, infant bedding and much more. Don't miss their limited selection of fine canvas luggage and baby items.

RUE DE FRANCE
Telephone: 800-777-0998
78 Thames Street
Newport, RI 02840
Catalog $3.00
Return policy: Money-Back Guarantee

Here, you'll find delicate French lace straight from the old "quartiers" of Paris and simple farmhouses of Provence; vibrant and earthy tones of Provence in the colorful cotton fabrics that first came to Marseille from India in 1664; subtle scents of a wonderfully fragrant soap made from original French 19th-Century molds - each in their own way a part of the traditions of France and brought to you exclusively by Rue de France. Also, there's a lovely selection of French tableware and decorative accents to further complete the look.

SPRINGMAID-WAMSUTTA FACTORY OUTLETS   Telephone: 704-298-3393
1340 Tunnel Road
Asheville, NC 28805   DISCOUNT
Free Catalog

Return policy: Exchanges Or For Credit Only.

Here you'll find the finest quality sheets and pillowcases, 100% cotton and blends, comforters and comforter sets and draperies, towels, placemats and napkins, table rounds Pacific Silvercloth and more at everyday tremendous savings. They will quote prices and will assist you with your decorating needs. Merchandise is shipped UPS within 24 hours if in stock. UPS charges only, no handling fee. There are 11 store location locations nationwide, call for the one nearest you. Receipts are needed for all exchanges.

THE COMPANY STORE   Telephone: 800-348-4000
500 Company Store Road   **Fax No:**   608-784-2366
La Crosse, WI 54601-4477   DISCOUNT
Free Catalog

Return policy: Money-Back Guarantee on regular-priced items only; saleprice items may be exchanged only.

If you relish the thought of slipping into a bed decked out in snuggly cotton linens and warm down-filled comforters, this is the mail-order guide for you! In addition to great buys on window treatments, linens and bath items, they specialize in down beddings in a broad spectrum of colors and styles. Speaking of down, they also carry a complete line of down-filled outerwear for the entire family. Don't miss their regular sales supplements for fantastic savings on these items and more.

THE GAZEBO OF NEW YORK   Telephone: 212-832-7077
127 East 57th Street
New York, NY 10022
Catalog $6.00

Return policy: Returns allowed for exchange only

Founded in 1971, The Gazebo of New York is America's premier country home furnishings retailer with stores in New York, California, Texas, Massachusetts and Virginia. Count them as your number one catalog resource for traditional handmade quilts, pillows, duvet covers, rag rugs, braided rugs, and curtains. They say that their ability to do custom work is unequaled and that there is generally no additional cost involved. Their broad collection of Christmas ornaments by Gladys Boalt is truly irresistible, including her Famous Historical Figures, Wizard of Oz, Nutcracker, Alice In Wonderland, and Peter Pan Series.

THE LINEN SOURCE   Telephone: 800-431-2620
5401 Hangar Court; P.O. Box 31151   **Fax No:**   813-882-4605
Tampa, FL 33631-3151   DISCOUNT
Free Catalog

Return policy: Money-Back Guarantee

The Linen Source is just that - a great source for the finest in discount bed linens and bath items. But they also sell richly colored, handcrafted accent rugs, pleated window shades and lovely table linens. There's a limited selection of stoneware, lamps and furniture to complement the beautifully designed soft goods. They've recently instituted a 4-month payment plan for credit card purchases totalling $100 or more.

BART'S WATERSPORTS CATALOG
P.O. Box 294
North Webster, IN 46555
Free Catalog

Telephone: 800-348-5016
Fax No: 219-834-4246
DISCOUNT

Return policy: Money-Back Guarantee if returned within 60 days

If you've sailed a sea of retail outlets searching for quality water sport equipment and accessories, Bart's is the discount resource you've been looking for. Water ski equipment is their specialty, including wetsuits, vests, inflatable tubes, skis, hydroslides, and ski roping. They also have quality swimwear and marine apparel - all endorsed by well-known professionals. A limited selection of boating equipment is also available, from boat seats and covers to inboard propellers and hydrofoil stabilizers.

DEFENDER INDUSTRIES
P.O. Box 820, 255 Main Street
New Rochelle, NY 10802-0820
Catalog $4.00

Telephone: 914-632-3001
Fax No: 914-632-6544
DISCOUNT

Return policy: Money-Back Guarantee if returned within 20 days

Wide product selection, enormous inventory, and low prices are the hallmarks of Defender Industries' 54-year history as a leader in boating and marine supplies, and a valued resource in product knowledge. Whether you're a beginner or a professional, they have every item you'll need to make your seafaring experience safe and enjoyable. The current catalog includes a wide variety of boats, boating equipment, heavy-weight sailing gear, fishing equipment and fishfinders.

E & B DISCOUNT MARINE
201 Meadow Road
Edison, NJ 08818
Free Catalog

Telephone: 800-533-5007

DISCOUNT

Return policy: Money-Back Guarantee if returned within 90 days

Buy marine accessories at discount prices from E & B's enormous selection "where America buys its boating supplies." Call or write for your 136-page catalog and receive fast, friendly and knowledgeable service when placing your order. Merchandise is shipped via UPS, parcel post or Federal Express, usually with 48 hours.

FOLLANSBEE DOCK SYSTEMS
State Steet, P.O. Box 610, Dept SBM
Follansbee, WV 26037
Free Catalog

Telephone: 800-223-3444
Fax No: 304-527-4507

Return policy: Returns are accepted, 10% Restocking Charge

The new 1993 "One Stop Shopping" catalog has great buys on Flotation Drums; Foam Filled, Swim Float Kits, Steel and Wool Floating Docks, Cantilever Docks, Stationary Docks, Wood Dock Hardware, Covered Dock Hardware, Handrails, Centrite Decking, Pipe Holders, Hoop Pile Holders, Wheel Docks, Aluminum Ramps, Dock Bench, Rubrail and Corners, Fasteners, Power Posts, Boat Lifts, Ladders and Boarding Steps, Cleats, and much more.

FREEPORT MARINE SUPPLY

47 West Merrick Road
Freeport, NY 11520

Catalog $2.00

Telephone: 516-379-2610
Fax No: 516-379-2909

DISCOUNT

Return policy: Money-Back Guarantee except on special-order or custom merchandise

They say that they carry "everything for your boat at discount prices." The latest Freeport Marine Supply catalog is a printed testimony to this claim with thousands of products for the aquatic sportsman - all at prices that are hard to beat. They have a bountiful stock of interior accessories including non-skid nautical dinnerware and moisture resistant teak accent pieces; plus a number of how-to marine videos, books, and manuals. Namebrands include engine parts by Chris Craft and Barr Marine; marine sanitation systems by Sealand and Par; replacement exchangers and oil coolers by Sen-Dure, and marine cooling pumps by Sherwood.

GOLDBERGS' MARINE

201 Meadow Road
Edison, NJ 08818

Free Catalog

Telephone: 800-BOATING

DISCOUNT

Return policy: Money-Back Guarantee

For over 45 years, Goldbergs' Marine has been serving boaters from coast to coast with their great discount prices, super fast service and convenient ordering. At Goldbergs' Marine your satisfaction always comes first. Call today them toll-free to receive the free catalog from the company "where thousands of boaters save millions of dollars!"

OVERTON'S

11 Red Banks Road, P.O. Box 8228
Greenville, NC 27835

Free Catalog

Telephone: 800-334-6541
Fax No: 919-355-6541

Return policy: Money-Back Guarantee if returned within 45 days

For the amateur or professional water sportsman, Overton's has a tremendous selection of the finest in boating equipment, accessories, electronics and clothing. They stock brand name items including Yamaha outboard motors, Penn fishing gear, Si-Tex marine electronics and O'Brien water-ski equipment. You'll also find great discounts on swimwear and protective clothing for men and women.

SKI LIMITED

7825 South Avenue
Youngstown, OH 44512

Catalog $2.50

Telephone: 800-477-4040
Fax No: 800-477-8080

DISCOUNT

Return policy: 1-Year Satisfaction Guarantee

Everything for watersport fun, except the water! Ski Limited has the guaranteed lowest prices in the country and same day shipping. If this isn't enough, they've got a huge catalog jammed with stuff for the avid waterskier, novice or plain old beach bum. Skis and accessories are here for all ages and skill levels. There are also beach games and blankets, even life vests for the pooch. Get throttled.

SKIPPER MARINE ELECTRONICS, INC.

3170 Commercial Drive
Northbrook, IL 60062

Catalog $3.50

Telephone: 708-272-4700
Fax No: 708-291-0244

Return policy: Money-Back Guarantee

They claim to be the world's largest supplier of boating electronics - no galley gadgets, hardware, boat shoes or anchors; just electronics. Skipper stocks the best in brand-name graph recorders, digital sounders, marine cb radios, antennas, fishfinders, digital compasses, marine stereos and solar panels; plus they offer free calibration and tuning on your own marine electronics, regardless of where they were purchased.

THE WOODENBOAT STORE

P.O. Box 78
Brooklin, ME 04616

Free Catalog

Telephone: 800-287-4651
Fax No: 207-359-8920

Return policy: Money-Back Guarantee

The WoodenBoat Store is the shop-at-home resource for quality building plans, books, videos and how-to guides for the boating enthusiast. Whether you're building a boat or learning how to sail the one you've got, you can answer all those important questions yourself with easy-to-read literature on catamarans, canoes, kayaks, and other boats. Also, check out the stock of good-looking apparel and boating accessories for the entire family.

WEST MARINE BOATING GEAR AND APPAREL

500 Westridge Drive
Watsonville, CA 95076

Free Catalog

Telephone: 800-262-8042
Fax No: 408-728-4360

Return policy: Money-Back Guarantee

With over 14,000 products listed in their latest catalog and new ones being added year-round, West Marine's selection of quality products is one of the best you'll find anywhere. Anchoring, electronics, outboard motors and accessories, maintenance gear, safety equipment and interior hardware are just some of the items you'll find at competitive prices. Also, don't miss the discounts on standard and safety marine apparel for adults and kids.

BARNES & NOBLE

Telephone: 201-767-8844

126 Fifth Avenue
New York, NY 10011

Free Catalog

DISCOUNT

Return policy: Money-Back Guarantee

Here's a book-lovers dream! Save up to 60% on hardcover books, current paperbacks, records, tapes and videocassetes. Whatever topic interests you, Barnes & Noble covers it; from sports to history, medicine to dinosaurs, flowers to science fiction. You'll find dictionaries, fine art collections, children's books, refernce materials and more. Well-over 350 new titles each season.

CHRISTIAN BOOK DISTRIBUTORS

Telephone: 508-977-5000
Fax No: 508-531-8146

137 Summit Street; P.O. Box 6000
Peabody, MA 01961-6000

Free Catalog

Return policy: Money-Back Guarantee

As one might imagine, their biggest seller is "the good book," but you'll also find a variety of Bible reference guides on parenting, evangelism, famous-author commentaries, and more. There's an interesting group of volumes on new age spiritualism, plus entertaining videos on parenting and dealing with tough issues such as abortion, divorce, etc. Don't miss select savings on gospel music recordings by big-name artists like Amy Grant, Susan Ashton and Sandi Patti.

COLLECTOR BOOKS

Telephone: 800-626-5420

P.O. Box 3009
Paducah, KY 42002-3009

DISCOUNT

Free Booklist

Return policy: Money-Back Guarantee

For avid bookworms, serious collectors, or people looking for some eye-catching coffee table titles, here's a great opportunity to get wholesale prices on both popular and rare book finds. They have a huge topic selection including period art, jewelry, furniture, toys, Americana and music. Order more than six books and receive up to 40% reductions on most titles. New titles are released each month so don't miss your chance to save big before current stocks are exhausted.

CREATIVE BEGINNINGS

Telephone: 914-476-3731

1085 Warburton Avenue, #426
Yonkers, NY 10701

Free Brochure

Return policy: Exchanges Only

Here's a place to order personalized children's books where your child becomes the main character of their own story. Books feature durable hard covers, beautiful illustrations and personalized information throughout. Fun and exciting stories include "The Teddy Bear Party," "The Birthday Wish," "A Christmas Story," "The Space Adventure," "The Dinosaur Adventure," "The Hanukkah Story," "The Little Mermaid" and "Baby's Book," which is a personalized, open-ended story where the parents complete the story as the child grows older.

DAEDALUS BOOKS
P.O. Box 9132
Hyattsville, MD 20781-0932
Free Catalog
Return policy: Money-Back Guarantee

Telephone: 800-944-8879
Fax No: 800-866-5578
DISCOUNT

Daedalus Books offers a tremendous selection of fine sale books at savings of up to 90%. There are hundreds of titles, subjects and famous authors to choose from by commercial publishers and university presses. Science & Nature, History, Art & Human Anthropology are just some of the fun subjects, while John Kenneth Galbraith, Ian Frazier and Christopher Isherwood head the list of authors.

DOVER PUBLICATIONS
31 East 2nd Street
Mineola, NY 11501
Free Catalog
Return policy: Money-Back Guarantee

Telephone: 516-294-7000
DISCOUNT

For over 50 years, Dover Publications has been supplying readers around the world with high-quality paperbacks and now over 4,800 titles can be purchased by mail at exceptional prices, most from $1 to $6. Virtually every subject is available, from Art to Zoology. Check out the Dover Thrift Editions, a unique collection of fiction, drama and poetry in complete, unabridged editions at only $1 each. There's also a fine grouping of greeting cards, labels, bookplates, stationery items, art prints, giftwrapping papers and post cards at great prices.

IDEALS PUBLISHING CORPORATION
P.O. Box 148000
Nashville, TN 37214-8000
Free Catalog
Return policy: Money-Back Guarantee if returned within 30 days

Telephone: 800-558-4343

Ideals Publishing offers a number of fantastic titles and topics in this catalog that features coffee table varieties, cookbooks and children's books. Religion, Holidays, Humor, Americana and Children's Interest are just a few of the topics. Also available is Ideals' own collection of commemorative books on photography, poetry, and essays by favorite authors. Orders for holiday gift-giving must be received by the specified deadlines.

LIBERTYTREE
134 Ninety-Eighth Avenue
Oakland, CA 94603
Free Catalog
Return policy: Satisfaction Guaranteed

Telephone: 800-927-8733
Fax No: 510-568-6040

If there is a book that is in anyway related to American culture or politcs, LibertyTree offers it. Contemporary discourses such as The Closing of the American Mind are offered along with popular commentary by Dave Barry and P.J. O'Rourke. While there are educational materials for children, we all can learn from historical works of political importance, such as Thomas Paine's Common Sense and the writings of Henry David Thoreau. Gift certificates are available.

B
O
O
K
S

MANDERLEY
13131 Highway 253, P.O. Box 880
Boonville, CA 95415-0880
Free Catalog

Telephone: 800-722-0726
Fax No: 707-895-3719

Return policy: Satisfaction Guaranteed.

Exotic settings, steamy plots and breathtaking fantasies. All this can be yours if you receive the Manderley catalog. This treasure trove for the avid fan of romantic fiction gives you access to what is essentially the largest romance bookstore around. All romantic genres are offered; fantasy, historical, contemporary and suspense, as well as all of the latest releases. With their Romance by the Dozen program, if you buy 12 books, the 13th is free. If you love romance, here's the place for you.

RAND MCNALLY WORLD ATLASES AND MAPS
8255 North Central Park Avenue
Skokie, IL 60076
Free Catalog

Telephone: 800-284-6565
Fax No: 708-673-7337

Return policy: Money-Back Guarantee

For over 130 years, Rand McNally has been bringing the world within reach through beautifully-detailed, full-color maps, atlases and globes of various sizes and styles for home, school, office or travel use. They have special edition atlases that focus on particular world areas, events and phenomenon. There are also maps and atlases designed especially for businesses, students and travelers of all ages.

READER'S DIGEST BOOKS, VIDEOS & MUSIC
Pleasantville, NY 10570
Free Catalog

Telephone: 800-345-6563
DISCOUNT

Return policy: Money-Back Guarantee if returned within 7 days

One of America's best-loved periodicals brings you many popular titles and topics in books, videos, and sound recordings. The collection includes a wealth of varied topics, from home improvement, gardening, household hints and hobbies, to environmental awareness, health, and Americana. The Music Collection features recordings by American favorites like Frank Sinatra, Henry Mancini, Nat King Cole, Elvis Presley, Willie Nelson and Kenny Rogers. In video, there are award-winning movies and documentaries on religion, nature, comedy and music; plus popular shape-up videos by Richard Simmons, Jane Fonda and Angela Lansbury.

RIZZOLI BOOKSTORES

300 Park Avenue
New York, NY 10010

Telephone: 800-52-BOOKS
Fax No: 212-387-3434

Free Catalog

Return policy: Money-Back Guarantee if returned within 30 days

Discover a wealth of international culture with intriguing books, music and distinctive gifts. There are lavishly illustrated book selections on fashion, fine art, photography, sports, cinema and other pleasures. Entertainment and travel books include bestselling collector editions from Rolling Stone, MGM Films, and Disney. Sound recordings exemplify sophisticated musical taste, renowned Broadway musicals, classics from the Big-Bands, and chilling operatic renditions head the list.

SOUNDPRINTS

165 Water Street, P.O. Box 679
Norwalk, CT 06856

Telephone: 800-228-7839

Free Catalog

Return policy: Money-Back Guarantee

Here's a fantastic selection of interactive children's books, audio tapes and stuffed toys that teach children about wildlife and nature through entertainment. A child can witness the prairie odyssey of a black-footed ferret family regaining freedom in the wild or learn about how Columbus reintroduced the horse to North America after its 8,000 year absence. The Soundprints "readalongs" are designed for kids of preschool to 5th grade age groups.

STRAND BOOK STORE

828 Broadway
New York, NY 10003

Telephone: 212-473-1452
Fax No: 212-473-2591

DISCOUNT

Free Catalog

Return policy: Money-Back Guarantee

Beginning in 1928 on New York's legendary Fourth Ave. "Book Row", Strand Book Store has grown to become one of the most unique book dealers in America. Millions of titles, recent and vintage, on every subject imaginable. Reviewer's copies of current titles are sold at half-price and Strand's Rare Book Department offers a wide varierty of hard to find treasures, many suprisingly affordable. Most of the books in the catalog are in new condition. A few are designated "Good Used Copies", drawn from their enormous stock of second hand books. These items have the same full return privileges that apply to new items.

TARTAN BOOK SALES

c/o Brodart Company, 500 Arch Street
Williamsport, PA 17705

Telephone: 800-233-8467
Fax No: 717-326-1479

Free Catalog

Return policy: Damaged Merchandise Returnable

Tartan Books are hardbound editions of fiction and non-fiction titles from major publishers, including many bestsellers, available at savings of up to 74%! Every book is protected by a plastic book jacket. Returns accepted on damages books or incorrect shipments only. No minimum order requirements.

TOTLINE & FIRST TEACHER BOOKS

P.O. Box 2250
Everett, WA 98203

Telephone: 800-334-4769

Free Catalog

Return policy: Money-Back Guarantee

Warren Publishing presents the Totline Resource Catalog loaded with fun learning aids for preschool and kindergarten-aged children. Music, language skills-building, art, self-concept development, and environmental awareness are just some of the varied themes. Turn up the quality level in quality time while opening up an enjoyable world of learning for your child. All themes incorporate skills-building exercises through drawing, coloring, writing, and even singing.

WORLD BOOK FAMILY CATALOG

2515 East 43rd Street, P.O. Box 182246
Chattanooga, TN 37422-7246

Telephone: 800-874-5885
Fax No: 615-867-5318

Free Catalog

Return policy: Money-Back Guarantee

You can open a world of learning possiblities for your child by buying from the World Book Family Catalog. For over 75 years, they've been an American institution, bringing high-quality, long-lasting learning aids to hundreds of thousands of children. Besides terrific books, they have games, toys and recordings that explore science, the environment, religion and others. Learning aids can be shared by generations and will truly make the learning experience fun.

BOOKS

CAMBRIDGE CAMERA EXCHANGE, INC.
Seventh Avenue at 13th Street
New York, NY 10011
DISCOUNT

Telephone: 212-675-8600
Fax No: 212-463-0093

Free Catalog

Return policy: Money-Back Guarantee if returned within 20 days

With nearly 30 years of dealership at the same New York City location, Cambridge Camera sells top brands at fantastic savings. Their catalog features cameras, camera equipment and accessories by Pentax, Olympus, Samsung, Rollei, Vivitar, Fuji and other brands. Those on a budget must check out the USED department, where they can find steals on used cameras and equipment in excellent working condition. They also buy and trade items.

CAMERA WORLD OF OREGON
500 SW Fifth Avenue
Portland, OR 97204
DISCOUNT

Telephone: 503-227-6008
Fax No: 503-222-7070

Free Information

Return policy: Returns accepted with a restocking fee, waived on defective items

Camera World of Oregon is the northwest's largest camera, video and camcorder dealer. Their policy is to try and meet or beat any advertised price on all equipment. They carry video camcorders, VCRs, cameras, photo and video accessories and peripherals, as well as a full line of Sony audio, including Walkman, Discman, boomboxes and telephones. Sony and JVC bookshelf stereo systems are also available. All merchandise is factory-fresh with full manufacturers' warranties and accessories. Extended warranties are available on certain items.

GOULD TRADING
7 East 17th Street
New York, NY 10003-9990

Telephone: 212-243-2306
Fax No: 212-243-2308

Catalog $2.00

Return policy: Money-Back Guarantee if returned within 10 days

Gould Trading promises a great deal on both new and used equipment.. They have a broad selection of instructional books and videos on virtually every type of photography, from outdoor to fashion to portraiture. Limited edition photo art books feature works by Robert Mapplethorpe, Helmut Newton, Paul Strand, Herb Ritts and other greats. Unheard-of prices on brand-name light boxes, waterproof camera cases, slide sleeving and other items.

PORTER'S PHOTO EQUIPMENT & SUPPLIES
P.O. Box 628
Cedar Falls, IA 50613
DISCOUNT

Telephone: 800-553-2001
Fax No: 800-221-5329

Free Catalog

Return policy: Money-Back Guarantee

Porter's catalog is loaded with impressive savings up to 80% on famous-maker cameras, studio & darkroom equipment, accessories and even do-it-yourself printing supplies. Trusted names like Tamron, Pentax, Canon and Vivitar head the list. They've got lots of necessities you may not find in other photo supply catalogs; retouching materials, mounting supplies and film by Kodak, Fuji, Polaroid,Scotch.

SUGRA PHOTOSYSTEMS
3045 West Liberty Avenue, Box 8051
Pittsburgh, PA 15216-8051

Telephone: 800-221-9695

Free Catalog

Return policy: 15% Restocking charge on returns.

Where can you obtain hard to find, unique camera equipment as well as standard items that every photography or camera hobbiest needs? Try Sugra Photosystems. They offer wooden tripods, studio camera stands, special filter systems and light diffusers. That is only some of the studio equipment available. They don't sell name brand cameras like most dealers, instead they market macro cameras for close-up photography. They also offer how-to video tapes.

ZONE VI STUDIOS, INC.
Newfane, VT 05345-0219

Telephone: 802-257-5161
Fax No: 802-257-5165

Free Catalog

Return policy: Lifetime Replacement/Repair Guarantee on Zone VI products

To professionals, they're known as 'field cameras' and their charming resemblance to the accordion pleated, free-standing models of the early days of photography adds to their value. Zone VI carries on the tradition by specializing in this model, complete with brass hardware and beautiful real-wood fittings. There's a selection of photo art books by contemporary masters such as Paul Strand and Ansel Adams, plus Zone VI's exclusive fine prints. They also offer instructional books and videos, lenses, filters and film by Kodak and Polaroid; as well as other accessories for field photography and studio work.

BEARDEN BROS. CARPET & TEXTILES
3200A Dug Cap Rd., Upper Level Dept 200
Dalton, GA 30720
Telephone: 800-433-0074
Fax No: 404-277-1754

Free Catalog
Return policy: No Refunds, No Returns

Bearden Bros.offers 3 major incentives to buy floor coverings by mail: 1) tremendous savings on 2) top quality name-brands along with 3) unbeatable service. Headquartered in the "carpet capital of the world" they have 1,850 shipping drop-off pointso. Vinyl floor coverings from top names like Congoleum, Armstrong, Johnsonite and Mercer; carpets from J.P. Stevens, Anso V and Galaxy, in addition to their own award-winning Elegante Showcase Carpet Collection.

BENINGTON'S CARPET & RUGS
1271 Manhein Pike
Lancaster , PA 17601
Telephone: 800-252-5060

Free Information
Return policy: Returns accepted for exchange or store credit only

With a little help from Benington's, you can buy to brand carpets and rugs and save up to 50% off the retail price! They carry most major mill brands and styles, residential or commercial; plus custom area rugs, imported handmade Orientals, braided rugs and more. Call them toll-free with the manufacturer's name, style number and color and get instant price quotes. No sales tax on purchases shipped outside of Pennsylvania and they offer same-day order processing.

CHARLES W. JACOBSEN, INC. ORIENTAL RUGS
401 North Salina Street
Syracuse, NY 13203
Telephone: 315-422-7832
Fax No: 315-422-6909

Free Catalog
Return policy: Exchanges Only

If you're serious about investing in top quality imported Oriental rugs, this is the mail order resource you've been searching for. Jacobsen's has been in the business for over 65 years and offers genuine handwoven rugs from India, Pakistan, Iran, Turkey, Afghanistan, China and Nepal. A magnificent array of styles and patterns to choose from include runners and floral designs. Their full-color catalog gives detailed information on how to find the right rug for your home and budget, as well as background on the quality of their product.

ELKES

Telephone: 919-434-4104

1585 Bethel Drive
High Point, NC 27260

DISCOUNT

Free Brochure

Return policy: Returns accepted with proper authorization

At this wholesale carpet mill outlet, save up to 50% and more on a large range of decorator colors and styles. Distributors for Evans Black Carpets, they feature Dupont Certified Stainmaster. They ship everywhere by truck or UPS, if in stock. If you need to return your purchase, they'll even pick it up after proper authorization.

FACTORY DIRECT CARPET OUTLET

Telephone: 800-225-4351
In MT 800-233-0208

P.O. Box 417
Miles City, MT 59301

DISCOUNT

Free Order Form

Return policy: No Refunds, No Returns

Add your name to the growing list of satisfied customers who've saved a bundle on quality, name-brand carpet from the Factory Direct Carpet Outlet. With well over 40 years in the retail carpet business, they sell every major brand of carpet at only $1 a sq. yd. over the dealer's cost. They can special order from the manufacturer and ship mill-direct to you. They carry brands like Coronet, Horizon, Galaxy, and Diamond Mill, Inc.

JOHNSON'S CARPETS

Telephone: 800-235-1079

3239 South Dixie Highway
Dalton, GA 30720

DISCOUNT

Free Information

Return policy: Returns subject to manufacturer's warranties

Buy carpet and custom area rugs direct from the manufacturer at savings of up to 80%. Johnson's Carpets will also quote prices on other name brands and offer residential and commercial carpets. Shipping is direct with no minimum quantities. Call them direct for price quotes, samples and their free brochure or custom rug pattern booklet.

S & S MILLS CARPET

Telephone: 800-241-4013

2650 Lakeland Road
Dalton, GA 30720

DISCOUNT

Free Catalog

Return policy: No Refunds, No Returns

Imagine being able to buy first quality carpet for 50% less than what you would pay at your local retail carpet store. That is exactly what you do when you buy carpet direct from the manufacturer - S & S Mills. Because they make all their own carpets and sell direct to the consumer market, you can take advantage of tremendous savings without added dealer charges. In fact, they've been helping homeowners across the country save money on premium quality carpets in a variety of styles, colors and textures for nearly two decades. Their selection includes soil and stain resistant carpets for long-lasting beauty and wear.

VILLAGE CARPET
Telephone: 704-465-6818

1114 Conover Boulevard West
Conover, NC 28613

Free Brochure

Return policy: No Refunds, No Returns

Village Carpet is a discount dealer in quality carpeting, providing reliable service to customers in all parts of the United States. They offer savings of up to 50% on several major brands including Aladdin, Diamond, Patcraft, Queen, Bigelow and Sutton. You'll also find soil and stain resistant brands like Weardated, Stainmaster by DuPont and Genesis. Home delivery is available.

WAREHOUSE CARPETS
Telephone: 800-526-2229

P.O. Box 3233
Dalton, GA 30721

Free Brochure

Return policy: Returns accepted on defective merchandise only

All major brands of rugs and carpets are offered by Warehouse Carpets at significant discounts. They carry merchandise from Philadelphia, Mohawk, Galaxy, Salem and over 25 other brands. Call or write them with the specific manufacturer's name and style number. They'll ship your order in under 2 weeks by truck.

YANKEE PRIDE RUGS
Telephone: 800-848-7610

29 Parkside Circle, Dept. MG2
Braintree, MA 02184

Free Catalog

Return policy: No Refunds, No Returns

If wall-to-wall carpet isn't your floor covering style, Yankee Pride Rugs can give you some beautiful alternatives in their handcrafted, quality rugs of richly-colored patterns and textures. The current catalog features their hand-woven and braided rugs available in your choice of size ranges (from 2'x3' to 11'x17') and shapes (from runners and half-circles to rounds, ovals and oblongs). In addition, they have handcrafted floral hooked rugs and rag rugs; plus Oriental and Persian reproductions - all available with optional Scotchgard protection. Samples are available for in-home inspection and believe it or not, they have a no-interest layaway plan to ease the purchase.

AFTER THE STORK
1501 12th Street NW
Albuquerque , NM 87104

Telephone: 505-243-9100
Fax No: 505-243-6935

DISCOUNT

Free Catalog
Return policy: Money-Back Guarantee

After the Stork can save you up to 60% and more on fun clothing and accessories for boys and girls. You'll find great values on school-time casuals, shoes, swimwear, sleepwear, outerwear and all the adorable trimmings in sizes to fit infants to preteens. They're a terrific shopping resource for back-to-school and holiday gift-giving. Gift certificates are available.

BABY BUNZ & COMPANY
P.O. Box 1717
Sebastopol, CA 95473

Telephone: 707-829-5347

DISCOUNT

Free Catalog
Return policy: Money-Back Guarantee

Baby Bunz & Company is celebrating 7 of years experience at "the art of diapering." The full-color catalog offers a complete selection of infant necessities including diapers, diaper covers, blankets, clothing and accessories for the baby. They also make great gifts for the mother-to-be. Don't miss all the facts and tips on newborn parenting, the benefits of cloth diapers over disposables, and even a detailed guide to proper diapering techniques.

BIOBOTTOMS
P.O. Box 6009
Petaluma, CA 94953

Telephone: 800-766-1254

Free Catalog
Return policy: Money-Back Guarantee

The best part about this quality selection of infant and children's clothes is that your youngster is guaranteed to love them as much as you will. You'll find great buys on the original Biobottom diaper cover made of super-absorbent wool. They also offer training pants, coveralls, rompers, and truly adorable accessories for your baby or great gifts for the mom-to-be. For toddlers and older kids, there's fun playwear, sleepwear, outerwear and dress clothes. They've also got some of the coolest school gear around including tie-dyed t-shirts, cuffed denim shorts, rugby pullovers and tons of other styles your kids will love. Infant/toddler sizes range from 6 months to 4T, while kids clothes are sized 4-14.

BRIGHTS CREEK
Bay Point Place
Hampton, VA 23653

Telephone: 804-827-1850
Fax No: 800-677-8687

Free Catalog
Return policy: Satisfaction Guaranteed

Here's a great collection of childrenswear at great prices. Choose from whimsical infant, toddler, girl's and boy's quality clothing accessories and baby essentials. Show off that special youngster in truly unique, yet affordable pieces. Orders are shipped in 2 days if they're in stock.

CHILDREN'S CLOTHING

CHILDREN'S WEAR DIGEST

2515 East 43rd Street; P.O. Box 22728
Chattanooga, TN 37422

Telephone: 800-433-1895
Fax No: 615-867-5318

Catalog $2.00

Return policy: Money-Back Guarantee if returned within 20 days

Talk about cool! If you're looking for big attitudes in small sizes, you'll find all the hottest trends in sportswear, sleepwear and accessories for kids. For boys, there are cotton pullovers with matching bottoms in hi-tech designs, plus denims, outerwear and shoes. For girls, they've got funky dresses, jumpers, blouses, skirts and pants in lots of hot prints, plus adorable hosiery, shoes and other accessories. Don't miss the special selection of great furniture and toys.

FLAP HAPPY

3516 Centinela Avenue
Los Angeles , CA 90066

Telephone: 800-234-FLAP

Free Catalog

Return policy: Money-Back Guarantee

Flap Happy is not just the company name, it also belongs to a too-cute hat specially designed to protect children from the sun. Other adorable designs for kids include the Infant Pilot, Vintage Rose, Flapper Cap and Lindbergh Cap designs. Some styles provide generous summer sun protection while others keep little heads toasty in the winter cold. They have wonderful childrens clothing in sizes to fit infants to toddlers; plus original accessories like Flap Happy Mittens and Booties.

JUST FOR KIDS

P.O. Box 29241
Shawnee, KS 66201-9141

Telephone: 800-443-5827
Fax No: 913-752-1095

DISCOUNT

Free Catalog

Return policy: Money-Back Guarantee

This might be the first time your kids enjoy shopping for themselves. Give them the Just For Kids catalog but don't be alarmed, though, by expressions like "Rad!", "Stylin'!" and "Cool!" These are signs of approval and the great prices will encourage similar responses from you, too. They've got a selection of funky, comfy school stuff like wildly printed tops, groovy little dresses, snappy denims, hot leggings, excellent accessories; plus great outerwear and shoes. Fun toys, games and stuff for kids rooms, like personalized bean bag chairs & sing-along stereos.

CHILDREN'S CLOTHING

MAGGIE MOORE
170 Ludlow street
Yonkers, NY 10705

Telephone: 914-968-0600
Fax No: 914-968-0754

Free Catalog

Return policy: Satisfaction Guaranteed.

Maggie Moore has come up with such unique clothing for infants and children. Words like "cute" and "adorable" just aren't enough to define the pure whimsy that inspire the crisp gingham jumpers, funky tees and shorts, picture-perfect hats and cuddly sleepwear. Matching girl/boy ensembles are so charming they'll truly break your heart! Sizes range from 6 months to 4T in infant wear and 2-14 in kids clothes. Gift boxes and personalized gift cards are available.

PATAGONIA MAIL ORDER, INC.
1609 West Babcock St., P.O. Box 8900
Bozeman, MT 59715-2046

Telephone: 800-523-9597

Free Catalog

Return policy: Satisfaction Guaranteed.

Activewear for the most active of all wearers; children. Patagonia offers the type of clothing that can stand up to the kind of punishment only kids can dish out during day-to day wear. Perfect for special activities, like rock climbing, kayaking or fishing, these clothes are stylish and built for comfort and are probably the one kind that will outlast a childhood. Iron-clad satisfaction guarantee.

RUBENS BABY WEAR FACTORY
P.O. Box 14900; 2340 N. Racine Avenue
Chicago, IL 60614

Telephone: 312-348-6200

DISCOUNT

Free Brochure

Return policy: No Refunds, No Returns

Here are great deals on basic infant clothing, backed by 100+ years serving hospitals all over the country. Chances are, the first clothes your little one wore or will wear were made by Rubens. 100% cotton baby shirts, gowns, kimonos, training pants, and diapers in first quality condition and seconds with small knitting flaws are guaranteed more durable than store-bought items. First quality baby linens, too.

STORYBOOK HEIRLOOMS
1215 O'Brien Drive
Menlo Park, CA 94025
Free Catalog
Return policy: Money-Back Guarantee

Telephone: 800-899-7666
Fax No: 415-323-9550

The Storybook Heirloom catalog features exquisite children's clothing and accessories that you won't see in other catalogs or retail stores. They offer high quality merchandise of painstaking workmanship that will endure and be treasured for years. Cute casual oufits, shoes and accessories, as well as charming dress-up ensembles are available in a full range of boys and girls sizes. They even have lovely girls' and boys' formal clothing for church, parties and other dressy occasions.

THE WOODEN SOLDIER
P.O. Box 800
North Conway, NH -3860-0800
Free Catalog
Return policy: Money-Back Guarantee

Telephone: 603-356-7041

Celebrating their 15th anniversary with the full-color Holiday 1992 Catalog, The Wooden Soldier offers some of the most beautiful, top-quality dress clothing for children of toddler to preten age groups. For girls, they carry exquisite confections of lace, velvet, tafetta, and silk among other fabrics. For boys, there are snappy tweeds, woolens, cottons and more. They also carry outerwear, sleepwear, and select school clothes of equally impeccable quality and style.

CHILDREN'S CLOTHING

TORTELLINI
P.O. Box 2615
Sag Harbor, NY 11963
Free Catalog
Return policy: Money-Back Guarantee if returned within 30 days

Telephone: 800-527-8725
Fax No: 516-725-9289

By no means will you classify this as just another mediocre kids' catalog. Tortellini offers classic designs and high-quality fabrics in all of its childrens' clothing. Fall in love with the picture-perfect floral dresses and jumpers in Liberty of London's finest Egyptian cotton. They also have crisp cotton shirts, roomy pullovers, pants, swimwear and outerwear for both boys and girls in traditional prints. In fact, most of the looks are unisex and make for effortless seasonal clothing transitions.

ALBERT S. SMYTH COMPANY, INC.
29 Greenmeadow Drive
Timonium, MD 21093

Telephone: 800-638-3333
In MD 410-252-6666

DISCOUNT

Free Catalog

Return policy: Money-Back Guarantee if returned within 30 days

Save up to 60% on beautiful china, crystal and silver items from Lenox, Waterford, Kirk-Stieff and more. Albert S. Smyth Company has been serving quality and value for well over 75 years. Price quotes can be given by phone, so give them a toll-free call. Orders are shipped conveniently by UPS.

BARRON'S
P.O. Box 994
Novi, MI 48376-0994

Telephone: 800-538-6340
Fax No: 313-344-4342

DISCOUNT

Free Catalog

Return policy: Money-Back Guarantee

Barron's offers significant savings on over 1,500 of the world's finest tabletop patterns, featuring famous names in fine china, porcelain, crystal, and silver dinnerware and giftware. Lenox, Noritake, Mikasa, Wedgwood, Royal Doulton, Oneida and Gorham are some of the designer names. You'll find all the right storage and maintenance accessories for your investment and they also offer a computerized bridal registry service.

BEVERLY BREMER'S SILVER SHOP
3164 Peachtree Road; Dept. S & B
Atlanta, GA 30305

Telephone: 404-261-4009

DISCOUNT

Free Brochure & Inventory

Return policy: Money-Back Guarantee

Missing a piece of your favorite silver pattern™? Now you can replace or add to your sterling silver collection at up to 75% off retail prices. They specialize in obsolete, hard-to-find, fine sterling silver. In fact, they now have well over 100,000 pieces of flatware in 950 patterns in stock. All their silver is in perfect condition with no mongram, unless noted. They also have goblets, tea sets, punch bowls, boxes, picture frames and centerpieces. Call or write for a free inventory of your pattern or send a photocopy and they'll identify it for you. Orders are shipped via UPS in 7-10 days.

CHINA CABINET, INC.
24 Washington St.
Tenafly, NJ 07670

Telephone: 800-545-5353

DISCOUNT

Free Brochures

Return policy: Satisfaction Guaranteed.

In your search to find tabletop items at wonderful prices, check out China Cabinet. They carry most brands of china, crystal and silver at discounts of 20%-60%. Their specialty is bridal registries and unique gifts for all your needs. Just call the 800 number for personal service. Let them help you with all your gift needs; corporate or personal.

GREATER NEW YORK TRADING
81 Canal Street
New York, NY 10002
Free Brochure

Telephone: 212-226-2808
Fax No: 212-334-1088
DISCOUNT

Return policy: Store Credit if returned within 10 days; No returns on special orders

Thanks to Greater New York Trading, you can now buy first-quality china, crystal and flatware - be it silverplate or sterling - at savings of up to 50%. Some of the best-loved names in crystal stemware are offered, including Kosta Boda, Orrefors, Baccarat, and Waterford. The flatware selection includes collections by Gorham, Reed & Barton, Tuttle and Wallace. The brand-name listings are always growing, so call them direct for such inquiries, as well as price quotes. Merchandise is shipped UPS.

KITCHEN, ETC.
P.O. Box 1560
North Hampton, NH 03862
Free Catalog

Telephone: 800-232-4070

DISCOUNT

Return policy: Satisfaction Guaranteed

The Kitchen, Etc. catalog features 20-50% savings on over 300 patterns and brands of dinnerware, including Noritake, Royal Doulton, Minton, Royal Albert, Villeroy & Boch, Wedgewood, Franciscan, Johnson Brothers, Nikko and Pfaltzgraff. Only first-quality merchandise is sold, including one of America's largest accessory selections. You can call their helpful china consultants for pattern inquiries. Merchandise is shipped via UPS in 7-10 days.

LANAC SALES
73 Canal Street
New York, NY 10022
Free Information

Telephone: 212-925-6422

DISCOUNT

Return policy: Money-Back Guarantee, if returned within 30 days

Lanac Sales offers a full selection of china, crystal silver and gifts at substantial savings on all major brands. They are exclusive sellers of Lladro figurines. Merchandise is first-quality only. Give them a call for discounted price quotes. Merchandise is shipped UPS in 7-10 days.

MAREL
6 Bond Street
Great Neck, NJ 11021
No Catalog

Telephone: 516-466-3118
Fax No: 516-468-7328
DISCOUNT

Return policy: Returns For Store Credit Only.

Make your china cabinet, hutch or table setting a masterpiece. Savings of up to a legitimate 50% on top brands of china, crystal and silver, including Royal Doulton, Wedgwood, Gorham, Reed & Barton, etc. No minimum order - returns accepted for store credit with authorization. Orders are shipped UPS right away if in stock.

CHINA CRYSTAL & SILVER

MICHAEL C. FINA

580 Fifth Avenue
New York, NY 10109

Telephone: 718-937-8484
Fax No: 718-937-7193

DISCOUNT

Free Catalog

Return policy: Money-Guarantee if returned within 3 weeks

For years, Michael C. Fina has been a household name for those who seek fine jewelry, china, glassware and decorative treasures for the home. Their catalog offers notable savings on well known brands like Lenox, Mikasa, Waterford, Gorham, Wedgwood, Oneida and Rosenthal. They guarantee you the lowest prices or they'll refund the difference if you find a higher price on the same item within 10 days of purchase. Gift certificates and custom engraving are available.

MIDAS CHINA & SILVER

4315 Walney Road
Chantilly, VA 22021

Telephone: 800-368-3153
In VA & MD 703-802-3233

DISCOUNT

Free Catalog

Return policy: Money-Back Guarantee on most items if returned within 30 days; earrings and closeout sale items are non-returnable

Midas China & Silver is a great source for a number of precious items from gold jewelry to silver flatware, china and crystal by famous makers such as Mikasa, Royal Doulton, Lenox, Spode and Noritake, all at savings of up to 70%. Choose from a selection of exquisite giftware by Towle, Kirk Stieff, Sheffield and others. A special offerings department features limited edition treasures like collector coins and estate silver. They offer optional engraving at additional cost.

MIKASA

25 Enterprise Avenue
Secaucus, NJ 07096

Telephone: 201-867-2354
Fax No: 201-867-4480

DISCOUNT

Free Catalog

Return policy: Exchanges and Strore Credit Only

In business for nearly 50 years, American-owned Mikasa is the largest tableware manufacturer in the world, setting a precedent for exceptional innovation in style, design and technology. They have the largest selection of fine china and crystal tableware to be found anywhere. Not to be missed are the beautiful china and crystal decorative accents including candlesticks, vases, clocks, picture frames and vanity sets. They can provide custom imprinting, engraving and etching to personalize your order. They also have an exclusive corporate gift-giving plan.

NAT SCHWARTZ & CO.

549 Broadway
Bayonne, NJ 07002

Telephone: 800-526-1440

DISCOUNT

Free Catalog

Return policy: Exchanges Only

Here's a place for big savings on fine china, crystal sterling and giftware. In their full-color catalog, you'll find pages of beautiful pieces at big savings. Top name brands in many patterns are available, and if you don't see what you're looking for, give them a call; they probably carry it.

PFALTZGRAFF

Telephone: 800-999-2811

P.O. Box 2048
York, PA 17405-2048

Free Catalog

Return policy: Money-Back Guarantee

You'll find a number of charming, affordable fine china patterns - from the simplistic to the elaborate - in Pfaltzgraff's latest mail-order catalog. The various collections include all the essential pieces; plus delightful teapots, canister sets, spice servers and candlesticks, among other extras. In some patterns, they offer decorative home accents like lamps, wall clocks, kitchen utensils and even bath accessories. Don't miss the popular "Christmas Heritage" and "Winterberry" holiday collections available year-round. Upon ordering, you'll also begin receiving the Pfaltzgraff Collector's Newsletter, filled with mouth-watering recipes and great entertaining ideas.

ROBIN IMPORTERS

Telephone: 800-223-3373
Fax No: 212-753-6480

510 Madison Avenue
New York, NY 10022

DISCOUNT

Send SASE For Catalog

Return policy: Returns Accepted For Exchange or Credit Only.

Robin Importers carries a complete selection of fine china, crystal, silver, flatware and giftware at 35-60% savings. Give them a call with the manufacturer's name and style/pattern number and they'll quote you a price. They ship anywhere in the US. Returns are accepted for exchange or store credit.

THE CHINA WAREHOUSE

Telephone: 800-321-3212

P.O. Box 21797
Cleveland, OH 44121

DISCOUNT

Free Brochure

Return policy: Money-Back Guarantee

Discount of 20% - 50% on most major brands of crystal, china, stainless, silverplate & sterling manufacturers. They also have substantial discounts on most major gift lines such as Lladro, Armetale, Nambe and Waterford. Some of the major china and crystal manufacturers carried are Lenox, Noritake, Royal Doulton, Spode, Wedgwood, Minton, Gorham, Rosenthal, Mikasa, Orrefors, Oneida, Sasaki, Villeroy & Boch and many more.

THE JOMPOLE COMPANY

Telephone: 212-594-0440

300 Seventh Avenue
New York, NY 10001

DISCOUNT

Free Information

Return policy: Exchanges Only; no returns on special orders

Savings of up to 50% and more are available on gorgeous china, flatware, crystal and watches from a wide assortmant of brand names. The Jompole Company can also special-order items not available in stock. Figurines and collectible items are available, as well. Price quotes can be given by phone and orders are shipped via UPS within a week.

THURBER'S

Telephone: 800-848-7237
Fax No: 401-732-4124

14 Minnesota Avenue
Warwick, RI 02888

DISCOUNT

Free Catalog

Return policy: Money-Back Guarantee if returned within 30 days

Compared with retail prices, Thurber's can save you money on their full selection of fine china, crystal sterling silver and stainless flatware. Name-brands include Royal Doulton, Gorham, Noritake, Towle, Wallace, Reed & Barton, Lenox, Wedgewood, Minton and others. They also have an outstanding selection of beautiful Christmas ornaments at similar savings. There's no sales tax issued on merchandise ordered outside Rhode Island and all items are shipped within 7-10 days.

VILLEROY & BOCH CHINA, CRYSTAL & GIFTS

Telephone: 908-788-5609

#97 Liberty Village
Flemington, NJ 08822

DISCOUNT

Free Information

Return policy: Money-Back Guarantee

This outlet resource carries overstocks and discounted patterns of famous names in china at tremendous savings everyday. Shop first, then call them with the pattern number you're looking for. Merchandise is shipped UPS in about 1 week. You might even live near one of their 8 outlet centers nationwide. For more information on the center near you, call (212)683-1747.

WINDSOR GIFT SHOP

Telephone: 800-631-9393

233-237 Main Street
Madison, NJ 07940

DISCOUNT

Free Catalog

Return policy: Money-Back Guarantee

Save up to 50% on many famous names in fine china, silver and crystal. Wedgwood, Coleport, Royal Doulton, Minton, Lenox and Gorham are just a few of the well-known brands they carry in china. They also offer comparable savings on silver by Towle, Gorham and Wallace, as well as crystal by Baccarat, Rosenthal & Edinburg, and more. No sales tax is issued on orders shipped outside of New Jersey.

C
H
I
N
A

C
R
Y
S
T
A
L

&

S
I
L
V
E
R

CHINA CHASERS

3280 Peachtree Corners Circle
Norcross, GA 30092

Free Information

Return policy: No Returns

Telephone: 404-441-9146

DISCOUNT

Replace the heirlooms you once thought were irreplaceable. China Chasers carries those out-of-production, hard-to-find china and crystal patterns from most major brands. All items are guaranteed new and unused - never seconds. Over 3,000 patterns are currently available in stock at discounts of up to 40%. Just call or send them the name of your pattern for a free inventory of pieces available.

JACQUELYNN'S CHINA MATCHING SERVICE

219 N. Milwaukwee Street
Milwaukee, WI 53202-5803

Free Brochure

Return policy: Money-Back Guarantee

Telephone: 414-272-8880

Complete and increase the value of the fine china service you thought was of limited use because replacement pieces were not available. For over 15 years, Jacquelynn's has helped thousands of customers worldwide add to or replace china services that were inherited, bought at auction or received as bridal gifts. They specialize in 13 English and American lines including Castleton, Coalport, Franciscan, Wedgwood and Royal Copenhagen. With over 5,000 patterns and a skilled sales staff, Jacquelynn's also specializes in the renewed art of pattern mixing.

PAST & PRESENTS REPLACEMENTS

65-07 Fitchett Street
Rego Park, NY 11374

Free Information

Return policy: No Returns

Telephone: 718-897-5515

DISCOUNT

Let Past & Presents Replacements make your tabletop dreams come true by replacing precious pieces. They carry discontinued, out-of-production and hard-to-find china, crystal and flatware at reasonable prices. Their large stock of discontinued tableware includes most major companies, like Lenox, Wedgwood, Denby, Franciscan, Mikasa, Noritake, Royal Doulton, Minton, Royal Worcester, Spode, Gorham, Metlox and others. Also, they have a large inventory of discontinued silverplated flatware.

REPLACEMENTS, LTD.

1089 Knox Rd., P.O. Box 26029
Greensboro, NC 27420

Free Information

Return policy: 30-Day Satisfaction Guarantee

Telephone: 919-697-3000
Fax No: 919-697-3100

Replacements, Ltd. has the world's largest inventory of obsolete, active & inactive china, crystal & flatware patterns. They carry all manufacturers of bone china, earthenware, crystal, sterling, silver plate & stainless flatware. Over 1.4 million pieces in 36,000 patterns available, with buyers across the country adding to their condition. Complete satisfaction guaranteed or you get a full refund!

HORIEN WREATH COMPANY

Telephone: 612-429-5569

3670 Auger Avenue
White Bear Lake, MN 55110

Free Brochure

COD

Return policy: No Returns

Horien Wreath Company can make sure you have a fresh, fragrant new wreath just in time for the holiday season, without having to resort to the plastic variety when you're short on holiday shopping time. Not just for Christmas anymore, wreaths and balsam door swags can look great year-round by simply trading the snow-covered pine cones, holly and red ribbonry for more neutral finishes that complement your home's decor. Horien Wreaths are shipped in bundles of 10, unless special ordered. They also give volume discounts for those planning to go on a decorating frenzy.

THE CRACKER BOX

Telephone: 215-862-2100

Route 202 & Aquetong Road
Solebury, PA 18963

Catalog $4.50 (can't be ordered by phone)

Return policy: Returns accepted only with written authorization

It's never too early to start planning for a spectacular Christmas and once you've seen the gorgeous tree ornaments you can make with Cracker Box kits, you'll want to 'plan' year-round! They have 250 exquisite designs; all originals and all backed by over 20 years in the holiday craft business. In fact, they say that one of their designs, "Crown Prince" took its rightful place on a tree in Buckingham Palace! Using delicate Austrian and Italian beads and jewels, some of the designs can be finished in as little as 2 hours. Most are ornate, if not baroque, but there are some more traditional styles like "Baby's First Christmas", "Wedding Ball", and "Here Comes Santa."

THE ORNAMENT RETAILER

Telephone: 800-524-6123

1231 East Main Street
Meriden, CT 06450

Free Brochures and Flyers

Return policy: Money-Back Guarantee

Hallmark Ornaments, Merry Miniatures, and Hallmark Gold Crown Galleries collectibles are now conveniently available by mail. Enesco, Carlton, Precious Moments and Coca-Cola ornaments are also offered, making The Ornament Retailer the place for Christmas ornament collectors. A secondary price guide shows the value of older ornaments and information on collector newsletters, magazines, etc. The Ornament Retailer sells at suggested retail prices, offers great customer service including layaways, and has early preview information on what's new for the upcoming season. Orders are shipped at once via UPS and reservations are available on "future releases."

47TH STREET PHOTO
36 East 19th Street
New York, NY 10003

Telephone: 800-847-4191
In NY 718-722-4760
Fax No: 212-353-8062

DISCOUNT

Catalog $2.00
Return policy: Money-Back Guarantee if returned within 30 days

Don't let the name fool you. Cameras and video supplies by Minolta, Canon, Pentax, Fuji and other famous makers are only the beginning. There's almost every electronic device imaginable, from TVs, VCRs, camcorders and stereo equipment to cordless phones, microwaves and calculators. Plus well-known names in watches, clocks, video games, electronic grooming aids! They have tons of computer supplies, with software, peripherals and accessories for nearly every major brand.

CELLULAR PHONE & ACCESSORY WAREHOUSE
934 Hermosa Avenue
Hermosa Beach , CA 90254

Telephone: 800-342-2336
Fax No: 310-379-5133

Free Brochure
Return policy: Money-Back Guarantee if returned within 30 days

Mitsubishi, Motorola, NEC, Panasonic and Audiovox are just a few of the trusted names you'll find at The Cellular Phone Warehouse. They have essential accessories for cellular phones like batteries, chargers, adaptors and carrying cases. They also carry portable and handheld phones under the same hi-end brands.

DAK INDUSTRIES, INC.
8200 Remmet Avenue
Canoga Park, CA 91304

Telephone: 800-888-7808
Fax No: 818-888-2837

Free Catalog
Return policy: Money-Back Guarantee

Even the most astute computer and electronics wiz will be amazed by the unheard-of electronic gadgetry found in the DAK Industries catalog. "Hi-tech" takes on a whole new meaning with their selection of cooking equipment, phone systems, computers, printers, stereos, speakers, CD players, CD ROM systems, software and more. If you're adiscriminating professional seeking the latest technologically advanced electronics, don't miss this remarkable resource. Music lovers will appreciate classical music collections offered on CD.

DAYTON COMPUTER SUPPLY
6501 State Route 123 North
Franklin, OH 45005

Telephone: 800-735-3272
Fax No: 513-743-4056

Free Brochure
Return policy: Money-Back Guarantee for 1 year from date of purchase

Dayton Computer Supply has earned a solid reputation as a nationwide distributor of quality computer supplies. They offer products from original manufacturers as well as compatible supplies, which include brands such as Verbatim, Apple, Canon, Epson, IBM, Panasonic, Toshiba and Okidata. A full range of supplies are available from diskettes and printer ribbons to copier, fax and computer paper.

COMPUTERS & ELECTRONICS

EASTCOAST SOFTWARE

422 Walton Avenue
Hummelstown, PA 17036

Telephone: 717-566-7240
Fax No: 717-566-1117

DISCOUNT

Free Catalog

Return policy: Money-Back Guarantee if returned within 30 days; entertainment products are returnable for Exchange Only

Get factory-direct prices on the computer software and accessory brands you trust, straight from the northeastern source. They've got hundreds of major brand-names to choose from including IBM, Apple, Microsoft and Panasonic. They also have a complete stock of fully integrated entertainment and educational programs, as well as graphics and desk-top publishing software.

ELEK-TEK

7530 North Linder Avenue
Skokie, IL 60077

Telephone: 800-395-1000
In IL 708-677-7660
Fax No: 708-677-7168

DISCOUNT

Free Catalog

Return policy: Defective merchandise replaced; otherwise all sales final

The world's best brands, the most current products, a superior selection and low, low prices highlight the pages of the Elek-Tek catalog of computers, computer accessories and supplies. Panasonic, Epson, Leading Edge, Okidata, Sharp and Verbatim head the list of top brands. Exceptional savings on personal computers, laptops, dot matrix printers, laser printers, fax modems, computer furniture, software; plus a full range of supplies and you've got a winning office combination.

FOCUS COMPUTERS & ELECTRONICS

4523 13th Avenue
Brooklyn, NY 11219

Telephone: 718-871-7600

DISCOUNT

Catalog $3.00

Return policy: Money-Back Guarantee, less 10% restocking fee

Focus Computers & Electronics can save you 20-50% on appliances, audio and video equipment, computers and related products, TV's and more. All major brands are available, so shop around, find the item you want and then give them a call for price quotes. Major items are dropped shipped.

FORDHAM-SCOPE

260 Motor Parkway
Hauppauge, NY 11788

Telephone: 800-695-4848
Fax No: 516-435-8079

Free Catalog

Return policy: Money-Back Guarantee if returned within 30 days

Get the most out of your electronics, increase the efficiency of your office, and save a bundle in electronic repairs by doing it yourself with audio/video supplies from the Fordham-Scope Catalog. Desktop laminators, indoor/outdoor surveillance equipment, dynamic stereo headphones, personal paper shredders, cordless phones, DJ equipment and even cordless shavers are all part of the diverse product line. If you know about the high cost of repairing electronics, you'll truly appreciate Fordham-Scope's huge assortment of repair equipment & supplies.

HEATH COMPANY
P.O. Box 8589
Benton Harbor, MI 49023-8589

Telephone: 800-44-HEATH
Fax No: 616-925-4876

DISCOUNT

Free Catalog

Return policy: Money-Back Guarantee if returned within 30 days

The catalog features an exclusive collection of unique products designed, developed and manufactured by the Heath Company, like Heath's House Sitter electronic security system, a talking alarm clock, clean-air machines and smoke detectors that attatch to your lightbulb's socket. Products also include computer software systems, books, stereo amplifiers and electronic datebooks.

JDR MICRODEVICES
2233 Samaritan Drive
San Jose, CA 95124

Telephone: 408-559-1200
Fax No: 408-559-0250

Free Catalog

Return policy: Money-Back Guarantee if returned within 30 days

Since 1979, JDR Microdevices has served the computer and electronics community with outstanding values on top-quality products, backed by impressive brandnames and superior service. They offer a toll-free technical support number, the own one-year warranty, and rigorous product testing, among other pluses. You'll also find a full range of hardware and software accessories, including integrated circuitry and repair equipment. for the serious "do-it-yourselfer."

LYBEN COMPUTER SYSTEMS
1150 Maplelawn
Troy, MI 48084

Telephone: 313-649-4500
Fax No: 313-649-2500

DISCOUNT

Free Catalog

Return policy: Money-Back Guarantee if returned within 30 days

This discount computer supply catalog offers up to 30% savings on a full range of software and hardware, computer maintenance products and office supplies. They have diskettes, computer paper and printers as well as efficient software systems by Avery, IBM and Macintosh. Helpful electronic products include keyboards, footpads, scanners, backup units and laser printer memory modules. Cleaning accessories, a wide array of storage cases and covers; plus sturdy machine stands round out the merchandise selection.

MACCONNECTION
14 Mill Street
Marlow, NH 03456

Telephone: 800-800-2222
Fax No: 603-446-7791

Free Catalog

Return policy: Money-Back Guarantee if returned within 30 to 60 days

MacConnection is more than a full-service computer supply resource. Their hallmark has been innovating the mail-order experience to make it easier for to get the supplies they want at competitive prices. You'll get discount prices on topbrand software, hardware and supplies, and you'll have access to a toll-free technical support hotline and recycled packaging that saves you money. There is a fun grouping of educational and entertainment program packages for computer buffs of all ages and levels of experience.

MACWAREHOUSE
P.O. Box 3013
Lakewood, NJ 08701-3013
Catalog $3.00
Return policy: Money-Back Guarantee

Telephone: 800-925-6227
Fax No: 908-905-9279
DISCOUNT

The current MacWarehouse catalog is jam-packed with the latest Macintosh computer products at unbeatable savings. Software systems by Adobe, Claris, Microsoft and Aldus can be in your hands by tomorrow using their innovative new Overnight Upgrade Service for just a $3.00 additional charge. They also offer state-of-the-art video imaging and desk-top publishing software, plus all the right business systems to keep your enterprise running at optimum efficiency. And of course, there are entertainment and computer game programs for those fanatics who just can't get enough from their Mac.

NEW MMI CORPORATION
2400 Reach Road
Williamsport, PA 17701
Free Catalog
Return policy: Exchanges Only

Telephone: 717-327-9200
Fax No: 717-327-1217

The New MMI Corporation claims to have pioneered the concept of a superstore in a catalog format. If the full-color catalog is any indication, that claim is true. There's a bountiful selection of nationally-known, name-brand products at superb discounts. Color monitors, disk drives, diskettes, keyboards, printers, fax machines; plus all the modern, hi-tech trimmings are available from manufacturers like Toshiba, Kodak, Microsoft and Quantum.

THE MAC ZONE
18005 NE 68th Street; Suite A-110
Redmond, WA 98052-9964
Catalog $2.00
Return policy: Exchanges Only

Telephone: 800-248-0800

Whether you're a computer wiz or you don't know a hard-drive from a hole in the ground, The Mac Zone has a trained, highly knowledgeable sales staff to help you with all your computer and electronic needs. They carry the best in famous-maker computer equipment from Macintosh, Microsoft, and Aldus, and others.Desk-top publishing and graphic design programs are their specialty. There are a number of integrated software packages and databases to choose from, not to mention monitors, keyboards, storage drives and all the accessories to make using a computer as easy as playing a video game. You'll also find a selection of your favorite games and educational programs, including Operation Desert Storm, Bungie Software and the Miracle Piano Teaching System.

A COOK'S WARES

Telephone: 412-846-9490

211 37th Street
Beaver Falls, PA 15010-2103

Catalog $2.00

Return policy: Money-Back Guarantee

Serving America's serious cooks and chefs since 1981, A Cook's Wares is a valued resource for fine gourmet cookware available worldwide. Prices are excellent, with savings of 20-40% on the best brands like Bourgeat, All-Clad and Cuisinart pans; Wüstof and Henckels knives; Michael Graves and Farberware cookery; plus utensils by Graham Kerr. Rare, name-brand kitchen appliances include Atlas Pasta Machines and food processors by Cuisinart and Krups. Don't pass up savings on famous-maker cutlery, spices, sauces, as well as the new cookbook selection.

ALESSI & BOURGEAT

Telephone: 508-990-2147

Howland Place, 651 Orchard Street
New Bedford, MA 02744

Free Catalog

Return policy: Refunds only on credit card orders returned within 30 days.

For those who love to cook, be it a large banquet or just supper for the family, Alessi & Bourgeat has a large inventory of imported French and Italian cookware. From huge chafing dishes saucepots, baking trays and casseroles to those hard-to-find items like fish poachers, wine coolers and crepe makers, you'll be amazed at the large selection. This distinctive, upscale cookery comes in heavyweight stainless steel, anodized aluminum or solid copper. There's also stainless steel coffeepots, table accessories and top quality utensils. Prices are a little higher, but longlasting, imported cookware like this is easily worth its weight in gold!

BAKER'S WRAP BY KAREN METZ & COMPANY

Telephone: 703-823-5647

P.O. Box 22008
Alexandria, VA 22304

Free Brochure & Pricelist

Return policy: Money-Back Guarantee

Here's a great way to present all your baked goods - from muffins and cookies to cakes and pastries. For holiday gift-giving or festive serving, they offer a number of patterned boxes that come with gift labels and waxed tissue to lock in that fresh-baked goodness. Red/white gingham check and multi-color confetti patterns are among the festive designs available.

CAPRILAND'S HERB FARM

Telephone: 203-742-7244

534 Silver Street
Coventry, CT 06238

Free Catalog

Return policy: Money-Back Guarantee

Deep in the heart of historic New England nestles Capriland's Herb Farm, offering everything for the herbal enthusiast, from gardening books, decorative baskets and crafts, to herbs, spices and seasonings. Don't miss the Christmas shop, handmade doll collection and exclusive Capriland's stoneware. They're unable to ship their live plants, but a selection of dried flowers and wreaths are available.

CHEF'S CATALOG

Telephone: 708-480-8312
Fax No: 708-480-8929

3215 Commercial Avenue
Northbrook, IL 60062-1900

Catalog $3.00

Return policy: Money-Back Guarantee

Your meals will echo the tastes of some of the best restaurants in the world when their prepared with cookware and kitchen aids from Chef's Catalog. Cutlery by Henckels, grills by Weber, cookware by Calphalon and appliances by Cuisinart, Krups and Kitchenaid are just some of the products you'll find in this full-color catalog. Missing an important appliance attachment? No problem. They offer a complete selection of attachments and accessories for all major models.

GRANDMA'S SPICE SHOP

Telephone: 410-672-0933

P.O. Box 472
Odenton, MD 21113

Free Catalog

Return policy: Money-Back Guarantee

As charming as it sounds, Grandma's Spice Shop brings you the very best in coffees, teas, herbs & spices at reasonable prices. Premium flavored, regular and decaffeinated coffees include delicious flavors like Mocha Java, Amaretto and Irish Cream. Loose black teas, rare estate teas and Benchley teas are available in hearty fruit and spice flavors. Add to all this a plethora of authentic herbs, spices and potpourri. Check out of natural plant oils, gift samplers, preserves and kitchen accents.

JESSICA'S BISCUIT COOKBOOK CATALOG

Telephone: 800-878-4264
Fax No: 617-527-0113

P.O. Box 301
Newtonville, MA 02160

Free Catalog

Return policy: 90-Day Satisfaction Guarantee

If it's edible, it's in here. Page after page of cookbooks for culinary artists of all styles and levels. There are books on French, German, Chinese, Greek, Hawaiian, Spanish and Brazilian cooking, only to name a few. Renowned TV chefs like Paul Prudhomme, Martin Yan and Julia Child fill you in their food secrets. This is a terrific way to expand your gourmet skills and spice up your diet. Why blindly experiment with unknown foods when you can be lead through the cooking process and avoid all of the problems most beginners face? Get this catalog and get cookin'!

PARIS INTERNATIONAL, INC.

Telephone: 202-544-6858

500 Independence Avenue, S.E.
Washington, D.C. 20003

Free Brochure

Return policy: Money-Back Guarantee

The folks at Paris International have select groupings of dependable, "tried & true" baking products that are hard to find elsewhere. Most of the products have been developed purely out of personal need, so you can be assured of their effectiveness no matter what you're baking. Choose from Paris Baguette French Bread Pans, San Francisco Sourdough Pans and 'Whole Oven' Baking Sheets. Each pan comes with distinctive baking recipes to guarantee success!

COOKING & KITCHENWARE.

PENZEY'S SPICE HOUSE, LTD.

Telephone: 414-768-8799

P.O. Box 1633
Milwaukee , WI 53201

Catalog $1.00

Return policy: Money-Back Guarantee

A family business since 1957, Penzey's Spice House grinds and blends high quality herbs & spices shipped direct to you to insure freshness. Herbs and delightful seasonings like adobo, basil, allspice, chervil and charnushka; as well as barbecue, chili pepper, and meat seasonings are available at great prices. Gift baskets include distinctive salad dressings, sauces and spice holders. Their catalog is seasoned with interesting tips on healthy cooking with spices and herbal extracts.

SAN FRANCISCO HERB COMPANY

Telephone: 800-227-4530
In CA 800-622-0768

250 14th Street
San Francisco, CA 94103

DISCOUNT

Free Catalog

Return policy: Money-Back Guarantee if returned within 15 days

Backed by over 19 years in the herb & spice industry, this is a great catalog of values on all the spices you need for cooking and crafts. Potpourri packages are a specialty here and they offer 33 recipes for your own scented concoctions. You'll also find fragrant oils, rare and exotic teas, nuts, seeds and herbal remedies. They offer volume discounts of 10-15% on orders of $200 or more.

SHIP TO SHORE, INC.

Telephone: 704-392-4740
Fax No: 704-392-4777

10500 Mount Holly Road
Charlotte, NC 28214-9347

Free Brochure

Return policy: Money-Back Guarantee

Hey mon! If you're looking for mouth-watering Caribbean recipes, herbs, spices, and colorful decorative accents for the home, look no further. Ship To Shore brings exotic treasures to you from the magical islands of the West Indies, including five books of tantalizing original recipes for main dishes, desserts, cocktails and hors d'oeuvres. Shrimp Cruzan, Champagne Framboise, Pina Colada French Toast and Paradise Pavlova are a few of the tempting delights. Tthe latest brochure gives information on booking a Caribbean holiday aboard a private yacht so that you can witness these island pleasures firsthand.

THE LITTLE FOX FACTORY

Telephone: 419-562-5420

931 Marion Road
Bucyrus, OH 44820

Free Information

Return policy: Money-Back Guarantee

The Little Fox Factory promises the most fun you'll ever have with bread and cookie dough this holiday season. They offer over 350 different cookie cutters, including miniatures. Along with conventional Christmas shapes, there are cutters shaped like kittens, pigs, cows, horses, mice, dogs, and even dog bones. Arrange assortments of your sweet treats in their decorative keepsake tins or wrapping paper for instant holiday gifts and crowd pleasers.

COOKING & KITCHENWARE

THE WOODEN SPOON
P.O. Box 931
Clinton, CT 06413-0931
Free Catalog
Return policy: Money-Back Guarantee

Telephone: 203-664-0303

Everything that is new and unique in specialty cookware can be found in the pages of The Wooden Spoon catalog. Gourmet cooking is easy and exciting given their clever cooking tools that'll help you win raves at the dinner table. Stainless steel cookware, European pressure cookers, Swiss salad spinners, Glass food steamers and cast-iron fajita skillets are just a few of the items offered. They also have attractive serving utensils and kitchen accents for the discriminating gourmet.

WESTON BOWL MILL
P.O. Box 218
Weston, VT 05161
Free Catalog
Return policy: Exchanges and Store Credit if returned within 30 days

Telephone: 802-824-6219
Fax No: 802-824-4215

If you're partial to wooden kitchen accents, decorative accessories and indoor/outdoor furniture, look to Weston Bowl Mill. They have all of these items and more at discount factory-direct prices. Hardwoods like maple, walnut and birch are offered, natural or finished. You'll also find high quality shelving, toys and country store items in the finest wood available by mail.

WILLIAMS-SONOMA
P.O. Box 7456
San Francisco, CA 94120-7456
Free Catalog
Return policy: Money-Back Guarantee

Telephone: 800-541-1262
Fax No: 415-421-5153

For years, Williams-Sonoma has supplied America's cooks with a select range of fine products, including the latest innovations in cookware, kitchen utensils and other food preparation items. Many of the items pictured in the full-color catalog come direct from recent European and American culinary trade fairs, while others are more specialized pieces that are hard to find elsewhere. Their Duotherm Plus Thermal Pot, a revolutionary pot for cooking  and keeping food warm for hours, and the Frieling Hot Rock Grill for tabletop or buffet grilling, are prime examples. They also have the Tortilla Chef tortilla maker, The Simac Ice Cream Machine, The Saeco Super Automatica Twin Espresso Machine and the Vitantonio Electric Pizelle Iron, among other cookware innovations.

AMERICA'S HOBBY CENTER, INC.
146 West 22nd Street
New York, NY 10011-2466

Telephone: 212-675-8922
Fax No: 212-633-2754
DISCOUNT

Catalog $1.00

Return policy: Money-Back Guarantee if returned within 14 days

Celebrating over 60 years in the discount hobby supply business, America's Hobby Center proudly presents notable savings on model locomotive sets, repair parts and a cargo of accessories. They specialize in steam and diesel engine trains by Tyco, Bachman, Atlas, Con-Cor and others. You'll also find life-like landscaping models to set the scene for hours of locomotive action and enjoyment.

AMERICAN COIN & STAMP BROKERAGE, INC.
45-A Merrick Avenue
Merrick, NY 11566

Telephone: 800-682-2272
Fax No: 516-546-2315

Free Catalog

Return policy: Exchanges In Certain Circumstances.

Buy U.S. and foreign coins, stamps and baseball cards at the same price as your dealer pays. Their catalog has over 5,000 individuals lots, or call for your specific "want" lists. They purchase for over 4,000 clients and frequently handle estate liquidations. Appraisals, consultations and estate planning available. Your satisfaction is always guaranteed.

ARTGRAFIX
15 Tech Circle
Natick, MA 01760

Telephone: 800-443-4421
Fax No: 508-655-3390
DISCOUNT

Catalog $3.00

Return policy: Money-Back Guarantee

You find stupendous savings of up to 70% on a vast assortment of art materials and supplies, and also see many items you wouldn't expect to find in the Artgrafix catalog. Of course they have the assorted art papers, choice paints, markers, specialized art equipment, frames, art furniture and portfolios as well as high quality computer furniture, office supplies and filing/storage systems. They have a knowledgeable customer service staff ready to help you with office and studio space planning, special orders and technical product information, among other needs.

BERMAN LEATHERCRAFT, INC.
25 Melcher Street
Boston, MA 02210-1599

Telephone: 617-426-0870
Fax No: 617-357-8564

Catalog $3.00   House Account

Return policy: Money-Back Guarantee ($15 restocking fee) within 14 days

Leathercrafters can get those essential, but hard-to-find supplies conveniently delivered by mail without setting a foot in a craft or hobby store. Beginners, professionals and instructors of the rewarding craft are the targets for this resource. It features shearlings, snake skins, rabbit skins and leather hides from fine tanneries around the world, easy-to-assemble kits from the Boston factory, plus the most economical line of hand tools, hardware, and solid brass belt buckles. If you've been searching for special leather dyes and preservatives, this is the place to find them at discount prices.

CHERRY TREE TOYS, INC.
P.O. Box 369
Belmont, OH 43718
Catalog $1.00

Telephone: 800-848-4363

Return policy: 30-Day Money Back Guarantee.

If you love to work with your hands, love knick knacks or have kids or grand-kids, you must get the Cherry Tree Toys catalog. Dollhouses, wild west wagons, whirligigs, clocks and toys in kits designed for all skill levels. In addition to unassembled kits, they offer tools and hardware so you can create your own wooden masterpieces. All the supplies necessary to build everything in this catalog are offered, so you can see what you want and make it happen.

CO-OP ARTISTS' MATERIALS
P.O. Box 53097
Atlanta, GA 30355
Free Catalog

Telephone: 800-877-3242
Fax No: 404-872-0294
DISCOUNT

Return policy: Money-Back Guarantee

Beginners and serious pros can use this one-stop-shopping resource for purchasing arts & crafts supplies - most at discount prices. They have virtually everything you'll need - from paints, markers, brushes and art paper, to name-brand airbrush equipment, artists' furniture and sturdy portfolios. You'll also find an assortment of how-to books and videos at exceptional discounts. They've even got a collection of frames to give whatever you're creating fine art finish.

COTTON CLOUDS
Rt. 2 Desert Hills #16
Safford, AZ 85546
$10, refunded with order of $50.00

Telephone: 800-322-7888
DISCOUNT

Return policy: Money-Back Guarantee

Cotton Clouds brings you high quality and big discounts on all your knitting needs. Specializing in luxurious cotton yarns in a spectrum of colors and textures, they offer samples of these yarns along with their informative catalog which features various project kits for knitting sweaters, scarves and accessories. As a catalog subscriber, you'll get regular newsletters with helpful hints and tips on new techniques, tools and machinery. They also have electronic knitting machines, looms, and weavers are available by the industry leader - Bond.

CRAFT KING
P.O. Box 90637
Lakeland , FL 33804
Free Catalog

Telephone: 813-686-9600
Fax No: 813-688-5072
DISCOUNT

Return policy: Refunds and exchanges when authorized only

Pick a hobby, any hobby! Craft King has the discount craft and hobby supplies to make the fun worth your while. For serious painters, there are paints by Signa-tex, Ceramcoat, Permalba and Bob Ross; as well as top-quality canvas, easels and brushes. For craft enthusiasts, there are quilting supplies, fabric paints, dyes, yarns, glass staining, latch hook kits and more. Plus, you'll find a bounty of dollmaking materials including complete kits, forms and stands.

DANIEL SMITH ARTISTS' MATERIALS
4130 First Avenue South
Seattle, WA 98134-2302
Catalog $3.00
Return policy: Money-Back Guarantee

Telephone: 800-426-7923
Fax No: 206-224-0404

This company's name graces a number of products including printmakers' inks, oil paints, acrylics, watercolors, easels and brushes. They specialize in hard-to-find papers such as papyrus, banana paper, Gogon grass paper and drawing paper by Strathmore. You'll also find tools and machinery for more involved works of art, from airbrush compressors and lucigraphs to Japanese block printing supplies. Canvas, canvas stretchers and designer frames come in a number of sizes.

DICK BLICK ART MATERIALS
P.O. Box 1267
Galesburg, FL 61401
Free Catalog
Return policy: Money-Back Guarantee if returned within 30 days

Telephone: 800-723-2787
Fax No: 309-343-5785

Even if you don't have an artistic bone in your body, you'll be amazed at the artful creations you can whip-up with supplies offered by Dick Blick. From the simple to the high-tech, their massive catalog has products for paper art, printmaking, painting, sculpting, jewelrymaking and other creative arts. They also carry durable art & drawing furniture that's equally versatile for home or studio. How-to books and videos take you from novice to master in less time than you'd imagine.

EDMUND SCIENTIFIC
101 East Gloucester Pike
Barrington, NJ 08007-1380
Catalog $3.00
Return policy: Money-Back Guarantee if returned within 45 days

Telephone: 609-573-6260
Fax No: 609-573-6295

The "mad scientist" in you will go into overdrive when you thumb through the pages of endless scientific wonders offered by Edmund Scientific. Here's a great resource for science project paraphernalia, from complete kits to compatible supplies. Robotic kits, prehistoric dinosaur models, human anatomy kits and working hot-air balloons are some exciting examples. You'll also find awesome projects that explore the hidden treasures of outer space, electronic wizardry, the environment and biology. High-tech microscopes, telescopes, video equipment and other marvels make this an excellent resource for teachers, too.

ENTERPRISE ART
P.O. Box 2918
Largo, FL 34649
Free Catalog
Return policy: Money-Back Guarantee

Telephone: 813-536-1492
Fax No: 813-536-3509

Whether you're crafting something special for gift-giving or just hoping to keep the kids busy after school, Enterprise Art has the supplies for months of fun projects. Craft beads, jewelry parts, fashion paints and iron-on transfers just scratch the surface. They also have lots of hard-to-find items, including latch hook grids, pottery supplies & fabric dyes. They gladly offer discounts when you buy in bulk.

HERRSCHNER'S CRAFTS
Hoover Road
Stevens Point, WI 54492
Catalog $2.00
Return policy: Money-Back Guarantee

Telephone: 715-341-0560
Fax No: 715-341-2250

America's foremost craft catalog has been offering the largest selection of needlework kits and other craft supplies since 1899. The latest issue contains pages of kits for afghans, tablecloths, sequin art, quilting, latch hook rugs and soft sculpture; plus a broad line of decorator Christmas kits.

HOBBY SURPLUS SALES
287 Main Street; P.O. Box 2170
New Britain, CT 06050
DISCOUNT
Catalog $3.00
Return policy: Money-Back Guarantee

Telephone: 203-233-0872

Hobby Surplus Sales' catalog of values brings quality discount hobby supplies to mail-order customers. Look for markdowns and discounts on model railroading kits, repair parts and accessories by Lionel, American Flyer, MDK, REA, Bachman, Lifelike, Atlas and Model Power. They have die cast, plastic and wooden replicas of the world's hottest cars, from the authentic 1959 New York Checker Cab to the 1970 Mustang Boss. Sci-Fi buffs, get awesome replicas from Star Trek, Star Wars, Bat Man, Ghost Busters, Back to the Future and RoboCop.

IVY IMPORTS, INC.
12213 Distribution Way
Beltsville, MO 20705
Free Catalog
Return policy: Returns accepted for exchange only.

Telephone: 301-595-0550

Order authentic French dyes and paints for "Silk Painting" on all fabrics. Some can be used on silk and wool only, while others are good for all fabrics and are the easiest and the most fun to use when painting on t-shirts and sweats. All dyes and paints are ready to use, easy to apply and long lasting. You can also purchase how-to books and videos; plus brushes and metal-tipped applicators.

JAN'S SMALL WORLD
3146 Myrtle
Billings, MT 59102
Free Catalog
Return policy: Money-Back Guarantee if returned within 10 days

Telephone: 406-652-2689

Now you can have the homes you've always dreamed about. Though you won't be able to live in them, these doll houses are truly awesome. Jan's Small World offers a huge assortment of doll houses and miniature furnishings that are so incredibly close to the original. Accuracy in design and detail will amaze you as you construct San Francisco-style mansions, New England colonials, English manors and other styles. Inside, furnish these 'homes' with beautiful Chippendale and Queen Anne miniature reproductions. They're truly heirloom treasures (not to be confused with mere toys) and will give you and your little one hours of play .

JERRY'S ARTARAMA

P.O. Box 1105
New Hyde Park, NY 11040
Catalog $2.50

Telephone: 800-U-ARTIST
Fax No: 516-328-6752
DISCOUNT

Return policy: Returns accepted with proper authorization only

Jerry's "ALWAYS SAVE" Catalog saves up to 70%. You don't have to be a wholesale buyer to save a bundle on paints, canvas, easels, artists' furniture, drawing pencils, brushes, special paper products, or specialized equipment like airbrushes and artograph projectors. They also have an extensive selection of instructional books and videos by well-known contemporary artists like Dana Jester, Gary Jenkins and Joyce Pike. They have a huge frame and mat grouping in an assortment of styles, sizes and colors.

KAYDEE BEAD & CRAFT SUPPLY

P.O. Box 07340
Fort Myers, FL 33919
Catalog $2.00

Telephone: 813-433-3606

DISCOUNT

Return policy: Returns accepted with proper authorization only

If your creative endeavors involve beading or other special trimmings, Kaydee Bead & Craft Supply has a fantastic array of styles to choose from. If you can string it, they've got it - beads of faux pearl, silver plate, plastic, synthetic gems and simulated bone. They also have leather lacing, nylon ribbon, jewelry clasps, earposts and more. Items are sold in bulk so you'll receive terrific savings over the retail prices. How-to books, beginner and advanced kits are available, too.

KIDSART

P.O. Box 274
Mt. Shasta, CA 96067
Free Catalog

Telephone: 916-926-5076
Fax No: 916-926-5076

Return policy: Money-Back Guarantee

Get those artistic juices flowing in your kids with entertaining, educational art and craft ideas specifically designed for young minds by KidsArt. Painting and drawing projects are only the tip of the iceberg! They can learn about printmaking, sculpture, origami and jazzying up their wardrobes with wearable art and fabric paints. They'll develop an appreciation for fine art given the informative historical books by Janson, Raboff other famous art historians. KidsArt also offers a wide assortment of essential supplies including paints, markers, specialized paper, art pencils and storage items for the young artist.

MARY MAXIM

2001 Holland Avenue; P.O. Box 5019
Port Huron, MI 48060-5019
Free Catalog

Telephone: 800-962-9504

Return policy: Money-Back Guarantee

Mary Maxim is the ideal place for buying exclusive needlework kits and other fun crafts. You'll find a wide selection of project kits, including adorable baby toys to make, beautiful table linens to embroider, exciting knitwear fashions to whip up, as well as all the essential supplies.

PASTIMES
Telephone: 800-372-5282

4844 Commerce Parkway
Cleveland, OH 44128

Free Catalog

Return policy: Money-Back Guarantee

If you've think the best you can expect from mail order craft & hobby supply is tired model vehicles and mediocre macrame, think again. You'll enjoy these projects to display or give as gifts. Classic antique clocks, Schwinn commemorative bikes, legendary model cars, kites, sailboats, and die-cast model planes are just great openers. Other treasures include working musical instruments and historical reproductions like Leonardo da Vinci's Flying Machine or the Guttenberg Printing Press. They've even got dinosaur kits and the intriguing doll houses.

PATTERNWORKS
Telephone: 914-462-8000
Fax No: 914-462-8074

P.O. Box 1690
Poughkeepsie, NY 12601

Free Catalog

Return policy: Money-Back Guarantee

Especially for the 'knit-picky', Patternworks has a wide range of hard-to-find products and accessories for knitting, crocheting, weaving, macrame. Handy helpers keep the fun ahead of the frustration - yarn holders, magnifying glasses, neat tools and the latest how-to books. Lace knitters will love the clever tools and supplies for their specialized craft. You'll also find home cleaning remedies to keep your knitted creations looking fresh, warm and cozy for seasons to come.

PEARL PAINT COMPANY, INC.
Telephone: 212-431-7932

308 Canal Street
New York, NY 10013

DISCOUNT

Free Catalog

Return policy: Exchanges only if returned within 14 days

Pearl Paint is a leader in art and craft supplies for beginners, professionals and students, offering discount of 20-70%. They've even added furniture to their catalog. Now you can buy drafting tables, ergonomically designed seating, lighting fixtures, taborets and artists' cabinets among other specialized furnishings. In addition, their technical department offers the lowest prices available on lucigraphs, opaque projectors, draft supplies and more.

S&S ARTS & CRAFTS
Telephone: 800-937-3482
Fax No: 203-537-2866

P.O. Box 513
Colchester , CT 06415-0513

Free Catalog

Return policy: Money-Back Guarantee

Inspire hours of creative genius in yourself and your kids with entertaining craft projects Lively home decorations, wearable art treasures, personalized gift items and more are at your mail-order fingertips. From paint-by-number kits to stained glass projects, they're challenging enough for even intermediate-level children. Whether you're planning rainy-day activities, children's club projects or travel-time 'busywork', you'll find everything you need in each kit.

SHILLCRAFT LATCH HOOK KITS

8899 Kelso Drive
Baltimore, MD 21221

Telephone: 410-682-3064
Fax No: 410-682-3130

Catalog $2.00

Return policy: Money-Back Guarantee

A leader in latch hook kits and other fine crafts since 1949, Shillcrafts offers challenging projects with the best materials and supplies. A rainbow of colors in imported wool or acrylic yarns match your every decorating need. The latest techniques let you make rugs, wall hangings and pillows. Select from a wide range of patterns like oriental designs, florals, landscapes, juvenile, and animal pattern kits. They also have cross stitch kits, beautifully designed on linen fabric, including floral and animal prints, plus their own Carousel Collection.

SUNCOAST DISCOUNT ARTS & CRAFTS

9015 U.S. Highway 19 North
Pinellas Park , FL 34666

Telephone: 813-577-6331
Fax No: 813-576-0835

DISCOUNT

Catalog $2.00

Return policy: Money-Back Guarantee

Professionals and hobbyists alike will appreciate the 30-60% savings on this gigantic assortment of craft supplies. They have the basics like paints, yarns, canvas and mounting boards. But they also have a tremendous selection of supplies for weaving, antiquing, macrame and jewelrymaking. There are cake decorating supplies, sculpting & casting tools, stencil kits and how-to books for every craft. One peek inside their latest 235-page catalog will make you creative.

THE FRUGAL FOX

P.O. Box 369
Fontana, WI 53125

Telephone: 414-275-9767

Free Brochure

Return policy: Satisfaction Guaranteed

If your hobby is custom-crafting pillows and stuffed toys, you know what a difference the right stuffings and fillings can make in the life of your creation. The Frugal Fox has polyester pillow forms, bonded polyester quilt batts and fiberfill for long-lasting fullness in whatever you're creating. These items are available loose or formed, and are safe and fully washable.

TOWER HOBBIES
P.O. Box 9078
Champaign , IL 61826-9078

Telephone: 800-637-6050
Fax No: 217-356-6608

Free Catalog

Return policy: Money-Back Guarantee if returned within 30 days

Little kids and 'big kids' alike will appreciate Tower Hobbies' tremendous assortment of model airplanes, boats, trucks and race cars with complete assembly equipment. These models are as much fun as you remember and Tower Hobbies can ship most parts already assembled so that the fun can begin sooner! For those who think half the fun is in the assembly, there are name-brand engines, parts, modeling essentials, controls and battery packs. Model vehicle enthusiasts will recognize top brands like Hobbico, ARF, Lanier, and Top Flite.

VAN DYKE'S TAXIDERMY SUPPLY
4th Avenue & 6th Street, P.O. Box 278
Woonsocket, SD 57385

Telephone: 605-796-4425
Fax No: 605-796-4085

Free Catalog

Return policy: Money-Back Guarantee if returned within 30 days

Since 1940, Van Dyke's has been the name in quality taxidermy supplies. For the sportsman who takes pride in preserving and displaying the catch, Van Dyke's has all the taxidermy tools, accessories and supplies for life-like results. From fish, reptiles and amphibians, to felines and game animals, they have mounting forms, artificial eyes, jaw sets, and ear liners to make your recreation come alive. They even have a unique assortment of leathers, vinyls and fake furs. For the less adventurous, there are wood carvings, lamps and wildlife prints to give your home the feel of the great outdoors.

WARNER-CRIVELLARO, INC.
1855 Weaversville Road
Allentown, PA 19103

Telephone: 800-523-4242
Fax No: 800-523-5012

DISCOUNT

Catalog $2.00

Return policy: Money-Back Guarantee

If stained glass is your hobby or business enterprise, don't buy another supply item until you've checked out the great savings on manufacturer-direct merchandise offered by Warner-Crivellaro, Inc. Their wholesale catalog features the most complete selection of glass, tools, and related supplies at unbeatable prices. Further discounts are available on quantity purchases. (See coupon at back of the book).

CAROLINE'S COUNTRY RUFFLES

Telephone: 704-867-4503

420 West Franklin Boulevard
Gastonia, NC 28052

Free Catalog

Return policy: Money-Back Guarantee if returned within 30 days

Put that cozy, "down home" feeling in your home with curtains from Caroline's Country Ruffles. Perfect for fans of frou frou, virtually all items have at least a ruffle or two. Simpler styles include straight panels with optional cascade or jabot valances. Mix and match solids with prints for distinctive results. They also have shower curtains, ruffled wreaths, pillows and lampshades.

COUNTRY CURTAINS

Telephone: 800-937-1237
Fax No: 413-243-1067

The Red Lion Inn
Stockbridge, MA 01262-0955

Free Catalog

Return policy: Money-Back Guarantee

A family-owned company started in 1956, Country Curtains is home to hundreds of curtain and drapery styles in a full range of fabrics, patterns and colors. Buzzwords like practical, energy-saving, economical and versatile describe the merchandise, while assuring you of quality that will grace your home for years. Designs range from simple, straight curtains to lace panels and elaborate ruffled varieties with curved valances and dressmaker details. They'll customize designs with matching bedding and linen accessories; plus rugs, pillows and lamps.

DANA'S CURTAINS & DRAPERIES

Telephone: 908-852-5812
Fax No: 908-852-2763

105 Mountain Avenue
Hackettstown, NJ 07840

Catalog $4.00

Return policy: Exchanges and replacements with return authorization

Here's a complete line of custom made curtains and draperies. When you open the full-color catalog, you'll see all the interesting and inventive accessories that can be made to accent or match your existing decor. They have traditional solids, stripes and florals in draperies, table linens, bedding and bath accessories. Fabrics can be purchased to cover walls, too, for a complete, picture-perfect look.

DIANTHUS, LTD.
P.O. Box 870
Plymouth , MA 02362
Catalog $5.00

Telephone: 508-747-4179
Fax No: 508-830-0313

Return policy: Money-Back Guarantee if returned within 10 days

For those who love classic country decor, Dianthus has a wonderful group of fine curtains and accessories Items shown in their catalog are handmade in the time honored way, at home, by "cottage craftspeople." We're not just talking curtains. They'll send you the fabric to make matching table linens, bed linen and slipcovers. Traditional curtain styles incude swaggers, valances, hourglass designs and shades. They can also provide you with all the tools to complete your decorating project including curtain rods, tiebacks and swag holders.

LINEN & LACE
4 Lafayette St.
Washington, MO 63090-2541
Catalog $2.00

Telephone: 800-332-LACE
Fax No: 314-239-0070

Return policy: Satisfaction Guaranteed

Linen & Lace provides just what the name says, lace window curtains that will look great in your kitchen, bath or bedroom. Pillow shams and doilies are also available, as are tablecloths, gloves and curtains for french doors. Their catalog is full of clear photographs that faithfully display the merchandise. The Color choices are white, off white or ivory, so don't expect to find bright colors. Expect high-quality window furnishings with simple designs.

ADELE-BISHOP

Telephone: 800-334-4186

P.O. Box 3349, Dept. SM 12
Kinston, NC 28502

Catalog $3.50, refunded with 1st order

Return policy: Satisfaction Guaranteed

Enjoy the charm of decorative stenciling in your home. Select from over 150 beautiful motifs, including Historic, Native American, Classic, Period and Children's Themes, as well as the new Adele-Bishop Designer Collection of Floral renditions. You'll decorate easily and professionally with these pre-cut stencils, how-to books, quality paints and brushes. All are beautifully illustrated in the full-color catalog.

AMERICAN HOME STENCILS

Telephone: 414-425-5381

10007 S. 76th Street
Franklin, WI 53132

Free Catalog

Return policy: Exchanges Only

Traditional, Cottage-Style, Country and Juvenile are among the themes that inspire the lovely, pre-cut decorative stencils offered by American Home Stencils. You'll find some very unusual and clever designs from ballet and circus motifs for the kids' rooms, to romantic floral motifs that bloom in the bath and bedrooms. They also have ceiling borders with corner stencils to match, as well as spot designs and religious motifs.

GAIL GRISI STENCILS

Telephone: 609-354-1757

P.O. Box 1263
Haddonfield, NJ 08033

Catalog $2.00, refunded with1st order

Return policy: Money-Back Guarantee if returned within 6 months

Intricate stenciling and border art - those finishing touches that add decorative interest to any room in your home. Gail Grisi offers an assortment of pre-cut stencils in colors and designs for every room in the house. There are Victorian and country florals, as well as sophisticated geometrics. For children, they have fun animal designs and circus themes. Use the catalog's tips on stenciling variations to produce one-of-a-kind decorative accents.

JEANNIE SERPA STENCILS

Telephone: 401-423-0230

Letourneau Center Rt. 202
Rindge, NH 03461

Free Brochure

Return policy: Money-Back Guarantee

Jeannie Serpa Stencils are laser cut from the finest stencil material - five mil mylar. You'll find them easy to use, complete with register guides for easy alignment and overlays for separate colors. Included in the current catalog are original designs used in the PBS television series "This Old House." Topiaries, cascading vines, and curling ribbon are among the motifs available. Stencils can be used for borders or painted all over the wall for striking trompe l'oeil effects.

**D
E
C
O
R
A
T
I
N
G**

STENART   Telephone: 609-589-9857
P.O. Box 114
Pitman , NJ 08071-0114
Catalog $2.50

Return policy: Money-Back Guarantee if returned within 30 days; custom
items are non-returnable.

From the basic to the elaborate, StenArt presents a generous assortment of stencil
kits, cross stitch kits and accessories to turn your decorating ideas in to real
works of art. Birds, florals, leaves and animals highlight many of the pattern
themes. The catalog offers helpful hints on achieving individual results by com-
bining patterns and colors for surprising effects. You'll also find the most charming cross stitch kits for wall accents, kitchen accessories and more. StenArt will
even custom-cut your own stencil designs at an additional cost.

STENCIL HOUSE OF NEW HAMPSHIRE, INC.   Telephone: 800-622-9416
P.O. Box 16109   In NH 603-625-1716
Hooksett, NH 03106
Catalog $2.50, refunded with 1st order
Return policy: Money-Back Guarantee

The decorative art of stenciling has been revived and is now a popular alternative
to the rising costs and tiresome application of paint and wallpaper. Stencil
House of New Hampshire has a selection of over 180 stencils, including those
traced from Old New England walls as well as Penn-Dutch motifs, Victorian,
children's patterns and Early American designs. The stencils are made of
durable, reusable mylar and can be used to stencil walls, staircases, fabric, paper
or just about any other paintable surface. The Stencil House also has just the
right colors and paintbrushes to give you perfect results.

BLOOMINGDALE'S BY MAIL, LTD.

Telephone: 800-777-0000

475 Knotter Drive
Chesire, CT 06410-1130

Free Catalog

Return policy: Money-Back Guarantee

Bloomingdale's is a household word, as is their unsurpassed style, quality and service. In the mail-order spotlight, they're an indespensible resource for the discriminating shopper with little time to cruise the retail circuit. Blockbuster clothing and accessories for women and men feature names like Norma Kamali, Ellen Tracy, Christian Dior, Claiborne Men and Pronto Uomo. Sophisticated home accents include tableware by Retroneu, linens by Ralph Lauren, crystal by Waterford.

JC PENNEY CO. INC.

Telephone: 800-222-6161

Circulation Dept. Box 2056
Milwaukee, WI 53201-2056

Catalog $5.00 (Mdse. Certificate $10)

Return policy: Money-Back Guarantee

JC Penney is like an old friend- someone you can trust and rely on. Their selection encompasses a wide array of merchandise from sneakers to clock radios to toys to strollers, but you know that. They carry lots of brand name merchandise as well as lots under their own label. If you haven't seen their catalog in a while it's time you called to start receiving it again as they have upgraded their look and are "looking smarter than ever - J C Penney". They are the source for almost all of your family's needs.

NEIMAN MARCUS

Telephone: 800-825-8000

P.O. Box 2968
Dallas, TX 75221-2968

Free Catalog

Return policy: Credit Only

All the fashion savvy and quality merchandise you've come to expect from the retail stores is also in the Neiman Marcus mail-order catalog. It features values on name-brand clothing, fragrances, & fashionable accessories for men and women. Well-known labels like Bill Blass, Perry Ellis, Anne Klein II, Alfred Sung and Leon Max adorn such products, most not available in Neiman Marcus stores.

SAKS FIFTH AVENUE FOLIO COLLECTIONS

Telephone: 800-322-7257

557 Tuckahoe Road
Yonkers, NY 10710

Free Catalog

Return policy: Money-Back Guarantee

An American retail legend, born on New York's famous thoroughfare, Saks Fifth Avenue Folio Collections offers you exquisite finds in designer clothing and accessories, jewelry, gourmet foods, fragrances and fantastic gift items for the whole family. Adolfo, Judith Leiber, Anne Klein by Louis Dell'Olio, and Joseph Abboud are just some of the famous makers. One-of-a-kind decorative treasures include delicate glassware, heirloom jewelry boxes, nostalgic artifacts.

D
E
P
A
R
T
M
E
N
T

S
T
O
R
E
S

SEARS, ROEBUCK & COMPANY

P.O. Box 740049
Atlanta, GA 30374-9812

Telephone: 800-366-3000

DISCOUNT

Catalog $5.00

Sears, 💳 〰️

Return policy: Money-Back Guarantee

America's oldest and most trusted name in mail-order merchandise keeps getting better and better. The Sears catalog of top-quality products denies categorization. They have virtually everything you want in family apparel, home decorating and improvement, automotive supply, gardening, electronics and recreation. Current styling and well-known name-brands highlight the family clothing collections, including sportswear separates, career clothing, formalwear, sleepwear, swimwear and activewear. For your home, there's everything to accent or completely remodel the interior, as well as gardening supplies and finishing touches for the exterior.

SPIEGEL

1040 West 35th Street
Chicago, IL 60609-1494

Telephone: 605-348-8100
Fax No: 800-422-6697

Free Catalog

💳 💳 ⚬ 〰️

Return policy: Money-Back Guarantee

Spiegel has for years been your number one resource for the essentials - be it clothing and accessories or home furniture and accents. In clothing, you won't make any 'irrational' purchases that'll end up in the back of your closet. The buyers at Spiegel have taken extra care in offering practical, versatile career suits and separates, sportswear, outerwear and the must-have accessories that pull it all together. Taking the concept a step further, Speigel has designed a series of specialized catalogs that 'zero-in' on the needs of specific consumers including Spiegel Talls, Spiegel Petites and For You From Spiegel (for sizes 14 and up). But, keep turning the pages. Pretty soon, you'll get to their sophisticated selection of home furnishings of the functional design you love most in colors and textures to enliven your existing decor.

THE ULTIMATE OUTLET

P.O. Box 88251
Chicago, IL 60680-1251

Telephone: 605-348-8100
Fax No: 800-422-6697

DISCOUNT

Free Catalog

💳 💳 ⚬ 〰️

Return policy: Satsifaction Guaranteed.

Here's The Ultimate Outlet, and you can browse through it on your own time at home. Brand name mens and womens fashions and shoes are offered at low prices. Great gift ideas like anniversary clocks, crystal lamps and antique reproductions can make shopping for special occasions easy. Owned by Spiegel, this catalog offers electronics by Sharp, GE and Emerson that are the same items for sale in other catalogs at 50% more!

DEPARTMENT STORES

ELDRIDGE TEXTILE COMPANY
277 Grand Street
New York, NY 10002

Telephone: 212-925-1523
Fax No: 212-219-9542

DISCOUNT

Catalog $3.00
Return policy: 10-Day Money Back Guarantee. Custom orders not returnable.

In business since 1940, Eldridge textile offers rock-bottom prices on most major manufacturers of sheets, pillowcases, comforters and towels, such as Fieldcrest, Martex, Revman, Springmaid, Stevens, Utica and Wamsutta. In addition, they carry a full selection of bedspreads, comforter sets, curtains and draperies from Blue Ideal, Cameo Interiors, Croscil, Crown Crafts, Dakota, Fashion Home Products and more, as well as bathroom accessories and shower curtains. Also, if there is a specific product you are looking for that is not in their catalog, just give them a ring. They'll do their best to find it for you.

FABRICS BY PHONE
P.O. Box 309
Walnut Bottom, PA 17286

Telephone: 800-233-7012

DISCOUNT

Free Information
Return policy: Money-Back Guarantee, less 25% restocking fee, with proper advance authorization

The name says it all, make a call to Fabrics By Phone and compare prices, selection and service on antique satins and decorative fabrics. Be sure to state the style of fabric you're looking for so they can send you free samples for your perusal. They also have a custom workroom for drapes, bedspeads and other decorative fabric accessories. Shipping is by UPS, usually in 2 weeks or less.

HOME SEW
P.O. Box 4099, Dept SB
Bethlehem, PA 18018

Telephone: 215-867-3833
Fax No: 215-837-9115

DISCOUNT

Free Catalog
Return policy: Satisfaction Guaranteed

Sew, where can you save up to 65% on sewing and craft supplies? In the Home-Sew catalog. Find thread (spools and cones) zippers & fasteners, quilting and needlecraft supplies, wreaths, doll parts, moving eyes, interfacing, pins and needles, lace galore and much more! Orders are shipped UPS or parcel post the same day as received. Complete satisfaction is guaranteed.

MARLENE'S DECORATOR FABRICS
301 Beech Street; Dept. 2J
Hackensack, NJ 07601

Telephone: 800-992-7325

DISCOUNT

Free Information
Return policy: Only damaged goods may be returned

Get 35-50% off retail prices on brand-name and designer fabrics from Ralph Lauren, Pierre Deveux, Mario Buatta, Burlington, Bloomcraft, and more. For do-it-yourself upholstery, creative decorating, home sewing or whatever your fabric need, they have a great selection. Wallpaper and trimmings are also available. Mininum yardage purchase is 4 yards and up to 25 yards on select fabrics.

MONTEREY MILLS OUTLET

1725 East Delavan Drive; P.O. Box 271
Janesville, WI 53547

Telephone: 800-438-6387
In WI 608-754-8309

DISCOUNT

Free Information and Price List

Return policy: Only damaged goods may be returned.

A longtime wholesale supplier to the toy, apparel and auto markets, Monterey Mills Outlet is also a smart source for unusual, hard-to-find fabrics like pile, fake fur and other novelties. Craft lovers and decorators who seek plush animal prints like dalmation and jaguar, or fun fakes of rabbit, fox, seal and mink will find this a superb mail-order find. Remnant selections are priced cheaply by the pound. Prices are 50% off retail; fabric can be shipped in quantities up to 500 yards.

NANCY'S NOTIONS

Dept. 54; P.O. Box 683
Beaver Dam, WI 53916-0683

Telephone: 800-833-0690

DISCOUNT

Free Catalog

Return policy: Satisfaction Guaranteed

Nancy's Notions' 160-page color catalog is like a sewing store that comes to you in the mail! Over 4,000 items comprise their diverse product selection, including sewing notions, books, video, quilting supplies and more. These and other products were featured on public TV's "Sewing With Nancy" program. Save even more money with their exclusive discount program.

NEWARK DRESSMAKER SUPPLY

6473 Ruch Road, P.O. Box 20730
Lehigh Valley, PA 18002-0730

Telephone: 215-837-7500
Fax No: 215-837-9115

DISCOUNT

Free Catalog

Return policy: Money-Back Guarantee if returned with 30 days

Newark Dressmaker Supply has every item imaginable for the seamstress, beginner or professional. There's a remarkably complete grouping of fabrics in patterns and colors to fit whatever you're sewing. There are also plenty of notions, tools and sewing machine accessories to keep your project moving to completion without a hitch. Check out the selection of bridal sewing supplies, children's patterns, dollmaking supplies, craft patterns, and quiltmaking supplies. There are hard-to-find items like dress forms, upholstery supplies & magnifiers, too.

SEWIN' IN VERMONT
84 Concord Avenue
St. Johnsbury, VT 05819

Telephone: 800-451-5124

DISCOUNT

Free Information

Return policy: Money-Back Guarantee

The nation's first and foremost discount sewing machine dealer has been serving America by mail since 1977. Sewin' In Vermont offers up to 40% savings on the world's best sewing machines. Whether you're a quilter needing a machine that can sew through thick batting or a stuffed toy maker sewing through thick pile fabrics, they can help you choose the right sewing machine and save you a bundle in the process. At Sewin' In Vermont, they have an experienced, knowledgeable staff ready to help you.

SUBURBAN SEW 'N SWEEP
8814 Odgen Avenue
Brookfield, IL 60513

Telephone: 800-642-4056

Free Information

Return policy: Money-Back Guarantee if returned within 3 days

If you're in the market for a new sewing machine, look to Suburban Sew 'N Sweep for the complete Singer and White lines. Whether you're a beginner or advanced pro, they carry the full range of sewing machines and sergers. They also carry irons by Singer Magic Press, Rowenta, plus Hy-Steam gravity feed irons.

THAI SILKS
252 State Street
Los Altos, CA 94022

Telephone: 415-948-8611

DISCOUNT

Free Brochure

Return policy: No Returns

Thai Silks offers a wealth of the world's most luxurious cloth - silk - in a wide variety of fabrications, from tissue-thin sheers to heavier weights . Some of the silks are available in broadcloth, chiffon, crepe de chine, georgette, silk linens, tweed and silk blends. By buying direct from foreign loomers, they save you over 50%. The full-color brochure includes many helpful hints on sewing with silk and how to care for silk at home and save even more on costly dry cleaning. Orders are shipped UPS or regular mail, depending on quantity.

THE BUTTON SHOP
P.O. Box 1065
Oak Park, IL 60304

Telephone: 708-795-1234

Free Catalog

Return policy: Returns Accepted within 30 days

Sew pros will welcome this selection of unique sewing accessories, notions and tools. From handy machine attachments like thread-cutting machine feet, to specialized notions like quality supplies and a full range of buttons - they are truly understated by their name. They also carry select supplies for knitting, jewelry-making and quilting.

THE FABRIC OUTLET

17 Mill Street; P.O. Box 2417
South Hamilton, MA 01982

Telephone: 800-635-9715

DISCOUNT

Free Information

Return policy: Returns and exchanges generally accepted

Offering up to 60% savings off suggested retail prices, The Fabric Outlet is home to a bountiful grouping of famous-maker and designer textiles. Stout Brothers, Ralph Lauren, Irvin Allen, Kravet and Bishops are a few of the well-known industry names in hard-to-find luxury fabrics available here. They say they'll ship anywhere. Professional and private buyers should take stock in this great resource, too.

THE PERFECT NOTION

566 Hoyt Street
Darien, CT 06820

Telephone: 203-968-1257

Free Catalog

Return policy: Money-Back Guarantee

Spend next to nothing, yet dress like the biggest spenders do when you sew beautiful fashions, accessories and home accents with supplies from The Perfect Notion. For beginners and pros alike, there are informative books, specialized machine parts, hard-to find notions, and handy gadgets that make home sewing faster and easier than ever. They have automatic cutting tools that make scissors virtually obsolete, special machine feet for applying fancy trim and a wide range of storage compartments for everything from needles to the machine itself. You'll also find great clothing and craft kits for rainy day enjoyment and creating those one-of-a-kind items you can't find in stores.

ARCTIC SHEEPSKIN OUTLET
Interstate 94 & Co. Road T
Hammond, WI 54015

Telephone: 800-657-4656
Fax No: 715-796-2295

DISCOUNT

Free Brochure

Return policy: Money-Back Guarantee if returned within 90 days

This mail-order outlet retailer offers fine quality sheepskin accessories for the entire family that cost so little for so much luxury. Imagine curling up on their soft sheepskin rug and you'll know where we're coming from. There's a great selection of slippers, trapper hats, earmuffs and gloves that are perfect for winter-time activities. They also have genuine sheepskin covers for your bicycle seats, car seats and even your steering wheel.

DAMART
3 Front Street
Rollinsford , NH 03805

Telephone: 603-742-4442

Free Catalog

Return policy: Money-Back Guarantee

Well known for their exclusive Thermolactyl cold-weather undergear for men and women, they now use the revolutionary fiber in sleepwear, hosiery, gloves and clothing. For all your winter sporting and everyday activities, you'll find practical, well-made insulated clothing that's guaranteed to last season after cold weather season. For women, there are traditional thermal basics, plus blouses, wool suits, sweaters, trousers and accessories. For men, there are durable thermal tops and bottoms, as well as handsome sportswear, work clothes and accessories.

DEERSKIN LEATHERGOODS
119 Foster St.
Peabody, MA 01961-6008

Telephone: 508-532-4040
Fax No: 800-933-3732

Free Catalog

Return policy: Money-Back Guarantee

Luxuriate in the sensuous look and feel of genuine leather and suede garments by Deerskin. For nearly 50 years, they've offered unbeatable quality and craftsman-ship at exceptional value to mail-order consumers across the country. For men, there's handsome leather and pigsuede crafted into shirts, bombers, sportcoats, pants, overcoats and accessories in contemporary styles and colors. For women, opulence is key. In addition to the traditional outerwear, they have gorgeous leather and suede suits, skirts, pants, dresses, handbags, boots and more.

EDDIE BAUER
Fifth & Union; P.O. Box 3700
Seattle, WA 98124-3700

Telephone: 800-426-6253

Free Catalog

Return policy: Money-Back Guarantee

The legend began in 1920; crisp, clean, all-American casual clothing and every-day essentials for men and women. They have all the clothes you count on for leisure living, including great swimwear, seasonless cotton knits, comfortable out-erwear, and durable footwear casuals. They also have a selection of outdoor and travel accessories like classic games, outdoor furniture and durable luggage.

J. CREW

Telephone: 800-932-0043

One Ivy Crescent
Lynchburg, VA 24513-1001

Free Catalog

Return policy: Money-Back Guarantee

Already an American tradition, the J. Crew catalog is as much a definitive guide to style as it is a shop-at-home resource. Every page features the very best in classic rugged outerwear, washed cotton twill shirtings, imported silk ties, seasonless khaki pants, durable leather accessories, flattering swimwear and comfy cotton boxers. You'll wear them year after year. Many looks are unisex, can be dressed up or down, and make easy transitional pieces for season-to-season style.

JAMES RIVER TRADERS

Telephone: 804-827-6000
Fax No: 800-955-0404

James River Landing
Hampton, VA 23631-2141

Free Catalog

Return policy: Money-Back Guarantee

Good-looking, practical, timeless sportswear for women and men are signatures of James River Traders. For the ladies, there are top quality separates including skirts, tops, shorts, denim and dresses, as well as dressier items for work or informal after-five wear. Choose from a superb grouping of finishing touches including shoes, belts and head gear. There's also outerwear and swimwear in flattering styles and colors. Men have fantastic options in sportswear staples including short and long sleeve cotton polos, oxford shirts, twill trousers, jeans and more.

JOS. A. BANK MEN & WOMEN

Telephone: 800-285-BANK
Fax No: 410-239-5911

500 Hanover Pike
Hampstead, MD 21074-2095

Free Catalog

Return policy: Money-Back Guarantee

This nationally known retail chain is also a mail-order resource for practical, high-quality executive apparel for men and women. Men will appreciate their finest quality suits, sportcoats, shirts, trousers, silk ties and leathergoods, plus great footwear by Kenneth Cole and other brands. They've also got sporty weekend looks for men in cotton shirtings, denim and more. For women, there's a catalog of smart, tailored separates, dresses, suits and special-occasion outfits. Versatile accessories include jewelry, shoes and leather goods.

L.L. BEAN

Telephone: 800-341-4341
Fax No: 207-878-2104

Freeport, ME 04033-0001

Free Catalog

Return policy: Money-Back Guarantee

As all-American as apple pie, the name is synonymous with superior quality, versatile sportswear and outdoor goods. Valued classics for men and women include 100% cotton mesh knit polos, leather boat shoes, Sperry Topsiders and Egyptian cotton sweaters. There's wrinkle-resistant Microfiber dress casuals for men and Sportif Interlock sportswear for ladies in soft, combed cotton. Both collrctions are great for travel and timeless in quality.

LAND'S END DIRECT MERCHANTS
1 Land's End Lane
Dodgeville, WI 53595
Free Catalog
Return policy: Money-Back Guarantee

Telephone: 800-356-4444
Fax No: 800-332-0103

How many hours have you spent in stores searching for just the right clothing items, only to return home frustrated and empty-handed? Land's End makes it easy and convenient at a price you can afford. Sportswear musts for women and men, including swimwear, sleepwear, outerwear, sweaters, jeans and all the finishing touches, are in the full-color catalog. They also carry sturdy luggage items available at competitive prices. A major resource of the time-conscious set, they can help you choose the right sizes over the phone and ship immediately.

LAUGHING BEAR
Box 732
Woodstock , NY 12498
Free Catalog
Return policy: Money-Back Guarantee

Telephone: 914-246-3810

Hunting high and low for something new and original in family clothing? Look no further. Laughing Bear has a complete assortment of the most comfortable 100% cotton styles for the whole family. They carry hooded tops, pants, leggings, t-shirts, sweats, and sleepwear for infants, children and adults, all hand-batiked from brights to muted pastel shades. They're guaranteed to turn heads and the discount prices will have you doing a double-take as well.

MID WESTERN SPORT TOGS
227 N. Washington
Berlin, WI 54923
Free Catalog
Return policy: Satisfaction Guarantee. Custom Orders Are Not Returnable.

Telephone: 414-361-5050

Mid Western Sport Togs offers over 50 different styles of leather coats, jackets and vests in a multitude of colors to fit everyone's taste, at factory direct prices. What truly sets Mid Western Sport Togs apart is the fact if you send them a deer or elk hide from an animal you hunted, they will transform it into one of their magnificent garments at a fraction of what it would retail for. If you're a deer hunter, don't waste that hide, make something of it at Mid Western Sport Togs.

OLSEN'S MILL DIRECT
1641 South Main Street
Oshkosh, WI 54901-6988
Catalog $2.00
Return policy: Money-Back Guarantee

Telephone: 414-233-7799
Fax No: 414-233-3755

Many of the items in the Olsen Mill Direct catalog are for kids, but there are some great selections for the rest of the family, too. Specializing in OshKosh B'Gosh sportswear, shoes and accessories for kids, they also carry select items by Carters', 60 D street, Spumoni, Good Lad, and Knitwaves. For men, there's traditional OshKosh B'Gosh workwear including their trademark bibbed overalls and cotton chambray shirts. Womens' clothes include denim jumpers, cotton pullovers, unconstructed blazers & Oshkosh bibbed overalls.

ORVIS

Telephone: 800-653-7635
Fax No: 703-343-7053

1711 Blue Hills Drive, Box 12000
Roanoke, VA 24022-8001

Free Catalog

Return policy: Satisfaction Guaranteed.

Orvis has items for everyone in the family, including fido! Casual sportswear for women, including denim skirts and coats, cotton shirts, sweaters and sweatshirts. Men can get raincoats, corduroy pants, boots and sportscoats. Gifts items include pet beds, jar openers, can holders for the car and travel shaving kits.

PATAGONIA MAIL ORDER

Telephone: 800-638-6464
Fax No: 406-587-7078

6109 West Babock Street; P.O. Box 8900
Bozeman, MT 59715

Free Catalog

Return policy: Money-Back Guarantee

A mail-order favorite among outdoor sports enthusiasts and the environmentally conscious, Patagonia Mail Order is a one-stop shopper's catalog resource. The very best in land and water sportsgear can be found - from featherweight nylon jackets to thermal underwear and insulated headgear; plus timeless sportswear for men and women. Champion rock climbers, surfers, skiers, canoers and rowers are among their valued customers, as are leisure sportsmen and everyday folks looking for great value from an earth-conscious merchant.

SHEPLER'S WESTERN WEAR

Telephone: 800-833-7007
Fax No: 316-946-3646

P.O. Box 7702
Wichita, KS 67277-7702

Free Catalog

Return policy: Money-Back Guarantee

For those who just can't get enough of the wild, wild west, here's the best of the west. Slip into Shepler's own line of proportioned-fit stretch jeans for men and women in the latest denim styles. They also have wonderfully printed Western-style shirts including the legendary embroidered, fringed and bib-front models. No Western look is complete without all the trimmings including cowboy hats, genuine leather cowboy boots, handcrafted sterling silver and stone jewelry; plus beautiful gifts and home accents with a distinctive Southwestern flair.

SMITH & HAWKEN CLOTHING

Telephone: 415-383-2000
Fax No: 415-383-7030

25 Corte Madera
Mill Valley, CA 94941

Free Catalog

Return policy: Money-Back Guarantee

Smith & Hawken of sportswear consists of classic, simplistic items for men and women. These clothes are meant to be worn, washed and worn again. The fabrics are dense, strong and durable - qualities you'll recognize as soon as you open their color catalog. Rugged chambray shirts, canvas pants, Japanese farmer's pants, classic denim jeans and reversible nylon windbreaker pullovers exemplify the earthy styles. These are clothes you'll count on year after year for hiking, gardening, camping, fishing, or whatever your active, outdoor lifestyle calls for.

THE PERFECT SHIRT COMPANY
1007 Johnnie Dodds Boulevard
Mt. Pleasant, SC 29464-6127

Telephone: 800-233-6365
Fax No: 803-881-6583

Free Catalog

Return policy: Money-Back Guarantee

Comfortable cotton novelty tees, sweatshirts, rugbies and other casual toppers are the true specialties of this catalog. Most of the logos and insiginia on these items are ficticious, but the all-American look is a casual hit with everyone in the family. Dressier pieces for men and women by Noble & Locke and British Khaki, include shirts, shorts, trousers & pullovers, all in seasonless, washable cotton.

THE RED FLANNEL FACTORY
Department B91; P.O. Box 370
Cedar Springs, MI 49319

Telephone: 616-696-9240
Fax No: 616-696-9261

Free Catalog

Return policy: Money-Back Guarantee

Almost nothing can compare to the feel of toasty flannel next to your skin on a frosty winter night. Almost nothing keeps you warmer on a cold winter day than sturdy flannel shirts and outerwear. The Red Flannel Factory has made a cold weather tradition of flannel fabrics in full-length underwear, sleepwear, sportswear and authentic lumberjack shirts. As the name implies, they stock a large amount of these items in the color red for fantastic holiday gifts.

TWEEDS
One Avory Row
Roanoke, VA 24012-8528

Telephone: 800-444-9449

Free Catalog

Return policy: Money-Back Guarantee

Fast becoming an American classic, Tweeds is a well-known favorite of the collegiate set. Comfortable, timeless sportswear for men and women. You won't find any trendy fads here, these looks are here to stay. For women - smart, versatile sportswear separates - fresh cotton crochet sweaters to loose, flowing trapeze dresses. Most of the men's looks are unisex but there's a handsome collection of trousers, unconstructed jackets and cotton oxfords that are undoubtedly male.

WATHNE CORPORATION
1095 Cranbury So. River Road, Suite 8
Jamesburg, NJ 08831

Telephone: 800-942-1166

Free Catalog

Return policy: Money-Back Guarantee

There's a certain appeal to clothing collections born of adventure and that's clearly what Wathne is all about. Open their full-color catalog and discover a wealth of superbly tailored clothes and distinctive accessories for men and women. Luxurious silk, cool cottons, wool gabardine and crisp linen highlight these high-touch vests, blazers, tailored shirts, polos, scarves, ties, braces and other items. There's also a wide range of outdoor sport clothing and accessories including oilcloth jackets, cotton sailing parkas, sleek swimsuits, safari jackets; plus durable canvas luggage with fine leather details.

WINTERSILKS

2700 Laura Lane; P.O. Box 130
Middleton, WI 53562

Free Catalog

Return policy: Money-Back Guarantee

Discover the incredible warmth and luxury of 100% pure knitted silk from Wintersilks. They carry luxurious silk thermal underwear, sleepwear and ski accessories for both men and women at up to 40% savings on retail prices. Their "Square Deal" guarantee means a prompt, courteous refund or exchange if you're in any way dissatisfied with your purchase.

FAMILY CLOTHING

CARROT-TOP INDUSTRIES, INC.
437 Dimmocks Mill Road; P.O. Box 820
Hillsborough , NC 27278

Telephone: 800-628-3524
Fax No: 919-732-5526

Free Catalog
Return policy: Money-Back Guarantee

Carrot-Top Industries provides a wealth of promotional items, including American flags for civic or commercial display, custom made flags and banners, flag accessories, supplies and novelties. There are convention decorations, bunting, traffic-stopper flags, weather resistant street banners and more. They can customize flags for you given size, color and fabric requirements. Whatever the cause, they've got a flag for you to wave at a cost conducive to your organization's budget.

FLAGS UNLIMITED
2035 28th Street SE; Suite I
Grand Rapids, MI 49508

Telephone: 800-649-3993
Fax No: 616-243-2969

Free Catalog
Return policy: Money-Back Guarantee

Providing valued service to churches, schools, government organizations and national groups, Flags Unlimited has a wide variety of international flags, novelty banners, accessories and mounting supplies. In addition to Old Glory, they have all the U.S state flags, novelty holiday and political flags, windsocks; plus red/white/blue fans and bunting. Their catalog also offers traditional facts and tips on proper etiquette an display of U.S. flags; plus handy accessories like no-flip flag poles and out-rigger poles. They can do custom flags for you to exact dimensions and color specifications.

FLAGS & BANNERS

1-800-THE ROSE

775 Park Avenue, Ste. 140
Huntington, NY 11743

Free Catalog

Return policy: Satisfaction Guaranteed.

Telephone: 800-THE-ROSE

DISCOUNT

Send your feelings with flowers. Across town or across the world, 1-800-THE-ROSE is your florist. One call says it all. Whether you choose to express your feelings with flowers, roses, tropical or mixed floral arrangements, plants, silk and dried arrangements, friut baskets or balloons, one call says it all!

BLUESTONE PERENNIALS

7211 Middle Ridge Road
Madison, OH 44057

Free Catalog

Return policy: Money-Back Guarantee

Telephone: 216-428-1327
Fax No: 216-428-7198

Bluestone Perennials offers its mail-order buyers a fantastic selection of the finest garden delights. Perennial bulbs are available including bearded iris, narcissus, daffodils, tulips and more. All plants are available in mixed groupings and are shipped immediately to insure quality and optimum conditions for growth.

BRECK'S

6523 N. Galena Road
Peoria, IL 61632

Catalog $2.00

Return policy: Money-Back Guarantee

Telephone: 309-691-4616

Breck's has been serving American gardeners with beautiful flowering bulbs since 1818. Their catalog gives you the unique opportunity to obtain Holland's finest bulbs at savings of as much as 50%. Their low sale prices are made possible by their ability to coordinate orders well ahead of the shipping season, therefore gaining volume discounts from growers and passing those savings on to you. Get savings on their complete selection of tulip varieties, hyacinths, daffodils, lilies, irises and wildflowers. They also carry their own line of garden maintenance products including the Breck's Dutch Bulb Handbook.

CALYX & COROLLA

1550 Bryant Street; #900
San Francisco, CA 94103

Free Catalog

Return policy: Exchanges on damaged goods returned within 3 weeks.

Telephone: 800-800-7788
Fax No: 415-626-3781

When was the last time you bought flowers that lasted five weeks? Sounds impossible? Well, Calyx & Corolla promises you flowers that are cut in the field (not the florist) and flown by Federal Express directly to your doorstep. This way, there are no warehouses, trucks or storerooms to wither away in. Choose from a variety of fragrant bouquets including holiday swags, wreaths and baskets. Perfect for gift-giving, they offer engraved champagne coolers brimming with mixed bouquets, orchid leis and juniper bonsais. Beautiful topiaries are also available in ivy, braided ficus and rosebud. Gift certificates are offered along with exquisite vases and pots to accent your floral purchase.

DUTCH GARDENS

Telephone: 908-780-2713

P.O. Box 200; Dept. SM
Adelphia, NJ 07710

Free Catalog

Return policy: Satisfaction Guaranteed

Gardening enthusiasts, Dutch Gardens has a huge assortment of bulbs and perennials at just above grower's prices. In addition to pages and pages of beautiful, colorful varieties, their catalog features tips on planning a successful and flourishing garden. Prices include shipping, handling and delivery. Their bulbs are guaranteed to grow and bloom in their first year after planting. Allow 6 weeks for delivery, as orders are shipped directly from Holland.

GARDEN SOLUTIONS

Telephone: 616-771-9540

2535 Waldorf Ct., NW
Grand Rapids, MI 49550-0724

Catalog $2.00

Return policy: Satisfaction Guaranteed.

Before you buy any perennial flowers for your garden, get this catalog. Unlike most mail order companies, Garden Solutions not only offers individual plants for sale, but also offers complete garden sets that are perfect for specific areas of the yard. There are gardens for shaded areas, gardens for sunny spots and gardens to provide a half-circle of color to beautify your mailbox. They also offer trees to provide shade and colorful foliage in the fall.

GILBERT H. WILD AND SON, INC.

Telephone: 417-548-3514

1112 Joplin Street
Sarcoxie , MO 64862-0338

Catalog $3.00

Return policy: Only faulty goods are returnable.

Currently shipping all over the United States and to 40 foreign countries worldwide, Gilbert H. Wild and Son, Inc. claims to be the largest grower of Daylilies and Peonies in the U.S. That's what they do best, so that's all they do! You won't need a green thumb to enjoy all the scrumptious varieties of these flowering plants, including the season's latest introductions. The full-color catalog includes facts and tips on background, proper care, growth cycles and more. Don't miss the special offers usually outlined on the order form.

GURNEY'S SEED & NURSERY CO.

Telephone: 605-665-1930

110 Capital Street
Yankton, SD 57079

Free Catalog

Return policy: One-Year Satisfaction Guarantee.

Gurney's Seed and Nursery Company has been helping gardeners grow for over 125 years. This catalog gets better and bigger each year. Page after page of perennials, plants and poplars for the home gardener or landscaper. Spruce up your yard with some spruce trees, or add some apples and pears to your pantry by planting them alongside your house. Garden helpers for the kitchen, such as apple parers and grain grinders, are also available.

HASTINGS NATURE & GARDEN CATALOG

1036 White Street; P.O. Box 115535
Atlanta, GA 30310-8535

Telephone: 800-285-6580
Fax No: 404-755-6059

Free Catalog

Return policy: Money-Back Guarantee

Hastings, the self proclaimed "Seedsman to the South", offers a complete assortment of seeds, perennial plants, herbs, organics, wild bird supplies, fruit and nut seeds, ornamentals and gardening tools by mail. Choose from fragrant tuberose bulbs to dahlias, lilies, daisies, sunflowers, poppies, culinary and medicinal herbs, as well as garden teas for you to grow. Get unusual items like hardy pond fish, rare 'antique' florals and essential supplies to keep your private garden blooming.

JACKSON & PERKINS

P.O. Box 1028
Medford, OR 97501-0702

Telephone: 800-292-GROW
Fax No: 800-242-0329

Free Catalog

Return policy: Money-Back Guarantee

Jackson & Perkins roses have been blooming across America since 1872. That's a reputation worth believing in! Their award-winning rose varieties are the beautiful, including hybrids named Barbara Bush, Lagerfeld (after the French couturier) and the Queen Elizabeth. Other floral species available include wysteria, hydrangea, dianthus and lace begonia. Fruit and herb plants like strawberries, raspberries, elephant garlic, and dwarf fruits are offered, too. Don't pass by their limited array of bed linens and garden furnishings usually found near the end of the catalog.

LOGEE'S GREENHOUSES

141 North Street
Danielson, CT 06239

Telephone: 203-774-8038
Fax No: 203-774-9932

Catalog $3.00

Return policy: Exchanges only for damaged goods returned within 30 days

Celebrating their 100th anniversary, Logee's Greenhouses provides a unique collection of rare plants including tropical specimens like Bougainvilleas, Jasmines, Camellias, Acacias, and Allamandas. A choice grouping of citrus varieties includes Valencia oranges, "limons" and kumquats. Begonia lovers will adore the many varieties including fibrous, rex, rhizomatous, procumbent and rose. There is a $20 minimum and items may be substituted if out of stock.

MELLINGER'S GARDEN CATALOG

2310 W. South Range Road
North Lima, OH 44452-9731

Telephone: 216-549-9861
Fax No: 216-549-3716

Free Catalog

Return policy: Authorized returns accepted with 10% handling charge

For all your gardening projects, Mellinger's large selection of landscaping plants include ornamental grasses, climbing vines, shrubs, trees and more. Dogwood, birch and bamboo trees; maiden, porcupine and pampass grass; bougainvillea, dwarf cypress and crape myrtle shrubs. There are also fruit vines and trees - from strawberries to grapefruit; plus hazelnut and almond. They also have garden care supplies from major tools to fertilizers and chemical deterrents.

MICHIGAN BULB COMPANY

1950 Waldorf, NW
Grand Rapids, MI 49550

Telephone: 616-453-8793
Fax No: 616-453-3560

DISCOUNT

Free Catalog

Return policy: Satsifaction Guaranteed

Michigan Bulb Company, America's leading direct-mail nursery, offers a wide variety of beautiful plants for value-conscious gardeners. Customers can order everything from colorful, carefree groundcovers to trees, shrubs, flowering bulbs, roses and more, all at bargain prices! Michigan Bulb also offers professionally-planned collections that take the guesswork out of gardening and put the fun back in. Everything they sell is covered by their exclusive 3-year double guarantee.

MILLER NURSERY

West Lake Road
Canandaigua, NY 14424

Telephone: 800-836-9630
Fax No: 716-396-2154

Free Catalog

Return policy: 30-Day Satisfaction Guarantee

If you have an edible garden, take notice of this nursery. Fresh fruits of all kinds, from apples to wine grapes, will help landscape your yard. Great memories come from picking blueberries, strawberries, blackberries and raspberries, or any of the huge variety of fruits that are available. The beautiful nut trees can be both awe-inspiring and productive. (When harvesting your nuts, remember you are what you eat!)

NOR'EAST MINIATURE ROSES

P.O. Box 307
Rowley, MA 01969

Telephone: 508-948-7964

Free Catalog

Return policy: Money-Back Guarantee

Their latest catalog's cover features 'Whoopi', a new variety of miniature rose, alongside the hilarious comedienne who lent it her name. In addition to this individual type, there is a full range of award-winning miniature rose varieties in a rainbow of colorations - from the red and white Whoopi to the bright-white Ice Queen. You can also purchase miniature tree roses of the same varieties; plus handy pruners, mini vases and how-to booklets on successful rose cultivation.

PARK SEED

Cokesbury Road
Greenwood, SC 29647-0001

Telephone: 800-845-3369
Fax No: 803-223-6999

Free Catalog

Return policy: Money-Back Guarantee

With hundreds of seed varieties to choose from, Park Seed can give you the lush garden flora you've been looking for. Flowering plants like tulips, crocus, daffodils and irises are here; plus rare and exciting selections including wood sorrel and the exotic scabiosa pincushion flower. There are bulbs available for late summer and early autumn bloom, as well as perennial dianthus, asiatic lilies, large-blooming peonies and daylilies.

PETER DE JAGER BULB COMPANY

188 Asbury Street; P.O. Box 2010
South Hamilton, MA 01982

Catalog $1.50

Return policy: Money-Back Guarantee

Telephone: 508-468-4707
Fax No: 508-468-6642

Flowering plants and bulbs are specialties of the Peter de Jager Bulb Company. Fragrant daffodils, hyacinths, tulips, crocus and lilies are available in nearly every perennial variety. There are also Christmas bulbs like Paperwhite narcissus and Christmas hyacinths ready for indoor planting. They have handy gardening tools like fool-proof bulb planters and how-to booklets available, as well. Gift certificates for your green-thumbed friends and relatives are offered, too.

PINETREE GARDEN SEEDS

Route 100
New Gloucester, ME 04260

Free Catalog

Return policy: Money-Back Guarantee

Telephone: 207-926-3400
Fax No: 207-926-3886

Pinetree Garden Seeds can provide you with a large selection of vegetable seeds, including little-known varieties from around the globe like Cucuzzi, an edible gourd from Italy, and China's zesty spring cabbage. They also have flower seeds, ranging from asters to zinnias. If you're in the market for root crops, check out the garlic bulbs, asparagus roots, horseradish and Jerusalem artichokes. Also worth mentioning is the collection of gardening products and kitchen gadgets for sale, including seed dispensers, standard and regional hand tools, composters, pruners, how-to guides, farmer's almanacs and more.

ROSEHILL FARM

Gregg Neck Road
Galena, MD 21635

Free Catalog

Return policy: Free one-year replacement on damaged goods

Telephone: 410-648-5538

Their specialty is miniature roses and if you're a fan of the regular variety, you'll love Rosehill Farm's selection of the little beauties in a plethora of colors and shapes. They offer how-to books and pamphlets on growing and care; plus generous discounts of up to 15% on large orders. They have valuable gift certificates in unlimited amounts for the gardener who has everything.

SMITH & HAWKEN
25 Corte Madera
Mill Valley, CA 94941
Free Catalog
Return policy: Money-Back Guarantee

Telephone: 415-383-2000
Fax No: 415-383-7030

The Smith & Hawken Bulb Book claims to be your best source for bulbs. Why? They sell only the most mature, healthy bulbs which in turn produce the most lavish flowers, giving you more bloom for the buck. What's more, they feel their service is unsurpassed in the realm of information and product knowledge. But the real proof is in their page-after-page presentation of your floral favorites including gorgeous tulips, lilies, allium, crocus, hyacinths, narcissus and other varieties.

STARK BROTHERS
Box 10
Louisiana, MO 63353-0010
Free Catalog
Return policy: One-Year Satisfaction Guarantee

Telephone: 800-325-4180

Thems good eatin'! You can say that about everything in the Stark Brothers Fruit Trees and Landscaping Catalog. Typical fruit trees, like apples, pears, apricots, plums and peaches are offered alongside hardy strains of exotic fruits like kiwis, figs, pawpaws, pluots, Asian pears and persimmons. All of these trees will beautify your yard and bring wholesome goodness to your table. Best of all, they do not use toxic pesticides.

THE VERMONT WILDFLOWER FARM
P.O. Box 5; Route 7
Charlotte, VT 05445-0005
Free Catalog
Return policy: Money-Back Guarantee

Telephone: 802-425-3931
Fax No: 802-425-3504

If you've got some extra outdoor space and have dreamed of a spectacular wildflower meadow, the The Vermont Wildflower Farm will mix wildflower seeds especially for your region, be it Northeast, Midwest, Southeast, West, Southwest or Pacific Northwest. Their seed collections include America's favorites like daisies, poppies, Queen Anne's Lace, wild cosmos and baby's breath. Also, get a jump on a season of savings with their excellent 'early bird' discounts.

VAN BOURGONDIEN BROTHERS
P.O. Box A, 245 Farmingdale Rd.
Babylon, NY 11702
Free Catalog
Return policy: Money-Back Guarantee

Telephone: 800-873-9444
Fax No: 516-669-1228

Hundreds of floral delights await your selection in the pages of this catalog. They carry a vast array of hardy perennials, peonies, tulips, crocuses, narcissus, daffodils, hyacinths and many other varieties. Don't miss the blockbuster savings on an extraordinary selection of bulbs. The catalog also offers a guide to the right sunlight and watering to keep your florals healthy throughout the season.

FLOWERS & PLANTS

W. ATLEE BURPEE & COMPANY

300 Park Avenue
Warminster , PA 18991-0003

Telephone: 215-674-4915
Fax No: 215-674-4170

Free Catalog

Return policy: Money-Back Guarantee

Burpee Ornamental Gardens has a colorful array of top-quality perennials, bulbs, shrubs, trees and supplies for all your green thumb needs. They carry many of your favorite floral creations - from tulips, daffodils and African Violets to Weeping Willows, Saucer Magnolias, Clump Birch and other ornamental trees. There are also hearty fruit plants like kiwi, raspberry, blackberry and blueberry offered. Among their varied supplies, you'll find modular yard composting bins, old-fashioned push mowers, and handy soil test kits.

WAYSIDE GARDENS

1 Garden Lane
Hodges, SC 29695-0001

Telephone: 800-845-1124
Fax No: 803-941-4206

Free Catalog

Return policy: Money-Back Guarantee

You can feel your thumb turning greener as you peruse the pages of floral wonders offered by Wayside Gardens catalog. Out of the temperate south comes an enormous selection of peonies, tulips, daffodils, irises, chrysanthemums, lilies and the list goes on and on. Don't miss the grouping of indoor plants, as well as gardening accessories like trellises, lighted greenhouse shelving, composters and electric sprayers. Bulbs and plants are shipped to you right out of the Carolina soil for guaranteed quality and growth capabilities.

F
L
O
W
E
R
S

&

P
L
A
N
T
S

BAKERS & BUILDERS
4851 Melvin Heights Road
Camden, ME 04843
Free Information
Return policy: Satisfaction Guaranteed

Telephone: 207-236-4871

From the balmy central coast of Maine comes a selection of baked goods by Bakers & Builders of Camden. Their popular, pastel-frosted Bunny Hutch gingerbread houses are the biggest sellers. Other sweet "real estate" includes The Maine Stay (a gable-roofed gingerbread house with Mr. Gingerbread Man himself tending a candied carrot patch), Rose Cottage (a cinnamon spiced gingerbread house with jelly bean chimney) and Miniature Gingerbread Lighthouses. All of these creative confections are wrapped in colorful ribbons.

BODACIOUS BUNS
10250 Santa Monica Boulevard; Suite M-12
Los Angeles , CA 90067
Free Information
Return policy: Satisfaction Guaranteed

Telephone: 310-470-0031
Fax No: 310-470-7522

The name will catch your attention every time, as will the large, mouth-watering cinnamon rolls and other baked goods they offer. Bodacious Buns come in a bodacious assortment of toppings, including frosted raisin, pecan, apple, orange and chocolate. They also have lighter alternatives to the cinnamon rolls including traditional English scones; plus oatmeal and wild blueberry muffins. Beautifully decorated gift baskets and boxes are available.

BOUDIN GIFTS
132 Hawthorne Street
San Francisco, CA 94107
Free Catalog
Return policy: Money-Back Guarantee

Telephone: 415-882-1810
Fax No: 415-882-1821

Famous for their fresh sourdough French bread since 1849, Boudin also offers sweet breakfast breads, garlic breads, cheeses, sourdough pizzas, smoked meats, cookies and croissants. Their packages come complete with wine and vinegars for wonderful hors d'oeuvres and fancy treats. Don't pass by the Fisherman's Wharf Soups or the romantic picnic food assortments, complete with baskets. They have gift samplers with personalized greetings and kitchen accessories, too.

BROWNIES ON TOUR!
P.O. Box 1277
Cutchogue, NY 11935
Free Brochure
Return policy: Money-Back Guarantee

Telephone: 800-736-4069
Fax No: 516-734-5415

Master chef Barbara Michelson has brought European panache to one of America's favorite homegrown desserts - Fudge Brownies. Michelson's luscious renditions include "Black Forest", a blend of tart cherries and bittersweet chocolate, and "Seville", a confection of sherry-soaked sultana raisins, lightly toasted almonds and orange. The brownies arrive in gift tins or stay-fresh wrapping, based on your preference.

DIVINE DELIGHTS
24 Digital Drive, Suite 10
Novato, CA 94949

Telephone: 800-4-HEAVEN
Fax No: 415-382-7599

Free Catalog

Return policy: Returns accepted on products damaged during shipment

Located in the culinary trend-setting San Francisco Bay Area, the Divine Delights pastry shop has, for over ten years, baked fresh, whole-grain breads, their signature petit fours and Mice-A-Fours, among other confections. You can experience the taste of their delicious cakes, chocolates, cookies and candied treasures that have been featured in Gourmet, Food & Wine, Victoria and House Beautiful. For the discriminating wedding planner, this is a great source for romantic dessert delights; baked, packaged and shipped to you within 48 hours.

FABULOUS FORTUNE BROWNIES
416 N. Adams Street
Glendale, CA 91206

Telephone: 800-869-0822
Fax No: 818-506-2567

Free Information

Return policy: Exchanges Only

When gift-giving calls for something a little out of the ordinary, surprise the lucky loved one with Fabulous Fortune Brownies. They're not just great tasting, they're the brownies with a clever fortune baked inside. The wonderful boxed gift assortments are custom decorated for informal wedding gifts, new baby congratulations, or for anyone who loves brownies. Six luscious flavors include Walnut, Peanut Butter, White Chocolate Almond, Chocolate Mint, Coconut , & Serious Chocolate.

FRENCH MEADOW
2610 Lyndale Avenue South
Minneapolis , MN 55408

Telephone: 612-870-4740
Fax No: 612-870-0907

Free Information and Price Lists

Return policy: Money-Back Guarantee

Master bakers and chefs at the French Meadow Traditional European Bakery prepare a unique line of organic sourdough breads. They bake in the true European tradition, naturally leavening the dough, which creates a superior texture and taste. French dill, Oatmeal Raisin and Brown Rice are some of the tasty flavors. The breads are certified organic and Kosher pavre.

MATTHEW'S 1812 HOUSE, INC.
P.O. Box 15; 250 Kent Road
Cornwall Bridge, CT 06754

Telephone: 203-672-0149

Free Catalog

Return policy: Money-Back Guarantee

They say that the wonderful aroma of freshly baked cakes permeates every post and beam of the Matthews 1812 House. The Chocolate Raspberry Liqueur Cake, Lemon Rum Sunshine Cake and Heirloom Fruit & Nut Cake could make a believer out of anyone. But don't stop until you've checked out the rich fruit sauces, Connecticut maple syrups and all-natural condiments. Smokehouse specialties include smoked turkey, salmon and ham. Chocoholics, don't miss the select grouping of Almond, Minted and Butterscotch varieties.

MISS GRACE LEMON CAKE COMPANY
422 N. Canon Drive
Beverly Hills, CA 90210

Telephone: 800-367-2253
Fax No: 818-995-2451

Free Catalog

Return policy: Money-Back Guarantee if returned within 30 days

If you're looking for a gift idea that practically screams "You're someone very special," Miss Grace can help you. Their Gracious Gifting catalog offers some of the finest quality desserts anywhere. Those accustomed to conventional sweets will adore Miss Grace's original Lemon Cake, a deliciously sweet, wickedly tart confection that'll make a  truly memorable gift or winning dessert for the family. Chocolate lovers will go wild over sinful selections like Chocolate Fudge Cake, Fudge Brownies and Chocolate Velvet Truffle Cake.

MOM'S APPLE PIE COMPANY
296 Sunset Park Drive
Herndon, VA 22070

Telephone: 703-471-6266

Free Brochure

Return policy: Money-Back Guarantee

For years, so-called "industry experts" have been urging Mom's Apple Pie Company to use cheaper ingredients and techniques to make their pies. But the fourth-generation, family-owned company has stuck to its original recipes. They still use tasty Shenandoah Valley Apples and other fresh fruits that are poured into pie crusts too good to be left on the plate. Great flavors include Rhubarb, Strawberry Cream Cheese, Pumpkin, Sweet Potatoe and Wild Blueberry.

MOTHER NATURE COOKIES
15437 Smithaven Place
Centreville, VA 22020

Telephone: 800-358-BAKE

Free Catalog

Return policy: Satisfaction Guaranteed

Mother Nature Cookies are rich, creamy gourmet renditions, delivered in unique gift packages, including keepsake tins, baskets, top hats, sports team hats Irish derbies, Christmas stockings and even bird feeders. These delicious cookies are baked fresh daily, using only the finest natural ingredients and no preservatives. Varieties include coconut macadamia nut, chocolate raspberry truffle, chocolate amaretto truffle and candy apple. All items shipped 1- or 2-day air to insure freshness.

THE GREAT VALLEY MILLS

Rd. 3; County Line Road; Box 1111
Barto, PA 19504

Telephone: 800-688-6455
Fax No: 215-754-6490

Free Catalog

Return policy: Money-Back Guarantee

"Superior foods from family-owned farms" - that's been their promise since 1710. And now, nearly 300 years later, you can buy real fruit preserves, freshly baked pretzels, muffins, pancake mixes, waffle mixes and more from The Great Valley Mills mail-order catalog. Old fashioned fruit butters, pure milk cheeses and smoked meats are specialties as well. Don't miss the bakery-fresh bread collection. Of course samplers are available for gift-giving or sampling for yourself.

WOLFERMAN'S FINE BREADS

One Muffin Lane; P.O. Box 15913
Shawnee Mission, KS 66285-5913

Telephone: 800-999-0169

Free Catalog

Return policy: Money-Back Guarantee

Who doesn't crave the taste of freshly baked breads? Well, if you can't bake it yourself, Wolferman's has already done it for you. In fact, they've been baking fine breads, muffins, crumpets, pastries and bagels since 1888. Your order is baked fresh and rushed to your table so you can catch the full flavor in every bite. Tasty English muffins come in apple streudel, blueberry, sourdough and other scrumptuous varieties. They're low in fat and cholesterol, while high in fiber and great taste. There are also delicious fruit crumpets, cinnamon rolls, tea breads, assorted bagels and a wide selection of great sandwich breads. If your mouth isn't watering by now, just check into the curd toppings, preserves and fruit spreads to complement these baked goods. But the best part of all is the unbelievably low price. You can join the Wolferman's Bakery Club and coordinate regular deliveries of their breads right to your doorstep. Samplers and gift orders are also available.

ALETHEA'S CHOCOLATES

Telephone: 716-633-8620

8301 Main Street
Buffalo, NY 14221

Free Brochure

Return policy: Exchanges Only

When only chocolate will do, Alethea's offers a wide assortment of candied gems featuring this worldwide favorite. These chocolates are all handmade, using only the purest of ingredients. Gourmet selections, chocolate cluster selections, nut varieties, mint chocolates, truffles, cherry cordials and even sugar-free chocolates are just some of the popular flavors. Other Alethea's services include corporate accounts, gift certificates and customized gifts for special occasions.

CLAIRE'S ANGELS

Telephone: 212-580-4700

60 West 68th Street; #5A
New York, NY 10023

Free Information

Return policy: Money-Back Guarantee

Cited by the New York Times as a one of the best foods to send as a gift, Claire's Angels offers their delicious chocolate treats in decorative tins, as well as festive boxes and baskets that highlight specific holidays. They have samplers for birthdays, St. Patrick's Day, Easter, Valentine's Day and Mother's Day. However, they can honor requests for custom-designed gift packages at an additional cost. Claire's Angels are shipped UPS second-day air to insure freshness.

GREAT SCOTT! FUDGE KITCHEN

Telephone: 406-728-3616
Fax No: 406-721-0609

3621 Brooks Street
Missoula, MT 59801

Free Information

Return policy: Money-Back Guarantee

Satisfied customers include a surfer from Australia who deemed the chocolates "...better than sex," and a four year old from Montana who told her parents "I hope I'm not dreaming!" Judge for yourself. Great Scott! offers regular and blended macadamia nut fudge chocolates individually wrapped and packed in Knotty Pine keepsake tins. They make great gifts for yourself or your truly loved ones.

GREENBERG'S DESSERTS

Telephone: 800-255-8278
In NY 212-861-1340

1377 Third Avenue
New York, NY 10021

Free Catalog

Return policy: Money-Back Guarantee

Well-known among New Yorkers and the international celebrities that frequent the famed metropolis, Greenberg's offers the finest dessert confections imaginable. If you're a sucker for elaborate sweet treats, then you'll love the chocolate carousels (complete with horses), danish pastries, buttercake squares and angel food cake. They also have dessert gift samplers available, filled with assorted brownies, fruit-filled butter cookies, schnecken and more.

Food

CANDY & CONFECTIONS

HERSHEY'S GIFT CATALOG

Park Boulevard; P.O. Box 801
Hershey, PA 17033-0801

Telephone: 800-544-1347
Fax No: 717-534-7947

Free Catalog

Return policy: Money-Back Guarantee

America's number one chocolate can now be purchased in decorative glass canisters and keepsake tins for memorable gifts and personal pleasure. Assorted Hershey miniature candy bar packages are available mixed with Reeses, Mr. Goodbar, Krackel and Hershey Kiss varieties. They also have a delicious new selection of chocolate truffles and personalized chocolate greeting cards that one wouldn't soon forget.

MARY OF PUDDIN HILL

4007 Interstate 30 Exit 95; P.O. Box 241
Greenville, TX 75403-0241

Telephone: 903-455-2651
Fax No: 903-455-4522

Free Brochure

Return policy: Money-Back Guarantee if returned within 30 days

Within their catalog of tasty gift creations, you'll find a selection of homemade cakes and candies for holiday treats or great gifts. These Mary of Puddin Hill favorites can be shipped year-round, too. There are fruit cakes, fruit cake miniatures, pies and cookies among other sweet delicacies. They welcome orders for samplers as well as requests for their very own Puddin Hill Cookbook.

THE POPCORN FACTORY

P.O. Box 4530
Lake Bluff, IL 60044

Telephone: 800-541-2676
Fax No: 309-691-9693

Free Catalog

Return policy: Money-Back Guarantee

Popcorn lovers, take special notice. Here you'll find natural flavors plus candied nut varieties like glazed almond and pecan. They also have decorator tins filled with tortillas, chocolate chip cookies, jellybeans and pretzels. The tins are keepsakes and make festive gifts for birthdays, graduations and holidays. They also do gift packages prepared in sturdy straw baskets.

FIGI'S GIFTS
3200 South Maple Avenue
Marshfield, WI 54449
Free Catalog
Return policy: Money-Back Guarantee

Telephone: 715-384-1327
Fax No: 715-384-1129

Sometimes the best gifts are the ones you can eat!. Figi's offers beautifully packaged gift samplers, stocked with premium cheeses, sausages, nut mixes and condiments; plus mini cakes, cookies, chocolates and other sweet treats. Check out the cheese logs of Port Wine, Swiss, Cheddar or Smoky, rolled in real shredded nuts. There are festive baskets and tins that they can fill with virtually any treat you can dream up, from candied popcorn to baklava. They also have charming commemorative crocks of favorite cheeses that you can keep year after year.

GIBBSVILLE CHEESE SALES
W2663 CTH OO
Sheboygan Falls, WI 53085
Free Information & Price List
Return policy: Money-Back Guarantee

Telephone: 414-564-3242
Fax No: 414-564-6129

Cheese lovers, this one's for you. Gibbsville stocks a full line of natural rindless cheeses including cheddar, mozzarella, parmesan, gouda, smoked string cheese and other favorites. If you like country fresh sausages, look once again to Gibbsville for delicious flavors like regular, beef and garlic. Gift boxes and economy packages combine selected cheeses and sauces for snacks and hors d'oeuvres.

HICKORY FARMS
P.O. Box 75; 1505 Holland Road
Maume, OH 43537
Free Catalog
Return policy: Money-Back Guarantee

Telephone: 419-893-5419
Fax No: 419-893-8068

A long-time leader in festive holiday gift packages of choice meats, cheeses and condiments, Hickory Farms now offers these items to you by mail as well. Aside from their gift samplers, they also have party cakes, choice fillet mignons, lobster tails, turkey, ham and sausages. For the sweet tooth, there are chocolate candies and those famous Melt Away Mints.

THE SWISS COLONY
1112 7th Avenue
Monroe, WI 53566-1364
Free Catalog
Return policy: Money-Back Guarantee

Telephone: 608-324-8000
Fax No: 608-242-1001

If you enjoy giving or receiving delicious gifts of cheese, chocolate, smoked meat, baked desserts or fruit, then here's a fine mail-order resource for such items. Swiss Colony provides scrumptious confections like holiday fruit cakes, chocolate truffles, macadamia nut chocolates and dried fruit ambrosia in reusable baskets and tins that are ready for gift-giving. Don't miss the charming gingerbread houses that come with little chocolate figurines or hard candies. There are also gifts of glittering crystal and glass, plus holiday centerpieces for your buffet.

Food

**C
H
E
E
S
E
S**

COMMUNITY KITCHENS

Telephone: 800-535-9901
Fax No: 800-321-7539

P.O. Box 2311; Dept. HR
Baton Rouge, LA 70821-2311

Free Catalog

Return policy: Exchanges and Credit only

Since 1919, Community Kitchens has defined the art of gourmet cooking with their distinctive line of foods, cookware and gourmet appliances. The food offerings run the gamut, from their signature coffee, tea and fresh fruit preserves to fresh bread mixes, breakfast cookies, blended salad dressings and authentic pasta sauces, and flavorful supper samplers. The cookware and appliance selections include coffee presses, wide-mouth toasters, vacuum-insulated crock pots and Krups coffee makers. Their Sample-of-the-Month Club features authentic Cajun fare.

NORTHWESTERN COFFEE MILLS

Telephone: 414-276-1031

217 North Broadway
Milwaukee, WI 53202

Free Catalog

Return policy: Money-Back Guarantee

In operation since 1875 and housed in a landmark mill listed in the National Register of Historic Places, Northwestern Coffee Mills offers some of the finest blends of American, South American, Italian and French coffees. They have a full range of regular and decaffeinated flavors including New Orleans Chicory, Mocha/Java Blend, Hawaiian Kona Extra Fancy, and French Altisimo, as well as all the right brewing filters for great results time after time. You can find a variety of herbal teas; plus gift samplers for the serious coffee lover to enjoy.

THANKSGIVING COFFEE COMPANY
COFFEE-BY-MAIL

Telephone: 800-648-6491
Fax No: 707-964-0351

P.O. Box 1918; Dept. SBM
Fort Bragg, CA 95437

Free Catalog

Return policy: Satisfaction Guaranteed

End the search for the perfect cup of coffee! Discover why the best restaurants and country inns in California's Wine Country serve Thanksgiving Coffee. Over 85 varieties are available, including special house blends, estate-grown Hawaiian Kona, organic coffees, half caffs and more - all custom roasted and blended, then vacuum packaged for optimum freshness and delicious aroma.

THE COFFEE CONNECTION

Telephone: 800-284-JAVA
In MA 617-254-1459
Fax No: 617-783-3683

119 Braintree Street
Boston, MA 0213

Free Catalog

Return policy: Satisfaction Guaranteed

Not only can you find a wide range of coffees from Latin America, Africa and France, but you can join The Coffee Connection's exclusive subscription service to receive these tasty blends regularly by mail. They also have an assortment of grinders, teapots, espresso makers, and coffee brewers by Rowenta, Bosch, Rotel and Krups. A $5.00 coupon toward your first purchase is included in the catalog.

THE HARRONS OF SIMPSON & VAIL, INC.
P.O. Box 309
Pleasantville, NY 10570

Telephone: 914-747-1336
Fax No: 914-741-6942

Free Catalog

Return policy: Money-Back Guarantee

If you enjoy the delicate taste of distinctive teas and coffees, the Harrons of Simpson & Vail have a tasty selection for you to sample. They have Black, Green, Oolong, Flavored and Decaffeinated teas, as well as American, African, and South American coffees. You simply can't miss the exquisite heirloom coffeepots and tea services they offer; plus select foods and condiments from around the world including Greek olives, Indian chutneys and English syrups.

Food

C
O
F
F
E
E
S

&

T
E
A
S

ALMOND PLAZA
1505 Holland Road; P.O. Box 75
Maumee, OH 43537
Free Catalog

Telephone: 419-893-7611
Fax No: 419-893-0164

Return policy: Money-Back Guarantee

Almond Plaza stocks the finest roasted almonds from the valleys of California. These quality nuts come in a full range of clever flavors like Honey Cinnamon, Sour Cream & Onion and Barbecue. In addition to the Almond Plaza name, they carry the Blue Diamond brand. But don't stop at almonds. They also have pistachios, macadamias, and cashews in similar flavors. You'll also find smoked meats, delicious cheeses, fresh baked desserts and sinfully sweet candies for holiday buffets or gift ideas. Samplers and corporate gift packages are available, too.

BATES BROTHERS NUT FARM, INC.
15954 Woods Valley Road
Valley Center, CA 92062
Free Brochure

Telephone: 619-749-3333

DISCOUNT

Return policy: Money-Back Guarantee

Nuts from all over the world meet at Bates Brothers Nut Farm! The Bates Family offers everything from walnuts, pecans, cashews, macadamias and pistachios, to the freshest dried apricots, prunes and dates; plus delicious old fashioned preserves, candies and honey. You can save up to 40% on these and other items. What's more, gift packages are available yearround for all occasions.

BLUE HERON
3221 Bay Shore Road
Sarasota, FL 34234
Free Brochure

Telephone: 813-355-6946
Fax No: 813-951-2672

Return policy: Money-Back Guarantee

They've been shipping fresh fruits since 1946, but they have other delicacies available by mail including Mayhaw Jellies, Southern Vinegars, Sarasota Stone Crab Claws, Smoked Catfish Pate, as well as hickory smoked holiday hams and turkeys. There are samplers and gift packages available for any occasion and most products are rush-shipped to insure freshness.

CAFE FANNY
1619 Fifth Street
Berkeley , CA 94710
Free Information

Telephone: 800-441-5413

Return policy: Exchanges available on damaged during shipment only

Cafe Fanny offers healthy, delicious loose granola by mail. They can ship it direct to you packaged in quantities of up to fifteen individual one-pound bags. They can coordinate a 'subscription' delivery plan for you to receive the granola in regular intervals, ranging from every two weeks to every two months.

CHUKAR CHERRY COMPANY
320 Wine Country Road; P.O. Box 510
Prosser, WA 99350-0510

Telephone: 800-624-9544
Fax No: 509-786-2591

Free Brochure
Return policy: Money-Back Guarantee

The bountiful orchards of Northwestern America are famous for yielding the world's finest cherries. Homegrown and preserved in over 20 delicious products, Chukar cherries and berries are as pure and wholesome as the mountain valleys from which they come. You can purchase dried pitted cherries, cranberries and blueberries; plus chocolate-covered varieties as well. Don't forget to check out the listing of special fruit toppings and sauces which are also available.

DUREY-LIBBY NUTS
P.O. Box 345
Carlstadt, NJ 07072

Telephone: 800-332-NUTS

DISCOUNT

Free Information
Return policy: Satisfaction Guarantee

Sometimes, you feel like a nut, right? Well, Durey-Libby sells mixed nuts, walnuts, almonds, pistachios, cashews, macadamias and pecans direct to you at up to 50% off what you'd pay in retail stores. Minimum orders are 3, 4 or 5 pound bags, depending on the variety ordered. Shipping prices are included on orders shipped within the U.S., which usually takes 2 to 3 weeks.

GRACEWOOD FRUIT COMPANY
P.O. Box 2590
Vero Beach, FL 32961-2590

Telephone: 800-678-1154
Fax No: 407-567-1160

Free Brochure
Return policy: Money-Back Guarantee

Regardless of the temperature outside or where you live, Gracewood can have Florida's best citrus fruits, melons, onions and mangos shipped to your home year-round. For grapefruit lovers, there are canned sections available already peeled. They also have Texas Gold Giant cantaloupes and delicious sweet onions. With the informative brochure, you'll also get a $5.00 coupon to use toward your first purchase.

HALE INDIAN RIVER GROVES
Indian River Plaza
Wabasso, FL 32970

Telephone: 407-589-4334

Free Information
Return policy: Exchanges available only for damaged goods

From the state that's home to hundreds of citrus groves and fruit farms comes a great alternative to store-bought fruit. Their shipping season runs from mid-November through June, which gives you plenty of time to stock up on delicious Florida Mangos, Valencia Oranges and other succulent fruits. They also have a limited selection of real-fruit cheesecakes, pies and other baked goods.

HARRY AND DAVID
P.O. Box 712
Melford, OR 97501
Free Catalog

Telephone: 800-345-5655
Fax No: 800-648-6640

Return policy: Non-perishable items may be returned for credit only.

Opening your cupboards to find these mouth-watering foods tucked away would be a dream come true! There are fruits like Rainier cherries, blush nectarines, Oregon peaches, giant kiwi and golden plums that are rare, even in season. There are also fresh baked goods, cheeses, smoked meats, luscious preserves and candies. The gift packages and picnic assortments run as large as you prefer, from one-pound decorative tins to giant picnic baskets. Their Veggie Club features unexpected items like Louisiana yams, tropical pineapple, Fuyu persimmons and baby French carrots, in addition to other nutritious garden selections.

MISSOURI DANDY PANTRY
212 Hammons Drive East
Stockton, MO 65785
Free Catalog

Telephone: 800-8-PANTRY
Fax No: 417-276-5187

Return policy: Money-Back Guarantee

They started out in 1946 processing black walnuts, and are now said to be the world's largest processor of these rich tasting nuts. That's only "the outer shell." They sell black walnuts, almonds, peanuts and pecans blended into rich candied confections. You'll also find pistachios, cashews and macadamia nuts here as well. If that's not enough, then look into their grouping of old fashioned fudge samplers and individually wrapped candies.

NUNES FARMS
P.O. Box 311
Newman, CA 95360
Free Brochure

Telephone: 209-862-3033
Fax No: 209-862-1038

Return policy: Money-Back Guarantee

Nuts are the specialty here. Nunes Farms has a number of Almond treats including Honey Glazed, White Cheddar and Spicy Cocktail renditions. Also, look for roasted pistachios and assorted nut candies blended with toffee, caramel or chocolate. Quantities are shipped in stay-fresh plastic bags, boxed decorator tins or handy single servings.

NUTS D'VINE
185 Peanut Drive; P.O. Box 589
Edenton, NC 27932
Free Brochure

Telephone: 800-334-0492

Return policy: Money-Back Guarantee if returned within 30 days

The name says it all. For nut lovers, there are jumbo peanuts from the Old South available in varieties to suit any palate like Raw Red Skins, Roasted-In-Shell, Salted-In-Shell, as well as more nutritious salt-free and cholesterol-free varieties. Order these nuts in burlap sacks, keepsake tins, or bushel baskets. They also have old fashioned peanut butter and peanut brittle for diehard fans of the nut.

RENT MOTHER NATURE

52 New Street; P.O. Box 193
Cambridge, MA 02238

Telephone: 617-354-5430
Fax No: 617-354-4951

Free Catalog
Return policy: Money-Back Guarantee

Here's a mail-order innovation! Rent Mother Nature cultivates a variety of agricultural crops. With their exclusive lease program, rent a New Hampshire Macintosh Apple Tree, Maple Tree, Sweet Cherry Tree, Pecan Tree, Peach Tree, Grapefruit Tree or Honey-Bee Hive and reap its harvest at the end of the season. Gift baskets are filled with cheeses, fruit preserves, syrups, nuts, popcorn, smoked meats and even lobster. Country cooking supplies include genuine soapstone griddles, ice cream makers and hardwood cutting boards.

SUNNYLAND FARMS, INC.

Wilson Road; P.O. Box 8200
Albany , GA 31706-8200

Telephone: 912-883-3085
Fax No: 912-432-1358

Free Catalog
Return policy: Money-Back Guarantee

Freshly harvested in the Old South is a plethora of delectable nuts including pecans, macadamias, cashews, peanuts, pistachios and nut medleys. These crops are available shelled or unshelled depending on how you like them. They can be conveniently packaged in plastic, boxes or reusable tins for instant holiday gifts or snacks. Don't miss the fruit cakes, cookies and dried fruits in season year-round. Country store treasures include select jams, jellies and condiments.

THE CHILDREN'S CATALOG

P.O. Box 15190
Seattle, WA 98115-0190

Telephone: 800-456-3338
Fax No: 206-527-1667

Free Catalog
Return policy: Exchanges available for damaged goods only

For almost 100 years, the Children's Home Society has been committed to supporting children and their families. Enjoy or send the gift that gives twice, once to the receiver of fruits and fine cheeses and again to the kids and families who benefit from the society's philanthropic activities. Granny Smith and Washington Red apples can be grouped  with Anjou pears and your choice of fine cheeses. They also have Walla Walla Sweet onions & gourmet candied apples.

Food

F R U I T S & N U T S

THE MAPLES FRUIT FARM
P.O. Box 167
Chewsville, MD 21721
Telephone: 301-733-0777

Free Catalog

Return policy: Money-Back Guarantee

All products from The Maples Fruit Farm are guaranteed to be of the highest quality available and very reasonably priced. For over 200 years, they've been producing quality custom blended dried fruit and nut baskets. There are raw nuts in salted and unsalted varieties, plus delicious dried fruit selections like apple rings, sweet raisins and unsweetened coconut. They also carry maple syrups and candied nuts, as well as 100% arabica bean coffees and herbal teas. There are gourmet gift baskets and specially arranged gift selections.

THE SQUIRE'S CHOICE
Suite 110; 2000 West Cabot Boulevard
Langhorne, PA 19047
Telephone: 800-523-6163
Fax No: 215-741-1799

Free Catalog

Return policy: Money-Back Guarantee if returned within 30 days

Specializing in tempting natural snacks like popcorn, nut medleys, pretzels, cookies and natural candies, The Squire's Choice is excellent for gift-giving. Their gift containers are perfect for any occasion - from birthdays to corporate events to Christmas. Choose centerpiece baskets, bushel baskets, decorative tins, boxes and glass jars - all in a full range of colors, shapes and sizes. Sin a little with hand-dipped candied apples, chocolate mushrooms and fudge brownies, among other devilish treats.

CAVIARTERIA

29 East 60th Street
New York, NY 10022

Telephone: 800-4-CAVIAR
In NY 212-759-7410

Free Brochure

Return policy: Satisfaction Guaranteed

Caviarteria is America's largest distributor of caviar and gourmet foods at savings of up to 65%. In their brochure, you'll find many varieties including Ultra, Sevruga Malassol, Imperial Golden, Beluga Prime, Oscetra Malassol, American Sturgeon; plus Scotch and Icelandic smoked salmon. Beautiful boxed assortments of fresh caviar and elegant temptations, like fresh French foie gras and Icelandic gravlax are available. There's a convenient West Coast location in Beverly Hills at (310)285-9773. All gifts delivered on the date you specify.

COYOTE CAFE GENERAL STORE

132 W. Water Street
Santa Fe, NM 87501

Telephone: 505-982-2454
Fax No: 505-989-9026

Free Catalog

Return policy: Returns allowed on damaged or defective items only

Southwestern food is known for its distinctive hot and spicy flavor, which many believe is a reflection of the region's hot and spicy weather. The Coyote Cafe General Store brings you the best of the Southwest's fiery food flair with a line of hot sauces, salsas, dried spices, pastas, tortilla mixes, preserves, candies and nuts that echo the taste of the region.They also have a hot selection of Cafe Coyote trademark clothing and Cocinaware cookery.

FERRARA

195 Grand Street
New York, NY 10013

Telephone: 212-226-6150
Fax No: 212-226-0667

Free Catalog

Return policy: Money-Back Guarantee on items returned within 10 days

Whatever your party food favorite, Ferrara's has it in the best tasting, best looking creations imaginable. The full color catalog features their selection of delicious cakes and pastries like Chocolate Black Velvet Cake, Tiramisu, and distinctive Ferrara cookies. Main dish items include their Pizza Rustica, Honey Cured Smoked Turkey and Smoked Norwegian Salmon. They also carry spaghetti by the yard, flavorful breads and candy samplers for sweet tooths.

HARRINGTON'S

Main Street
Richmond, VT 05477

Telephone: 802-434-3415
Fax No: 802-434-3166

Free Catalog

Return policy: Money-Back Guarantee

Harrington's special "corn cob" smoked hams are the centerpiece of this fine collection of gourmet meats, cheeses, condiments and dessert dishes. You can outfit your party buffet with maple-glazed party ham, smoked turkey, zesty aged cheddar cheese, French brie cheese and Danish saga blue cheese. Add rich plum pudding, chocolate cake with raspberry melba sauce or any other Harrington's baked confection, and you've got a guaranteed holiday crowd-pleaser!

Food
GOURMET
FINE
FOODS

K-PAUL'S LOUISIANA MAIL ORDER

824 Distributors Row; P.O. Box 23342
New Orleans, LA 70183-0342

Telephone: 800-457-2857
Fax No: 504-731-3576

Free Catalog
Return policy: Money-Back Guarantee

Chef Paul Prudhomme offers the finest ingredients for cooking up your favorite Cajun cuisine. When you're in the mood for something new and exciting suprise yourself with Jambalaya, Etouffee, Cajun Gumbo, or New Orleans Beans & Rice. Add a spark to your regular meals with Magic Seasoning Blends for poultry, pork, veal, seafood, vegetables and pasta. There are flavorful condiments, coffees and even great gift ideas in authentic Cajun cookware, music and K'Paul's signature clothing items. Check out Prudhomme's best selling cookbooks as well.

PEACHTREE SPECIALTIES, LTD.

P.O. Box 19511
Atlanta, GA 30325

Telephone: 404-875-0773
Fax No: 800-527-4306

Free Catalog
Return policy: Money-Back Guarantee

Peachtree Specialties, Ltd. offers its premier catalog filled with delicious, cholesterol-free, low-fat products available with the ease of phone or mail order. The healthful gourmet selections include cholesterol-free sweet sauces, baking mixes, fruity salad dressings, oil-free marinades and other delights. They also have specially hand-picked seasonal baskets for thoughtful gifts or the products can be packed individually for personal pleasure.

R.S.V.P.

Bridge Street
Waitsfield, VT 05673

Telephone: 802-496-RSVP

Free Information
Return policy: Exchanges allowed on damaged goods

Pizza lovers, Repondez s'il vous plait and receive information on Richard's Special Vermont Pizza by mail. The dough is a nutty blend of King Arthur unbleached white and stone ground whole wheat flours. Chock-full of delightful ingredients like Vermont mozzarella, Vermont "corn cob" smoked bacon and ham, it makes a hearty dinner for 4 and serves 12 for hors d'oeuvres. Try it as a birthday alternative to cake, or the corporate gift that says "job well done."

ROWENA'S GOURMET FOODS
758 West 22nd Street
Norfolk, VA 23517

Telephone: 800-627-8699
Fax No: 804-627-1505

Free Catalog

Return policy: Money-Back Guarantee

Just look at some of the names given to their delectable food items and you'll see why they're known as a true gourmet delight. There's "I Love Peanut Butter" Pound Cake, Rowena's Dark Delicious Chocolate Pound Cake and Luscious Lemon Pound Cake. But that's just dessert! You'll also find cooked Virginia hams, delicious tea breads; plus all the right fruit sauces and savory condiments to accent these and other foods. Gift samplers are available, ready to give.

SAN ANTONIO RIVER MILL
P.O. Box 18627
San Antonio, TX 78218-0627

Telephone: 800-627-6455
Fax No: 512-662-6914

Free Catalog

Return policy: Money-Back Guarantee

Treat yourself and your family to a wealth of good Texas eating with delicious gourmet food products by San Antonio River Mills. Just open the full-color catalog and you can almost smell the aroma of country-style biscuits, muffins, pancakes, cinnamon rolls, and Southern cornbread baking in your oven. They also offer mouth-watering gravies, fruit preserves, smoked meats and snack foods that'll leave you longing for more. Not to be missed are the unique decorative accents and cooking gadgets for your kitchen or sending as gifts.

SUSAN GREEN'S CALIFORNIA CUISINE
3501 Taylor Drive
Ukiah, CA 95482

Telephone: 800-753-8558
Fax No: 707-463-5512

Free Catalog

Return policy: Money-Back Guarantee

If you enjoy good eating and don't mind spending a little extra for the most tempting condiments, pastas, pastries, cakes and prepared vegetables, then look no further. For at-home entertaining, gourmet dinners or whatever the occasion, California Cuisine presents a mouth-watering selection of choice specialty foods that you'd never dream of buying by mail, including fine pastas and pasta sauces, balsamic vinegars, olives, apple strudel, corned beef hash, Belgian waffles and other delicacies. The selection of sourdough breads and California sundried fruits and nuts is not to be missed. They also have a variety of gourmet cookware and appliances including automatic bread makers, pressure cookers and earthenware dishes.

Food
GOURMET FINE FOODS

BETH'S FARM KITCHEN

Telephone: 518-799-3414

P.O. Box 113
Stuyvesant Falls, NY 12174

Free Information

Return policy: Returns allowed on damaged or defective items only

Delectable fruit condiments, including chutneys that range from "demure to demonic", reflect the range of products offered by Beth's Farm Kitchen. Chutneys include mild "Delta Road" with peaches and apples; exotic and tangy "Green Tomatoe"; and mean, ornery "Blazing Tomatoe Chutney." Raspberry Jam, Sour Cherry Jam, Triple Fruit Marmalade and Apple Butter are other tasty selections.

MAVERICK SUGARBUSH

Telephone: 802-763-8680
Fax No: 802-763-8684

P.O. Box 99
Sharon, VT 05065

Free Information

Return policy: Money-Back Guarantee

If you like maple syrup, then you know where to look for the best; Vermont. From 500 acres of painstakingly managed sugarbush, comes the highest grade, 100% organic syrup Vermont has to offer. Maverick Sugarbush oversees the complete development of its product, from sap to syrup. You can be assured of syrup that's free of chemicals from inorganic fertilizers, among other benefits. The syrup is available in a range of quantities from 8.5 to 34 fluid ounce bottles.

MCCUTCHEON'S APPLE PRODUCTS, INC.

Telephone: 800-875-3451

13 S. Wisner St.; P.O. Box 243
Fredrick, MD 21701

Free Brochure

Return policy: Money-Back Guarantee

They started out producing premium apple products in 1938. Pretty soon, they began using other fresh fruit varieties in their spreads, preserves, butters and syrups. Peach, Black Raspberry, Cherry, Strawberry, Blueberry and Pumpkin round out the fruit flavor selection. They have a selection of no-sugar items for the calorie conscious, as well as a grouping of vegetable condiments and salad dressings. All products are packed in sealed jars of up to 20 ounces in size.

Food

J
A
M
S

J
E
L
L
I
E
S

R
E
L
I
S
H
E
S

STONEHILL FARMS
Telephone: 800-776-7155
P.O. Box 158
Schwenksville , PA 19473

Free Brochure

Return policy: Money-Back Guarantee

Stonehill Farms produces a variety of deliciously thick and rich fruit butters. Their consistency and unique taste are achieved through a very special cooking process which has been in use for nearly a century. The butters are 100% fat-free, cholesterol-free and salt-free. Three to five pounds of fruit are used in the preparation of each 11-ounce jar of apple, blueberry, pumpkin, plum and peach, among other flavors. Their brochure also offers a few clever recipes that show you how the condiments can be used in main dishes.

WOOD'S CIDER MILL
Telephone: 802-263-5547
RFD #2, Box 477
Springfield, VT 05156

Free Brochure

Return policy: Money-Back Guarantee

From a small family farm in southern Vermont that's been in the Wood family since 1798, comes a unique grouping of fine ciders, jellies and syrups. They grind and press fresh apples on the original screw presses, then process the juices in a wood-fired stainless steel evaporator to make their Boiled Cider and Cider Jelly. They have a plentiful supply of Grade A Dark and Grade A Medium Amber Maple Syrup in all sizes, as well as Grade B, a stronger, darker cooking syrup available in gallons. They also have a small flock of sheep that produces wool which is spun locally into soft, water repellent yarns. Samples of this top-grade yarn are available. Wood's can send gift packages directly to your loved ones, with personalized greetings enclosed if you prefer.

Food

JAMS

JELLIES

RELISHES

AIDELLS SAUSAGE COMPANY

Telephone: 415-285-6660

1575 Minnesota Street
San Francisco, CA 94107

Free Brochure and Price List

Return policy: Money-Back Guarantee

Bruce Aidells, owner of this fine establishment, is a former chef at Berkeley, California's famed Poulet Restaurant. The same hearty, full flavored sausages used in many of his dishes are available by mail. They have low-fat poultry sausages, in turkey or chicken, that are 88% lean. There's also Cajun Style Andouille, Creole Hot, Hunter, Whiskey Fennel & Mexican Chorizo, and other mouth-watering varieties. Chef Aidells sends you tantalizing recipes with each order.

BURGER'S OZARK COUNTRY CURED HAMS,

Telephone: 800-624-5426
Fax No: 314-796-3137

Highway 87 South
California, MO 65018

Free Catalog

Return policy: Money-Back Guarantee

This family-owned and operated business located on a 350-acre working farm in the Ozarks of Missouri has been offering a high-quality selection of meats for over 40 years at competitive prices. They combine old fashioned curing processes with modern packaging and shipping techniques so that their products arrive on your table "smokehouse fresh." There are country hams, hickory smoked sausages, smoked turkeys, choice steak cuts, hamburger patties and more. They also have original baby swiss cheese and rare German sausages.

FISHERMAN'S FINEST

Telephone: 206-759-7163

3318 North 26th Street
Tacoma, WA 98407

Free Information

Return policy: Money-Back Guarantee

From Alaska's pristine waters comes the perfect gift for that special friend or business associate...or yourself. Fisherman's Finest has succulent full sides of Sockeye Salmon that are carefully hand-trimmed, lightly brined and cold-smoked overnight for a rich, silky texture and light, smoky flavor. The fish is then sealed in gold foil pouches and heat processed in all its natural juices. What's more, absolutely no preservatives or anything artificial is ever used.

FOLK'S FOLLY PRIME STEAK HOUSE

Telephone: 800-467-0245
Fax No: 901-762-8287

551 South Mendenhall Road
Memphis, TN 38117

Free Information

Return policy: Money-Back Guarantee

Folk's Folly has a special way of sharing good taste. If you're preparing a holiday feast, informal summertime gathering or sending gifts of gourmet food, the Folk's Folly menu will impress the most discriminating palate. Their products are all seasoned with 14 years of experience, insuring the highest level of quality. Choose from choice beef, lamb, veal and pork cuts. Whether you're serving 2 or 200, they'll ship the quantities you need and even offer a new.

GRAFFAM BROTHERS

Central Street
Rockport, ME 04856

Telephone: 207-236-3396
Fax No: 207-236-2569

Free Brochure

Return policy: Money-Back Guarantee

Serious seafood lovers know Maine is the best place to look for the world's best-tasting lobster. These lobsters are caught by independent fishermen who work through even the fierce northeastern winters. They are brought to Graffam Brothers tanks in Rockport, then shipped directly to you by overnight ground or air mail. Their prices are a little steep, but if you know Maine lobster, you know its truly worth it. They also have clams available, priced by the pound.

JAMISON FARM

171 Jamison Lane
Latrobe, PA 15650-9400

Telephone: 800-2237-LAMB
Fax No: 412-837-2287

Free Brochure

Return policy: Money-Back Guarantee

John and Sukey Jamison raised sheep as a hobby for 15 years in the lush pastures of western Pennsylvania. In 1985, they decided to go into the mail-order business as suppliers of top-quality lamb products, including choice cuts of the tender meat and their very own "Sukey's Lamb Stew." They have other stew bases, condiments and selected gift items like aprons and t-shirts with the Jamison logo.

NEW BRAUNFELS SMOKEHOUSE

P.O. Box 311159
New Braunfels, TX 78131-1159

Telephone: 512-625-7316
Fax No: 512-625-7660

Free Catalog

Return policy: Money-Back Guarantee

Superior quality meats and food gifts have been New Braunfels Smokehouse traditions since 1945. Their latest full-color catalog features smoked turkeys, hams, briskets, beef jerkeys and Canadian bacons. They also offer tasty sausage varieties, smoked sockeye salmon and fully prepared party platters that are sure-fire crowd pleasers. Nut lovers appreciate the Pecan Fruitcake and Texas Chewie Pecan Pralines. If you're into samplers, then they've got customized packages already prepared for memorable breakfasts, picnics and other occasions.

OMAHA STEAKS INTERNATIONAL

4400 South 96th Street
Omaha, NE 68103

Telephone: 800-228-9055
Fax No: 402-597-8120

Free Catalog

Return policy: Money-Back Guarantee

Since 1917, Omaha Steaks International has supplied corn-fed Midwestern beef to a number of the finest restaurants nationwide. Since 1952, they've offered these choice meats to consumers by mail. Whether you frequent America's best restaurants or not, you can enjoy delicious filet mignons, strip sirloins, tenderloin kabobs and prime rib. What's more, there's a bounty of fresh seafood available, including lobster tails, Alaskan King crab legs, swordfish, halibut, cod, salmon, shrimp and more. At your request, they'll also prepare surf 'n turf combinations.

PFAELZER BROTHERS

281 West 83rd Street
Burr Ridge, IL 60521

Telephone: 800-621-0202
Fax No: 708-325-0117

Free Catalog

Return policy: Money-Back Guarantee

What could be more impressive than serving the finest steaks you can buy to dear friends, family, and valued business colleagues? How about elegant Beef Wellington, tender veal, lobster tails or stuffed chicken breasts? Since 1923, Pfaelzer Brothers has been a well known resource, catering the most extraordinary meats and seafood to be found anywhere. They can also help you coordinate clever and unusual gift packages with their fine gourmet foods. What's more, there's a limited selection of fully-prepared hors d'oeuvre items including petite quiche, patrician canapes and the finest caviar.

SEA ISLAND MERCANTILE & PROVISIONING

928 Bay Street; P.O. Box 100
Beaufort, SC 29901

Telephone: 800-735-3215

Free Catalog

Return policy: Money-Back Guarantee

South Carolina's historic Lowcountry has a distinctive style all its own which includes a number of foods and special dishes unique to this area. Sea Island Mercantile & Provisioning, Ltd. offers delectable She-Crab Soups, Sweetmarsh Oyster Stew and Vidalia Onion Relish, among other specialties. They also have food assortments named for the big-budget movies filmed in the area, like "The Prince of Tides Assortment." You can stock your pantry with delicious southern condiments, seafoods, preserves and more. They also have select home accents made from fragrant Charleston Cypress wood.

SPECIALTY SEAFOODS

P.O. Box 898; 605 30th Street
Anacortes, WA 98221

Telephone: 800-645-3474
Fax No: 206-293-4097

Free Information

Return policy: Money-Back Guarantee

Specialty Seafoods began as a small custom smokehouse in the fishing port of Anacortes, Washington over 25 years ago. They use no chemicals, artificial preservatives or added oils to preserve the full, rich flavor of their famous smoked salmon. Instead, they use the same time-honored process that seals the flavor into a multi-layered pouch. These pouches can be stored at any temperature, almost indefinitely. This way, no matter where you are, you can appreciate that great Northwestern salmon flavor.

DIAMOND ORGANICS
Freedom, CA 95019

Telephone: 800-922-2396

Free Catalog

Return policy: Exchanges available on damaged during shipment only

Only 1% of the fresh produced in America is organically grown, while a whopping 99% is subject to normal chain-store distribution methods, including the use of chemical pesticides and synthetic ripening agents. A purveyor of organically-grown specialty lettuces, greens, herbs, roots and fruits to top-quality restaurants and hotels for 8 years, they can deliver goods to you overnight, year-round..

FINES HERBES COMPANY
16 Leonard Street
New York, NY 10013

Telephone: 212-384-9022
Fax No: 212-334-9116

Free Catalog

Return policy: No Returns

Join the ranks of chefs from famous restaurants like The Rainbow Room, Le Bernardin, 21 Club and Canyon Ranch Spa in receiving the herbs, spices and produce that meet the approval of discriminating palates in the food industry. In response to frequent requests, they offer an entire line of organic, pesticide-free culinary herbs, specialty produce and salad greens, shipped overnight from their farms to your kitchen. A 10%-off coupon is in the catalog to benefit your 1st purchase.

JAFFE BROTHERS NATURAL FOODS, INC.
P.O. Box 636
Valley Center, CA 92082-0636

Telephone: 619-749-1133
Fax No: 619-749-1282

Free Catalog

Return policy: Money-Back Guarantee

You don't have to be a die-hard health fanatic to enjoy delicious and nutritious organic dried fruits, nuts and condiments from Jaffe Brothers. They're great vitamin and mineral sources and make tasty snacks or party mixes. Dried fruits are organically grown, unsulphured and unfumigated. There are apples, apricots, cherries, black mission figs, peaches, pears, prunes and fuyu persimmons Tropical delights include dried mangos, pineapple, papaya and bananas. Other specialties are peas, beans, rice, whole wheat pasta and dehydrated veggies.

WALNUT ACRES
Penns Creek, PA 17862
Free Catalog

Telephone: 800-344-9025
Fax No: 717-837-1146

Return policy: Money-Back Guarantee

When you place an order with Walnut Acres, you can be assured of receiving the freshest, most nutritious foods possible by mail. Many of the 'certified organic' foods in the catalog are grown and prepared right there on Walnut Acres in Pennsylvania. The full-color catalog alone gives new meaning to the word "wholesome" offering 100% natural, 100% organic foods including cereals, condiments, fruit juices, smoked meats, coffees, cheeses, pancake mixes, fresh breads, dried fruits and the like.

CUSTOM WINE CELLARS & RACKING BY VINOTEMP INTERNATIONAL

Telephone: 800-777-VINO
Fax No: 213-719-9500

134 West 131st Street
Los Angeles, CA 90061

Free Catalog

Return policy: Returns Not Accepted.

Here's where to get all-wood winecellers and fur vaults at the very best prices. They sell factory direct-to-you. Over 28 models, featuring individual redwood racking for each bottle, the Rolls Royce of cooling systems by Breezaire, all-wood construction, 46 types of beveled doors/windows. Optional features include etched glass windows, 98 types of carved doors, 18 types of see-through doors with double thermal panes. Full 1-year warranty. The very best in Amerca for the lowest prices; largest handmade wine cellar factory in the US.

E.C. KRAUS HOME WINEMAKING EQUIPMENT AND SUPPLIES

Telephone: 816-254-7448

9001 East 24 Highway; P.O. Box 7850
Independence, MO 64053

Free Catalog

Return policy: Money-Back Guarantee on nonperishable items only

For those daring enough to try their hand at home beer brewing or winemaking, EC Kraus offers a complete line of tools and supplies. Beginners will appreciate informative books that give step-by-step instructions, as well as recipes for award-winning beers and wines. Once you're ready to begin, choose from a selection of yeasts, wine clarifiers and fining agents, fruit acids, and dried winemaking ingredients. Hydrometers, filtering equipment and fermentation gadgets round out the list of supplies. In the back of their catalog, you'll also find a number of convenient resources for purchasing liquid malt extracts and other supplies. Consult your local legal codes for any restrictions on the purchase of these products.

INTERNATIONAL WINE ACCESSORIES, INC.

Telephone: 800-527-4072
Fax No: 214-349-8712

11020 Audelia Rd.; Suite B-113
Dallas, TX 75243

Catalog $3.00

Return policy: Money-Back Guarantee on items returned within 30 days

If you're a connoissuer of fine wine, or just beginning to enjoy the art of collecting, International Wine Accessories, Inc. has an incredible range of wine supplies - from the basic to the extraordinary. The full-color catalog displays their wood, glass and wrought iron wine racks. Most of these racks are expandable to grow with your budding collection. They also have the most beautiful glass tables which rest on natural grapevine bases. There are coffeetable books on wine collecting, as well as elegant gifts for wine aficionodos, like quality crystal stemware, personalized English pub signs and marble serving accessories.

A BRASS BED SHOPPE
Telephone: 216-371-0400

12421 Cedar Road
Cleveland Heights, OH 44106

DISCOUNT

Free Catalog

Return policy: Money-Back Guarantee if returned within 10 days

There are many furniture styles which are cherished and constantly sought after for timeless beauty. The brass bed is one of them. A Brass Bed Shoppe has the bed you want in an assortment of sizes and styles, at an unbelievable price. They have genuine brass beds of high quality construction, with designer styling and extra heavy duty framework. Also available with or without a superior baked epoxy finish that keeps the brass from tarnishing, so it never needs polishing. Contemporary models include matte black finish and charming daybeds of white iron.

ADIRONDACK DESIGNS
Telephone: 800-222-0343

350 Cypress Street
Fort Bragg, CA 95437

Free Catalog

Return policy: Money-Back Guarantee

For the finest Redwood outdoor furniture, check out Adirondack Designs. Their catalog features chairs, loveseats, footrests, lounges, tables, swings, planters, benches and modular units direct from the manufacturer at great prices. Preassembled components with predrilled holes allow for easy assembly.

BARNES & BARNES
Telephone: 800-334-8174

190 Commerce Avenue
Southern Pines, NC 28387

DISCOUNT

Free Information

Return policy: Only damaged merchandise accepted for return

The Barnes & Barnes toll-free number is your direct contact with America's leading furniture manufacturers at superlative savings of 40-50%. Call for price quotes and information. Of the 180 manufacturers they stock, names like Lexington, American Drew, Stanley, Richardson Brothers, Classic Leather, Pennsylvania Classics and Universal Furniture head the list. Shipping is via in-house trucking in approximately 8-10 weeks.

BLACKWELDER'S INDUSTRIES, INC.
Telephone: 704-872-8921

Highway 21 N; RR 18-8
Statesville, NC 28677

Catalog $5.00

Return policy: Money-Back Guarantee

Blackwelders offers a huge assortment of fine furniture styles and brands, including leather furnishings by Leathercraft, chairs by Century, modern pieces by Thayer Coggin and French Provincial bedroom groups by Henry-Link. Each manufacturer has been thoroughly researched to insure that their merchandise meets with the Blackwelder's tradition for excellence and superior craftsmanship in fine furnishings. The merchandise is generally delivered by household mover, with smaller items shipped by common carrier.

BOSTON & WINTHROP
35 Banks Terrace
Swampscott, MA 01907
Free Brochure
Return policy: Money-Back Guarantee

Telephone: 617-593-8248

After searching for the right furnishings for their kid's rooms, the owners of Boston & Winthrop created the pieces they envisioned. They guarantee you'll love them as much as they did. This wide selection of children's furniture is individually handpainted and custom decorated to fit specifically in your home. They'll coordinate pieces to match walls, wallpaper - even your child's bed linens. Dressers, bed frames, table and chair sets, desks and baby cradles are crafted in carefully selected hardwoods. The paints are non-toxic Benjamin Moore products, protected by two coats of clear polyurethane for lasting beauty.

BRENTWOOD MANOR FURNISHINGS
317 Virginia Avenue, Dept. SBM
Clarksville, VA 29327
DISCOUNT
Free Brochure
Return policy: Returns accepted, excluding special orders.

Telephone: 800-225-6105

Brentwood Manor can save you upwards of 50% on fine furnishings for your home. They have famous-name furniture, draperies and other accessories at factory-direct prices. Call for price quotes and information on the specific brand names. They ship nationwide, usually by in-home delivery in 6-14 weeks.

CANDLERTOWN CHAIRWORKS
P.O. Box 1630
Candler, NC 28715
Free Catalog
Return policy: Money-Back Guarantee if returned within 7 days

Telephone: 704-667-4844

How's this for southern charm? Candlertown Chairworks is located at the foot of Mount Pisgah, in Hominy Valley, near Asheville, in the Smoky Mountains of North Carolina. With local character this strong, they can't help but turn out a superior product. Chairs are made of hickory, oak, walnut or maple; each chair post is carefully turned and each 'mule ear' is steam-bent to a form. Chairs are assembled without screws, nails or fasteners that can loosen with time. Styles range from children's heirloom highchairsto pilgrim ladderback and Mt. Lebanon chairs. Each seat is handwoven in their trademark herringbone pattern.

CAROLINA INTERIORS
115 Oak Avenue at Cannon Village
Kannapolis, NC 28081
DISCOUNT
Free Brochure
Return policy: Only damaged merchandise is returnable.

Telephone: 704-933-1888
Fax No: 704-938-2990

High quality standards and low prices are the foundations upon which Carolina Interiors sells all of its fine home furniture. They're known by the "companies they keep", including Wellington Hall, Wildwood Lamps, Hancock & Moore, Craftique and American Drew. All furniture orders require a 1/3 deposit.

CHERRY HILL FURNITURE, CARPET & INTERIORS **Telephone: 800-328-0933**
Box 7405 at Furnitureland Station   **or 919-882-0933**
High Point , NC 27264   **Fax No:**   919-882-0900

DISCOUNT

Free Brochure
Return policy: Satisfaction Guaranteed

Save up to 50% on more that 500 of America's finest brands, directly from the
furniture capital of the world. Call toll-free for price quotes on Cherry Hill's elegant furniture, carpet and decorative accent collections or to order a free
brochure. Their merchandise is shipped via van line service for extra-careful
handling, usually within 8-14 weeks. Cherry Hill has been serving thousands of
satisfied customers since 1933.

DOUGLAS ASSOCIATES, INC.   **Telephone: 800-732-5661**
14 Duck Pond Road
Norwalk, CT 06855
Free Catalog
Return policy: Money-Back Guarantee

They call the look "Neoferric," translated "new iron." Douglas Associates, Inc.
has put together a unique collection of iron furnishings and decorative accents
that are as timeless in design as they are in versatility. The collection features
innovative designs in chairs, dining tables, consoles, end tables, beds, and cande-
labras. All-iron and all-handmade in America, these products are a true reflection of the quality workmanship, materials and value they offer.

EDGAR B. FINE FURNITURE   **Telephone: 800-255-6589**
P.O. Box 849   **Fax No:**   919-766-8308
Clemmens, NC 27012   DISCOUNT
Catalog $15.00
Return policy: 25% Restocking Fee For Undamaged Merchandise.

Choose from over 130 top brand name manufacturers at savings of up to 50% off
retail prices. Their toll-free number connects you with an expert sales consultant
ready to assist in selecting the finest home sampling of America's most popular
collections. Delivered nationwide; guaranteed satisfaction with the quality and
price you need.

ELLENBURG'S FURNITURE   **Telephone: 800-841-1420**
I- 40 at Stamey Farm Rd.; P.O. Box 5638
Statesville, NC 28687   DISCOUNT
Catalog $6.00
Return policy: Returns accepted on damaged merchandise only.

From choice wicker and ruttan collections to some of the finest wood and uphol-
stered furniture available today, Ellenburg's has it all at tremendous savings!
SAVE UP TO 50% on some of America's most famous brand names in home
furnishings, like Lexington, Henry Link, Lane, Hooker, Highland House, Bob
Timberlake, Pulaski, National Mt. Airy, Charleston Forge, Yield House, Capel
Rugs, Yorkshire Leather and many others.

FURNITURE "AT A DISCOUNT"

Telephone: 704-376-6518

P.O. Box 6005
Charlotte, NC 28207

DISCOUNT

Free Brochure

Return policy: Satisfaction Guaranteed

Superior quality and unbeatable service, backed by over 50 years in the business are the hallmarks of this discount furniture and upholstery retailer. They stock well-known name brands like Craftique, Broyhill, Ficks Reed, Habersham Plantation, Stanley, Pennsylvania Classics and hundreds of others. They also have lighting and decorative accessories by Stiffel, Virginia Metalworks and Waterford. On shipping, the word is "everywhere", including Canada and Puerto Rico.

HARVEST HOUSE FURNITURE

Telephone: 704-869-5181

P.O. Box 1440, Highway 109 South
Denton, NC 27239

DISCOUNT

Catalog $7.00

Return policy: Returns accepted on damaged merchandise only

Check out the prices before you buy! Harvest House carries over 200 lines and offers savings of 50% or more. When ordering, your payment is automatically secured by surety bond. For price quotes, just give their knowledgeable customer service representatives a call.

HOUSE DRESSING

Telephone: 800-322-5850

2212 Battleground Avenue
Greensboro, NC 27408

DISCOUNT

Free Brochure

Return policy: Returns accepted on damaged merchandise

Give your house a new wardrobe of the most beautiful furnishings now available by mail from House Dressing. They offer big discounts on exquisite and fine furniture and represent over 200 major manufacturers. In 8 weeks or less, you can have superior quality furniture in your home by merely placing a telephone call. Save 50% and more by purchasing furniture direct, thereby avoiding the local furniture dealer's added cost and local sales tax.

J. JENKINS BEDS

Telephone: 508-336-4480
Fax No: 508-336-4884

600 Taunton Avenue
Seekonk, MA 02771

Free Brochure

Return policy: Money-Back Guarantee

For nearly 50 years, the Jenkins family has been in the business of buying, restoring and selling antique beds. To date, the firm has one of the largest collections of antique beds in the country and now offer beautiful heirloom reproductions to you by mail. Each bed is constructed with the same materials and in the same manner as its antique predecessor. The J.Jenkins finish has been developed to match the patina and color found on antique pieces. Some reproductions include the New Hampshire Acorn Bed, circa 1830; the Pine Tree Top Bed, circa 1850; and the Sheraton Field Bed, circa 1800. J.Jenkins exercises a rigid "cut a tree/plant a tree" policy so the environment isn't sacrificed for this lasting beauty.

LAURA D'S FOLK ART FURNITURE, INC.

Telephone: 914-228-1440

106 Gleneida Avenue
Carmel, NY 10512

Catalog $2.00

Return policy: Returns accepted for exchange only

Looking for funky, creative designs to perk up the kids' rooms or add a spark to drab decor throughout the house? Laura D's Folk Art Furniture has a few ideas that are truly innovative. Featured in major retailers like FAO Schwartz, Neiman Marcus, Macy's and The Horchow Collection, artist Laura Dabrowski  personally designs and signs all of these fun pieces, made of genuine hardwoods. They're crafted with the sturdiest hardware to last a lifetime. Designs include handpainted rocking horses, chairs that resemble storybook animals and a range of other patterns on tables, storage bins and bookshelves.

LEONARD'S ANTIQUES

Telephone: 508-336-8585
Fax No: 508-336-4884

600 Taunton Avenue
Seekonk, MA 02771

Free Catalog

Return policy: Money-Back Guarantee

If you've dreamed of waking up one glorious morning in a big, four-poster canopy bed of the finest antique wood, then stop dreaming. Leonard's can make your fantasy a beautiful reality. They have antique beds gathered from old New England homes and estates, each available in its original condition or sized, restored and refinished to your specifications. They have other antique and reproduction furniture including headboards, dressers and storage chests, too. Also available are odd-size bedding and charming fabric canopy covers.

LOFTIN-BLACK FURNITURE

Telephone: 800-334-7398

111 Sedgeville Drive
Thomasville, NC 27360

Free Information

Return policy: Returns accepted on damaged merchandise only

Here's your opportunity to purchase major brands of furniture at great prices, including bedroom, dining room and livingroom styles. They offer nationwide home delivery in about 8-10 weeks. They carry over 300 lines, so chances are they'll be of help to you in searching for that special pattern.

MARION TRAVIS

Telephone: 704-528-4424

P.O. Box 292
Statesville, NC 28677

DISCOUNT

Free Catalog

Return policy: Money-Back Guarantee if returned within 30 days

Think genuine, handcrafted hardwood furnishings have to be expensive? Guess again! Marion Travis offers folksy country chairs, tables, swings and benches of white hardwoods, at great prices. Chairs feature wood or handwoven backs and seats and are crafted using a special "natural lock" joint that insures an everlasting tight fit. All items available unfinished, with a clear protective gloss, or in your choice of oak or walnut stains.

MECKLENBURG FURNITURE SHOPPE

Telephone: 704-376-8401

520 Providence Road
Charlotte, NC 28207

Free Information

Return policy: Money-Back Guarantee

If you're searching for a one-stop decorating resource, just relax and put yourself in the hands of the specialists at Mecklenburg Furniture. You can choose from their vast selection of beautifully crafted furniture in styles to suit any decorating scheme. From Queen Anne and Chippendale to contemporary designs, you can't beat the assortment. Oriental carpets, wall coverings, antique clocks, wall art, bedding and other necessities round out their array of upscale decorating items.

NEVER PAY RETAIL, INC.

Telephone: 214-748-8721

1525 Dragon Street
Dallas , TX 75207

DISCOUNT

Free Information

Return policy: Returns accepted for exchange only

The folks at Never Pay Retail offer mail-order shoppers 40-70% savings on one-of-a-kind fine furnishings and decorator accents. In addition to their 3 showrooms, they market surplus items out of the Dallas World Trade Center, direct to you. Their wide assortment of designer pieces includes sofa sectionals, chandeliers, dining sets, canopy beds and more. Be assured of quality service as they employ only non-commissioned, degreed interior designers to assist you.

PLEXI-CRAFT

Telephone: 212-924-3244

514 West 24th Street
New York, NY 10011

Catalog $2.00

Return policy: Returns accepted for credit only

Perhaps you're only familiar with Lucite/Plexiglas as a glass alternative for patio doors, picture frames and the like, but this revolutionary material has long been used to make beautiful furnishings for your home or office, as well. It's cheaper and safer than glass and adds the illusion of space in tight quarters. Plexi-craft designs can be traditional or modern in tables, chairs, wall units, rolling bars, bar stools, desks or virtually any other type of furniture. Combine clear Lucite/Plexiglas with other innovative surfaces for striking contemporary effects.

PRIBA FURNITURE

Telephone: **919-855-9034**
Fax No: 919-855-1370

210 Stagecoach Trail; P.O. Box 13295
Greensboro, NC 27415

DISCOUNT

Free Brochure

Return policy: Damaged merchandise returnable

Priba Furniture represents over 300 major furniture and decorative accessory lines. You can expect savings of 50% or more off the manufacturer's suggested retail prices on names like Broyhill, Thomasville, Burnhart and other quality lines. Call one of their experienced creative designers or visit the beautiful new showroom in Greensboro, conveniently located near the Triad Int'l Airport.

QUEEN ANNE FURNITURE COMPANY, INC.

Telephone: **919-431-2562**

Route 2; Box 427
Trinity, NC 27370

Free Brochure

Return policy: Money-Back Guarantee

Queen Anne Furniture Company has sought to preserve the illustrious heritage of 18th Century style. Queen Anne and Chippendale sofas, loveseats, chairs and ottomans are available in a delightful array of upholstery fabrics - from the neutral to the baroque. The Queen Anne sofas come in lengths of 72" to 82". Wing chairs have been designed to accentuate their sculpted form with full wings and high backs. Other styles include hostess chairs, George & Martha Washington chairs, executive desk chairs and swivel rockers. Wooden leg styles vary in design and are available in cherry or medium oak finish.

ROOM & BOARD

Telephone: **800-486-6554**

4600 Olson Memorial Highway
Minneapolis, MN 55422

Free Catalog

Return policy: Money-Back Guarantee

Decidedly functional and uncontrived, this selection of versatile metal and wood furniture is made to complement any decor - from the classic to the most contemporary. The 'Ashley' bed is a prime example in bent raw steel, individually crafted for twin, full, king and queen sizes. A handcrafted steel table collection combines the same modern material and classic style with your choice of tops in glass, birch, cherrywood, granite marble or travertine. Other furnishings are available at equally understated prices, given their quality and innovative design.

SHAW FURNITURE GALLERIES

Telephone: **919-498-2628**
Fax No: 919-498-7889

P.O. Box 576
Randleman, NC 27317

DISCOUNT

Free Brochure

Return policy: Damaged Merchandise Returnable

Shaw Furniture Galleries offer more than 300 brands of furniture at up to 47% savings. They've been in business for 48 years. Great service and selection from hundreds of the best furniture and rug manufacturers. Visit their showroom or call for information on ordering by mail. You can find anything from armoires, sofas to bedroom suites.

F
U
R
N
I
T
U
R
E

STUCKEY BROTHERS FURNITURE, INC.
Route 1, Box 527
Stuckey, SC 29554
Free Brochure

Telephone: 803-558-2591
Fax No: 803-558-9229

DISCOUNT

Return policy: Money-Back Guarantee with written authorization only

Stuckey Brothers Furniture stocks a complete line of famous-maker fine furnishings, backed by a reputation of quality service and discount prices. Choose from a broad selection of furniture items by Broyhill, Ficks Reed, Hickory Chair, La-Z-Boy, Southwood, Stanley, and Conover, among others. Indoor, outdoor and baby furniture is available, as are lamps, bedding and other accessories.

THE BARTLEY COLLECTION, LTD.
29060 Airpark Drive
Easton, MA 21601
Free Catalog

Telephone: 800-787-2800
Fax No: 410-820-7059

Return policy: 30-Day Satisfaction Guarantee

Bartley offers an alternative to high-priced colonial furniture. Antique reproduction furniture kits include everything necessary for construction; from nails and glue,to hinges and hardware. Instructions make assembly quick and easy. If you're not the handy type, purchase any of these exquisite pieces of furniture preassembled, for a higher price than for the kits. Besides tools, the only thing not included is finishing material, but they sell dozens of colors of stains and varnishes.

THE BED FACTORY
112 Harding Way East
Gallon, OH 44833
Catalog $2.00, refunded with 1st order

Telephone: 419-468-3861

DISCOUNT

Return policy: Money-Back Guarantee

Whatever your bed preference is gleaming brass, iron, daybeds, wooden, upholstered or juvenile style, The Bed Factory can fulfill your dreams at factory-direct savings up to 50%. They've got nearly every style - from traditional to contemporary. They also have special payment plans to make your "dream bed" a reality.

THE BOMBAY COMPANY
P.O. Box 161009
Fort Worth, TX 76161-1009
Free Catalog

Telephone: 800-829-7789
Fax No: 817-347-8291

Return policy: Money-Back Guarantee

Top quality and superior craftsmanship abound in this sensational selection of furniture and home accents by The Bombay Company. Whether you're looking to redecorate or just add a few heirloom pieces to your current decor, you'll find a wealth of antique reproductions like gold leaf mirrors, Queen Anne consoles and buffet tables, beautifully framed art prints and more. Not to be missed is the collection of small accents like ivory porcelain, fine crystal and brass accessories. The prices are great for the quality and beauty you'll get.

THE HORCHOW HOME COLLECTION
P.O. Box 620048
Dallas , TX 75262-0048
Free Catalog
Return policy: Money-Back Guarantee

Telephone: 800-456-7000

A legendary source for the most imaginative upscale decorative treasures, The Horchow Collection is a great mail-order catalog for gifts, as well as items you wouldn't dare part with. They have an exquisite collection of fine furniture, mostly classic in design, in fabrics and materials for indoors and out. There are porcelain, glass, pewter, and wooden accents to complement these furnishings; plus select handcrafted soft goods, like heirloom quilts, durable canvas outdoor seat covers, fresh cotton table linens and 100% wool rugs of Oriental and European design.

THOMAS H. KRAMER, INC.
805 Depot Street, Commerce Park
Columbus, IN 47201
Free Information
Return policy: Money-Back Guarantee

Telephone: 812-379-4097

If Early American is a fair description of your favorite decorating style, then you'll appreciate the Thomas H. Kramer Farmhouse Furniture Collection. All of the furniture is built of the finest wood nature has to offer, including pine, oak or cherry. They have a range of stains to choose from, plus a selection of furniture paint colors to complement your existing decor. The furnishings include pencil-post canopy beds, armoires, modular bookcases and American Windsor chairs. Aside from the standard wooden knobs, they offer other hardware, like porcelain knobs and Chippendale batwing brasses, where appropriate.

WELLINGTON'S FURNITURE
902 Blowing Rock Road; P.O. Box 2178
Boone, NC 28607
Free Catalog
Return policy: Money-Back Guarantee

Telephone: 704-262-5511
Fax No: 704-265-1049

If you love the look and feel of smooth, sumptuous leather in furniture for your home or office, then the Wellington's Furniture Catalog is a mail-order "must see." It displays the most beautifully crafted leather furniture - from sofas and sectionals to executive chairs and ottomans - in designs that'll match any decor. They feature leathers by McKinley of Hickory, Emerson, Distinction, Leathercraft and Wellington's own top grain varieties. They have a wonderful selection of decorative colors and patterns. They can even custom blend the unusual shades you might be hunting for elsewhere. What's more, they deliver anywhere in the U.S., right to your home or office door.

F
U
R
N
I
T
U
R
E

DALTON PAVILLIONS, INC.

Telephone: 215-342-9804

7260-68 Oakley Street
Philadelphia, PA 19111

Free Brochure

Return policy: Money-Back Guarantee

Add an elegant touch of Colonial styling, not to mention considerable value to your home and property, with these beautiful Western Red Cedar gazebos, pagodas, and 'architectural' birdhouses. The charming gazebos and pagodas come in sizes ranging from 9-26 feet, from point to point. Often commissioned for town squares, public parks and campground facilities, these structures are useful additions to backyard pool sites, decks or patios, too. Optional screening and concealed electrical kits are available. The gazebos and pavillions can be shipped to you prefab or unassembled. The birdhouses are equally attractive blends of function and design. The nesting compartments and holes are well suited for small songbirds and look great on your lawn or hanging from a terrace or patio.

LEISURE WOODS, INC.

Telephone: 815-784-2497
Fax No: 815-784-2499

P.O. Box 177
Genoa, IL 60135

DISCOUNT

Free Brochure

Return policy: Manufacturer's Warranty

Leisure Woods manufactures cedar gazebo kits that come with optional screening. They offer unbelievable quality at unheard of prices. Thay have many attractive styles to choose from and are rumored to be the most versatile gazebo manufacturer in the U.S. Orders are shipped anywhere in the country, usually delivered in 2-3 weeks. No returns are accepted, but if kits arrive with parts omited, they will be replaced at no charge.

VIXEN HILL GAZEBOS

Telephone: 215-286-0909
Fax No: 215-286-2099

Vixen Hill Manufacturing Company
Elverson, PA 19520

Free Catalog

Return policy: Money-Back Guarantee

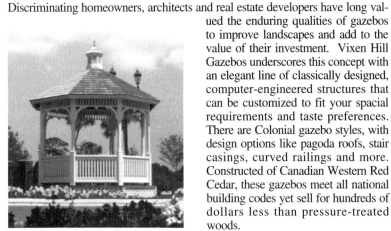

Discriminating homeowners, architects and real estate developers have long valued the enduring qualities of gazebos to improve landscapes and add to the value of their investment. Vixen Hill Gazebos underscores this concept with an elegant line of classically designed, computer-engineered structures that can be customized to fit your spacial requirements and taste preferences. There are Colonial gazebo styles, with design options like pagoda roofs, stair casings, curved railings and more. Constructed of Canadian Western Red Cedar, these gazebos meet all national building codes yet sell for hundreds of dollars less than pressure-treated woods.

SegmentE

DAMARK
6707 Shingle Creek Parkway
Minneapolis, MN 55430
Telephone: 612-566-4940
Fax No: 612-560-1644
DISCOUNT
Catalog $3.00
Return policy: Money-Back Guarantee if returned within 14 days

Damark has such varied merchandise, it's hard to generalize the selection. There are computers, fax machines, telephone systems, camcorders, typewriters, and stereos by Xerox, Emerson, Sharp and Magnavox. But you'll also find leather furniture, sheepskin car seat covers, hi-tech exercise equipment, vaccums, portable fireplaces, luggage, bikes and a myriad of unexpected items. Save over 50% off on these products. Join the Preferred Buyer's Club for even greater discounts.

HEARTLAND AMERICA
6978 Shade Oak Road
Eden Prairie , MN 55344-3453
Telephone: 800-966-1233
Fax No: 612-943-4096
DISCOUNT
Free Catalog
Return policy: Money-Back Guarantee if returned with 30 days

The best values in general merchandise "straight from the Heartland". They supply the latest in automotive, electronic, office and recreational accessories for the hi-tech consumer. Hard-to-find items, like high-pressure home car wash systems, outdoor stereo speakers, electronic language translators and home lamination machines can be found in their catalog. Collectors of fun recreational equipment should check out the Wurlitzer jukeboxes; plus slot machines by Mills Hightop and Golden Nugget. The best part, though, is the substantial savings up to 60%.

HOME SHOPPING VALUES
11851 30th Court N
St. Petersburg, FL 33716
Telephone: 813-572-6859
DISCOUNT
Free Catalog
Return policy: Money-Back Guarantee if returned within 30 days

This catalog is loaded with "as seen on TV" products endorsed by name-brands and well-known Hollywood stars. It features a many household gadgets like Singer's Hand-Held Sewing Machine, The Welbilt Bread Baker and Soundesign's Air Purifier/Ionizer. There are great fashion & beauty buys; plus fitness products like The Thigh Master endorsed by Suzanne Somers, Jack Lalanne's Fit Over 50 Vitamin Supplements, and Richard Simmons' Deal-A-Meal Program.

SERVICE MERCHANDISE
P.O. Box 25130
Nashville, TN 37202-9863
Telephone: 800-251-1212
Fax No: 800-962-4329
DISCOUNT
Free Catalog
Return policy: Money-Back Guarantee if returned within 30 days

Known as America's Leading Jeweler, they have Lifetime Diamond and Gold Chain Warranties. But they have much, more than jewelry; like Xerox's 5220 Personal Copier, Waring's Professional Juice Extractor, Samsonite Luggage and IBM's PS Notebook Computer with an 80MB Hard Drive. A very helpful Manufacturers' Assistance section provides you with all of the numbers to call when you need to talk to a manufacturer directly about a product.

ABBEY PRESS

344 Hill Drive
St. Meinrad, IN 47577-1001

Telephone: 812-357-8393
Fax No: 812-357-8260

Catalog $1.00
Return policy: Money Back Guarantee

While Abbey Press proclaims themself "The Christian Family Catalog," many of the gifts are perfect for persons of every faith. Personalized ice cream and pop-corn bowls, lemonade stands, stars and stripes windsocks and personalized door mats make great gifts for anyone. A percentage of all of the proceeds helps support St. Meinrad College. No matter if you're religious or not, you will enjoy this catalog.

AMIGOS

P.O. Box 720024
McAllen, TX 78504

Telephone: 512-687-1813

Free Brochure
Return policy: Money-Back Guarantee with proper authorization

If you haven't already heard of Amigos, read on! They're tiny handmade dolls of brilliant Guatemalan colors that are cleverly grouped onto earrings, necklaces, pins, hats, picture frames, headbands, hair combs, sunglasses, purses and many other accessories. Legend has it that people tell their worries to their Amigos. These adorable little friends come in varying sizes depending on what they're crafted onto, from 1 to 4 inches. Each one is wholly unique.

ANTICIPATIONS

9 Ross Simons Drive
Cranston, RI 02920-9848

Telephone: 800-521-7677
Fax No: 401-463-8599

Free Catalog
Return policy: 30-Day Money Back Guarantee

Why not make your home as delightful a place as possible. Anticipations makes this easy to accomplish with their marvelous vintage-style merchandise. Furniture, home accents, trinkets and seasonal decorations are just an overview of the varied inventory of tasteful items available. Silver flatware and china dinnerware in shapes and styles to complement your dining room table. Anticipations helps you make the most of your home.

CHARLES KEATH, LTD.

P.O. Box 48800
Atlanta, GA 30362-1800

Telephone: 404-449-3103
Fax No: 404-447-1357

Free Catalog
Return policy: Unlimited Satisfaction Guarantee

Add a slice of whimsy to your home. Fun and folksy, frisky and functional, all the items in the Charles Keath, Ltd. catalog are a perfectly elegant way of making life just a little nicer. From the high-quality antique bank reproductions to classic wicker Chippendale-styled stacking end tables, you know that these aren't just a bunch of cheap imitations. There's definitely something for everyone, and perhaps several things for you!

CHIASSO
P.O. Box 10399
Chicago, IL 60610-9002
Free Catalog
Return policy: Money-Back Guarantee

Telephone: 800-654-3570
Fax No: 312-419-8179

This innovative gift and accessories retailer out of Chicago offers its products to you by mail. They have a clever assortment of modern objets d'art in accent furniture, tableware, and office accessories. Most are created by well-known artists like Lorenzo Porcelli, Philippe Starck, Nathalie du Pasquier and Matteo Thun. Many of the photo props that you'll find in the catalog are for sale too.

COLLECTABLES ON CALL
1231 East Main Street
Meriden, CT 06450
Free Brochures and Flyers
Return policy: Money-Back Guarantee

Telephone: 800-622-4114

Collectibles On Call sells Precious Moments, all Dept. 56 Villages and Snowbabies, Swarovski Crystal and David Winter Cottages. Layaways, reservations, special requests and the latest in product information are commitments to the best in customer service for serious collectors. Selling at suggested retail only, Collectibles On Call is an authorized collectibles retailer for Madame Alexander and Annalee Dolls, Byers' Choice, All God's Children, Cairn Gnomes, Hallmark Galleries and Ornaments, Maud Humphrey, Memories of Yesterday, Lowell Davis, M.I. Hummel and more - all just a phone call away.

FORTUNOFF
P.O. Box 1550
Westbury, NY 11590
Free Catalog
Return policy: Money-Back Guarantee within 10 days, Credit cards 30 days

Telephone: 800-937-4376
Fax No: 516-873-6984
DISCOUNT

Fortunoff, the world-famous company known for years as "the source" for precious jewelry and silver tableware, also offers beautiful bed linens, bath items and window treatments. They even sell contemporary outdoor furniture and accessories in your choice of materials (from genuine hardwoods to cast aluminum) at great prices. All items are of superior quality and brought to you by a name that's been tops in the mail-order business for years.

FRATRACK FACTORY
981 First Avenue; Suite 137
New York, NY 10022
Free Information
Return policy: Satisfaction Guaranteed

Telephone: 212-755-1679
Fax No: 212-223-4752

Sherryl Fratell has come up with and ingenious gift idea for the golfer who has everything. She's put real golf balls on the pegs of acrylic racks for hanging coats, hats, ties or ties. The white or multi-colored golf balls rest on tubular silver-finished pegs. Choose from clear or black bases to match any decor. You can buy the racks with one ball or four, and the folks at the Fratrack Factory can customize the balls or acrylic base with a company logo for corporate gifts.

GEARY'S
351 North Beverly Drive
Beverly Hills, CA 90210-4794
Free Catalog

Telephone: 800-227-6488
Fax No: 213-858-7555

Return policy: 30-Day Money Back Guarantee

Exclusive and lavish objects from Beverly Hills can beautify your home. Geary's has been presenting tasteful and elegant items for over 60 years. The outstanding art reproductions, Waterford crystal pieces and mahogany desk accessories will instantly upgrade your home or office. Endearing porcelain bookends, night-lights and teddy bears are perfect for your child's bedroom.

GUMP'S
250 Post Street
San Francisco, CA 94108
Free Catalog
Return policy: Money-Back Guarantee

Telephone: 800-284-8677
Fax No: 214-228-0397

The rare, the unique and the imaginative have been Gump's trademarks since 1861. They search the world over for creative ideas to help with last-minute shopping and the most original decorative accents for your home. You'll ooh and aah at the turn of every page. They have fine porcelain treasures, pillows made of antique Oriental rugs, handblown tortoiseshell glassware and the most charming selection of handpainted Christams ornaments. Also worth mentioning is a festive grouping of holiday clothing, from opulent eveningware to lovely silk dresses.

HANOVER HOUSE
P.O. Box 2
Hanover , PA 17333-0002
Catalog $1.00
Return policy: Money-Back Guarantee

Telephone: 717-633-3366
Fax No: 800-338-1635

Here's one of America's best known shop-at-home resources, not just for gift items, but for a myriad of clever household gadgets that you never knew existed. From ultrasonic outdoor pest repellers to convenient tool holders, you'll find literally everything to keep those annoying household frustrations at bay. No longer will you have to ask question's like the classic "Where'd I put it?!" They have attractive and discreet storage racks and compartments for everything from thread to video cassettes. There's a great selection of home accents, clothing and personal items for the one on your list who supposedly has everything.

HARTS ENTERPRISES
PO Box 6132
Lubbock, TX 79493
Free Brochure, flyers
Return policy: Returns accepted within 45 days

Telephone: 800-873-2755

Beautiful "Memories of Yesterday" figurines at special prices. Harts has access to craftsmen who specialize in stain glass butterfly suncatchers, brass and copper flowers, fish and trees. Also, display cases and shadow boxes show and protect your treasures whether they be figurines, plates, spoons, ornaments, military medals, or even golf balls! Excellent gifts for someone who has "everything"

I. MAGNIN
Telephone: 800-227-1125

P.O. Box 2096
Oakland, CA 94604

Free Catalog

Return policy: Satisfaction Guaranteed

I. Magnin has excquisite giftware for everyone. Quality crystal creations by Hoya Museum Crystal, watches by Cartier and robes by Polo. Oversized tee shirts for her and cashmere sweaters for him. Gold-plated razors and classic fragrances for both husband and wife. You can't "I.magnin" how terrific these gifts are. There's even a dog collar with a gold vermeil buckle and matching leash! When they say something for everyone, they mean everyone.

KENTUCKY ART AND CRAFT GALLERY
Telephone: 502-589-0102

609 West Main Street
Louisville, KY 40202

Free Catalog

Return policy: Money-Back Guarantee

Representing over 400 of the most talented artists and craftspeople in Kentucky, this catalog features a unique collection of handmade wonders. The Kentucky Art and Craft Gallery catalog features Native American-inspired pottery, sterling silver jewelry, hand-pieced quilts, hand-carved wooden home accents and much more. Some of the prices are a little exorbitant, but the craftsmanship is truly unsurpassed for this type of merchandise.

LEFTHANDED SOLUTIONS, INC.
Telephone: 516-474-0091

P.O. Box 617
Port Jefferson Station, NY 11776

Free Brochure

Return policy: Satisfaction Guaranteed

Talk about frustrating, lefty's don't have it easy. While Einstein figured out the theory of relativity, it's probably true that he had a rough time figuring out how to get along in a right-handed world. If he had only known about Lefthanded Solutions, purveyors of the most extensive selection of products provided exclusively for lefties. Items like lefty corkscrews and can openers make the kitchen a better place to be, especially when your viewpoint is from the left!

LENOX
Telephone: 800-225-1779

1170 Wheeler Way
Langhorne, PA 19047

Free Information

Return policy: Money-Back Guarantee

You've seen what they can do with fine china, glassware and other table accents. Now see their wonderful selection of gift ideas, including The Lenox Garden Bird Sculpture, Nativity and Floral Sculpture Collections. Crafted of the finest materials, like bisque porcelain and fine bone china, these and other collections are guaranteed to apppreciate in value with each year. Every charming creation comes with a signed Certificate of Authenticity attesting to its Lenox exclusivity.

LILLIAN VERNON

Telephone: 804-430-1500

510 South Fulton Avenue
Mount Vernon, NY 10550

Free Catalog

Return policy: Money-Back Guarantee

Call Lillian Vernon to receive full-color catalogs chock-full of merchandise at the best prices. They've traveled far and wide to find the things you need for home maintenence, decorating and recreation. Most items can be personalized.

LOUISIANA GENERAL STORE

Telephone: 800-237-4841
Fax No: 504-482-3922

620 Decatur Street at The Jackson Brewery
New Orleans, LA 70130

Catalog $1.00

Return policy: Money-Back Guarantee

We've classified it as giftware, but some of this stuff is just too cool to give away! Aficionados of the Cajun region will love the selection of fun memorabilia by McIlhenny Tobasco and the New Orleans School of Cooking. There's also a wide range of food items, seasonings, spices and entertaining cookbooks to give your special dishes Cajun country flavor. They offer barbecue sauces, coffees, teas and preserves. Don't miss the music collection from Louisiana's own Mardi Gras Records, bringing you the spirit of the annual tradition in Cajun & Zydeco, Rhythm & Blues, Dixieland and Traditional Jazz.

MUSEUM COLLECTIONS

Telephone: 800-442-2460

921 Eastwind Drive
Westerville, OH 43081-3341

Free Catalog

Return policy: Money-Back Guarantee

If you've ever walked through a museum and wished you could take home some of the wonderful treasures on display, this is your chance. Here's a sophisticated grouping of replicas and reproductions from actual museum artifacts. Original works of art that inspire these items can be found in museums all over the world, including The Acropolis Museum in Athens, The British Museum in London and the Cooper-Hewitt Museum in New York. Home accents, jewelry and furniture are as mysterious and intriguing as the originals that inspired them.

NATIONAL WILDLIFE FEDERATION

Telephone: 800-432-6564
Fax No: 703-442-7332

Order Dept., 8925 Leesburg Pike
Vienna, VA 22184-0001

Free Catalog

Return policy: Money Back Guarantee

The wonders of the natural world meet the commercial world. The result is a unique selection of items that could only come from the National Wildlife Federation. Children can lather up with a soap egg that has a soft dinosaur inside. Full color prints of wolves, foxes and other members of the forest community can decorate your walls. There are solar battery chargers, 20- year coffee filters and other unique solutions to waste disposal and environmental problems. You can save something else besides the world—save up to 65% on sale items.

G
I
F
T
W
A
R
E

PIECES OF OLDE

Telephone: 301-366-4949

P.O. Box 65130
Baltimore, MD 21209

Catalog $3.00

Return policy: Money-Back Guarantee if returned within 10 days

If you crave handmade crafts or love assembling your own for gift-giving, then you'll enjoy thumbing through this catalog. They have a number of soft dolls that you can purchase ready-made, in unassembled kits, or as a pattern to customize with your own fabric. There's an artful variety of clothing made from antique fabrics, soft cotton fleece, white lace and elegant brocade, as well as needlepoint pillows, kilim accents, crocheted lace tablecloths; plus a full range of craft supplies.

SHANNON DUTY FREE MAIL ORDER

Telephone: 800-223-6716
Fax: 011-353-61-363182

c/o Aer Lingus - Irish Airlines;
Building #87; JFK Airport
New York, NY 11430

Catalog $2.00

Return policy: Money-Back Guarantee

Shannon specializes in duty-free, imported giftware from Ireland. They carry limited edition replicas of 18th and 19th century weaponry and "character jugs" by Royal Doulton. They have world-famous porcelain Hummel figurines, Irish linen handkerchiefs, Waterford Crystal glassware, and precious jewelry by Claddagh, Jacques Esteve and Swarovski. French perfumes offered include Dior's Poison, Van Cleef & Arpels' Gem and L'Air du Temps by Nina Ricci.

SIGNALS

Telephone: 800-669-5225
Fax No: 612-659-4320

1000 Westgate Drive
St. Paul , MN 55114

Free Catalog

Return policy: Money-Back Guarantee

Signals mail-order service offers a number of entertaining products for fans of public television. They have video collections of the best-loved episodes from your favorite PBS series including "The Cases of Sherlook Holmes", "Agatha Cristie's Poirot" and "I Claudius". The catalog also features jewelry, personal artifacts, and clever electronic gadgets like The Crossword Puzzle Solver by Franklin and Infrasound's cordless tv/stereo headphones. A unique assortment of games, books and videos that revel in the mysteries of the spiritual world, too.

SUNDANCE GENERAL STORE

Telephone: 800-422-2770

780 West Layton Avenue
Salt Lake City, UT 84104

Free Catalog

Return policy: Money-Back Guarantee

The best of the American West is what you'll find in Robert Redford's Sundance General Store catalog. From the desert plains of Utah is a collection of Western favorites including handmade patchwork quilts, earthenware pottery, terracotta, wrought iron fireplace accessories, Western clothing, jewelry, & Native American artifacts. The Sundance Wildflower Farm offers you the same organically-grown flowers and herbs they send to their famous restaurant clients out west.

G
I
F
T
W
A
R
E

THE COCKPIT
P.O. Box 019005
Long Island City, NY 11101-9005
Catalog $3.00
Return policy: 60 Day Money Back Guarantee

Telephone: 800-272-WING
Fax No: 718-472-9692

You can hear the airplanes roar as you browse through this exceptional collection of aviation clothing, artifacts and novelties for both the air memorabilia collector and the man who wants classically styled leather bomber jackets. Own authentic and replica flight bags, insignia and flying helmets, as well as military styled shirts, boots and watches. There's even an actual World War II B-25 bomber for sale. Fly high without leaving the ground.

THE DANCING DRAGON
5670 West End Road, #4
Arcata, CA 95521
Free Catalog
Return policy: Money-Back Guarantee

Telephone: 707-826-0189
Fax No: 707-826-1370

If you love this mythical, fire-breathing creature from the Orient, you'll appreciate the fine quality workmanship that went into the creation of these artful renditions. You'll find many beautiful dragon items, from brass dragon pins to medieval lithographs to red glass dragon charms. Some items are just plain fun and whimsical, like the 'Dragons in the Attic' sculpture. Others are works of art to be treasured, such as a River Dragon sculpted of colored glass. They also have imported cloisonne pocket watches and reproduced ceremonial Samurai swords.

THE ENGRAVER'S BLOCK/INITIALLY YOURS
P.O. Box 678
Brookfield , CT 06804
Catalog $1.85
Return policy: Money-Back Guarantee except on personalized items

Telephone: 203-775-5998

You might never see your name in lights, but they can immortalize it on anything in their catalog of gift items and personal collectibles. Elegant business card holders, clocks, brass letter openers and other office necessities can be engraved for perfect corporate gifts. They also have bookends, large 'initial' paperweights, brass money clips and even stainless steel engraved pet feeders. Or congratulate someone you love on their first "big break" with an engraved nameplates.

THE FARMER'S DAUGHTER
P.O. Box 1071
Nags Head, NC 27959
Catalog $2.00
Return policy: Money-Back Guarantee

Telephone: 919-441-1077
Fax No: 919-441-4220

Folksy giftware, country home accents and casual clothing are just a few of the items you find in this fascinating catalog. From Nags Head, NC comes a number of handmade country decorations for your home including beautiful patchwork quilts, wood & metal light fixtures, country art lithographs and more. They carry a handsome selection of accent furniture pieces crafted of ponderosa pine.

G
I
F
T
W
A
R
E

THE HEMMETER COLLECTION
1999 Avenue of the Stars
Los Angeles, CA 90067
Free Catalog
Return policy: Money-Back Guarantee

Telephone: 800-533-9660
Fax No: 310-768-2063

Turn your home into a cornucopia of museum-quality artifacts from an extraor-dinary collection of exotic decorative accents made from the finest materials. Charming cloisonne animal figurines, hand-painted cotton pillows with authentic African beading, a copper-plated cast iron table that evokes hyroglyphic themes and exquisite earrings crafted of tourmaline cabochons, amethyst, and citrines are just a few of the breathtaking treasures. You'll also find flattering women's fashions and beautifully-crafted furniture.

THE HOUSE OF TYROL
P.O. Box 909; Alpenland Center
Cleveland, GA 30528
Free Catalog
Return policy: Money-Back Guarantee if returned within 30 days

Telephone: 404-865-5115
Fax No: 404-865-7794

For 21 years, The House of Tyrol has spanned the globe to bring you quality gifts. They began as a specialty shop of imports from the Alps. Today, in addition to charming steins, cuckoo clocks, wood carvings, dolls and ornate textiles from that region, they also carry treasures from the American Southwest, Germany and Great Britain. Note their stained glass decorations and baroque tapestries.

THE JOHNSON SMITH COMPANY
4514 19th St. Court East; P.O. Box 25500
Bradenton, FL 34206-5500
Free Catalog
Return policy: Money-Back Guarantee

Telephone: 813-747-2356
Fax No: 813-746-7896

Since 1914, they've searched the world for "Things you never knew existed...and other items you can't live without." They're referring to everything from voice change megaphones and life-size "stand-ups" of your favorite NBA basketball stars, to high protection sunglasses and unheard-of electronic gadgets. Don't miss the most complete collection of Star Trek memorabilia from the 60s and 90s, plus great stuff from big screen hits. Halloween will be a night to remember with cos-tumes, masks, life-like plastic "body parts" and other gruesome fare.

THE MUSIC STAND
1 Rockdale Plaza
Lebanon, NH 03766-1585
Free Catalog
Return policy: Satisfaction Guaranteed

Telephone: 802-295-9222
Fax No: 802-295-5080

Music calms the savage beast, but it doesn't help with your gift shopping. The Music Stand is a cornucopia of music-oriented items suitable for the musician, composer or that special note of music in your life. The largest collection of pen-dants, tee shirts, boxes, and novelties with a note-worthy touch. This large cata-log will provide at least something for everyone.

THE PARAGON
89 Tom Harvey Road
Westerly, RI 0289
Free Catalog
Return policy: Money-Back Guarantee

Telephone: 800-343-3095
Fax No: 401-596-6104

Given on finding a one-stop-shopping resource for gifts? Don't throw in the towel until you've checked out The Paragon's catalog of clever gift ideas Or, forget the list and treat yourself to their festive holiday clothing, jewelry, table accessories, fine furnishings, and rare musical recordings. Sportsmen will love classic golfing accessories, baseball memorabilia, sports-inspired desk accessories and mind-challenging games.

THE SAN FRANCISCO MUSIC BOX CO.
P.O. Box 7817
San Francisco, CA 94120-7817
Free Catalog
Return policy: Moeny-Back Guarantee

Telephone: 800-227-2190

Each and every musical item in their catalog plays a tune you select from a list of well-known favorites. Holiday will ring memorable selections from famous Broadway shows, classical composers or popular films They also have silk flowers that add musical charm to a bouquet, stuffed toys that lull kids to sleep, plus paperweights, bookends and collector porcelain figurines.

THE SOURCE FOR EVERYTHING JEWISH
P.O. Box 48836
Niles, IL 60648
Free Catalog
Return policy: Money-Back Guarantee

Telephone: 708-966-4040
Fax No: 708-966-4033

The name implies a serious challenge, which they exceed in bringing you a tremendous assortment of products that celebrate the rich heritage of the Jewish faith. Wonderful holiday trimmings for the home include beautifully sculpted menorahs, decorative draydels and hand-painted ceramic sederware. There are also great bar mitzvah and bat mitzvah gift items; plus a library of books, videos and musical compositions on the Jewish experience.

THINK BIG!
16249 Stagg Street
Van Nuys, CA 91406
Catalog $2.00
Return policy: Money-Back Guarantee if returned within 30 days

Telephone: 800-676-6523
Fax No: 818-373-7949

In an era when excess is generally frowned upon, its nice to know that someone out there realizes that bigger will always be better. Think Big! is a giftware catalog that's based on this concept. Followers of the "less is more" school need not apply! We're talking BIG 12 x 6 inch pasta holders fashioned like salt 'n pepper shakers; BIG 15 x 6 inch wall hangings that look like bagels; and a BIG 12 inch Oreo cookie that's great for serving party snacks. These and other BIG items are available for fun gifts and intriguing conversation pieces for your own home or office.

G
I
F
T
W
A
R
E

TRIFLES

Telephone: 214-556-6055

P.O. Box 620048
Dallas, TX 75262-0048

Free Catalog

Return policy: Money-Back Guarantee

Just when you thought you'd seen all there was to see in unusual home accents and gift ideas, along comes Trifles, and you realize you ain't seen nothin' yet! Their selection is simply tremendous and the only way to describe the quality of the merchandise is "upscale". When only a gift of the highest taste will do, check into their stained crystal glassware, exquisite porcelain dinnerware, silver serving pieces, designer luggage, lovely linens and personalized stationery. The flattering women's clothing selection in sumptuous fabrics and colors is a must-see.

WESTMINSTER PEWTER & GIFTS

Telephone: 215-322-5925

37 Bellwood Drive
Langhorne, PA 19053

DISCOUNT

Free Catalog

Return policy: Money-Back Guarantee

Fine quality pewter and sterling giftware is available from Westminster Pewter and Gifts at wholesale prices. Their large selection of baby items are perfect for new arrivals or the mom-to-be. They also carry a complete selection of holloware - from coffee sets to after-dinner cordial services. For Christmas, a large selection of pewter ornaments available, too. Orders are shipped UPS.

WHALE GIFTS

Telephone: 800-227-1929

P.O. Box 810
Old Saybrook, CT 06475-0810

Free Catalog

Return policy: Money-Back Guarantee

Sponsored by the Center For Marine Conservation, this catalog of collectibles and gift items promotes the appreciation and preservation of the world's marine wildlife. There's an interesting mix of clothing items including sweatshirts, ties, and outerwear, all with endearing animal motifs. There are charming animal sculptures, jewelry, posters, bed & bath accessories and stuffed animals for the kids. About 15% of the proceeds from merchandise sold benefits the CMC and there's a 10% product discount for current members of the nature conservancy.

WILD WINGS

Telephone: 800-445-4833
Fax No: 612-345-2981

South Highway 61
Lake City, MN 55041-0451

Free Catalog

Return policy: Money-Back Guarantee

Bring the adventure and wonder of the great outdoors into your home or office with worldly creations offered by Wild Wings. You won't be able to resist their cozy, animal-print furniture, decorative accents, hunting gear, jewelry and dinnerwear, among other objects. Their colorful assortment of framed lithographs captures the natural beauty of every variety of flora and fauna imaginable. If you're searching for the right gift for the adventurer in your life, look no further!

G I F T W A R E

WIRELESS

Telephone: 800-669-9999

1000 Westgate Drive
St. Paul, MN 55114

Free Catalog

Return policy: Money-Back Guarantee

For fans and friends of public radio, or for people who just love collecting fun bits of cultural nostalgia, this is a fantastic mail-order guide. They have sound recordings of the comedy team Bob & Ray, Broadway's "Phantom of the Opera", Frank Sinatra, Victor Borge, Woody Allen, Glenn Miller and other classic attractions. You'll also find collector's treasures like historic porcelain enameled signs, commemorative t-shirts, jewelry and rare books. Beyond this, there's still a bountiful selection of hard-to-find items, like wonderful wildlife memorabilia, cross-cultural relics and decorative accents inspired by old Hollywood.

WORLD WILDLIFE FUND CATALOG

Telephone: 800-833-1600

P.O. Box 224
Peru, IN 46970

Free Catalog

Return policy: 30-Day Money Back Guarantee.

If you love animals, or fun and colorful things, the World Wildlife Fund Catalog is for you. Everything that growls and grunts can be purchased in some form or another. Pandas, pachyderms and porpoises grace t-shirts, ties and towels. Really want to make an impression? Send animal greeting cards instead of ordinary cards. We'd all like to do something to save animals, and by purchasing any of the products offered here you will be doing yourself and the animals a favor.

ADAPTABILITY
P.O. Box 515
Colchester, CT 06415-0515
Free Catalog
Return policy: Money-Back Guarantee

Telephone: 800-243-9232
Fax No: 203-537-2866

This catalog offers ingenious products that help disabled consumers become more able. Items are designed to promote comfort and an independent lifestyle, from everyday helpers to tools that aid in physical therapy and rehabilitation. They have specially designed furniture, tableware, kitchen utensils, personal care items, medical supplies and games and challenging activities to keep the mind active and alert.

MEDI-MAIL PHARMACY
P.O. Box 98520
Las Vegas, NV 89193-8520
Free Brochure and Pricelist
Return policy: Unopened Merchandise Returnable

Telephone: 800-RX-DELIVERY

The rising costs of prescription drugs and over-the-counter pharmaceuticals is enough to make anyone sick! Stop paying high prices with this mail-order service by Medi-Mail, Inc. They offer outstanding savings on a wide range of the health products. These include generic drugs, vitamins, name-brand cold and allergy products, sleeping aids and antacid remedies. They also have an assortment of indispensible personal care products by Oil of Olay, Vaseline and Keri.

PHARMAIL
87 Main Street; P.O. Box 1466
Champlain, NY 12919-1466
Free Information
Return policy: Money-Back Guarantee

Telephone: 800-237-8927

If you've been paying entirely too much for prescription or over-the-counter drugs (and chances are you have), Pharmail can get them to you at or below wholesale prices. They also offer substantial savings on generics. There are no age or membership requirements and they can dispense any "mailable" prescription pharmaceuticals, except for narcotics. Pharmail enters into preferential agreements with groups and social welfare organizations, and will negotiate additional incentives based on size and purchasing volume.

STAR PROFESSIONAL PHARMACEUTICALS
1500 New Horizons Boulevard
Amityville, NY 11701
Free Catalog
Return policy: Money-Back Guarantee if returned within 30 days

Telephone: 800-274-6400

You and your family can be fit and healthy without spending loads of money on health care products. They offer their own line of products, fully comparable to the well-known, high-priced brands on drug store shelves. Star has been providing consumers with high quality, affordably priced over-the-counter drugs for 38 years.Cold & allergy products, dental care products, pain relievers, vitamins, kids' health products and diet aids are just a small representation of the items offered. They also have health care books and easy-living aids for the whole family.

HEALTH & MEDICAL

129

VITAMIN POWER HEALTH & FITNESS

Telephone: 616-429-3352

1588 Cardinal Drive
St. Joseph, MI 49085

Free Catalog

Return policy: Money-Back Guarantee

To help meet the specific nutritional needs of a healthier America, this comprehensive line of over 300 functional nutrition and health products is manufactured under the Vitamin Power label. The top-quality products are manufactured using only bio-nutrients derived from foods - no drugs, chemicals, artificial coloring agents or artificial flavors. Whether you're rethinking an existing health and fitness regimen or finally beginning one, stock up on specialized vitamin supplements, muscle anabolic formulas, all-natural diet aids, energy boosters and pain remedies. You'll also find a wide assortment of "nutritious" skin care products by GreatWay; plus a number of informative health and fitness manuals.

VITAMIN SPECIALTIES COMPANY

Telephone: 800-365-8482
Fax No: 215-885-1310

8200 Ogontz Avenue
Wyncote, PA 19095

DISCOUNT

Free Catalog

Return policy: Money-Back Guarantee on unopened merchandise only

Here is your chance to compare prices and then save big on generic health products, natural cosmetics and drug items. Now in their 51st year of unbeatable service, Vitamin Specialties Company offers every vitamin on the market, from A to Zinc, plus exotic herbal extracts like Ginseng, Bee Pollen and Apple Pectin. Don't miss the selection of specialized cosmetic healers for hair, eyes, skin and overall well-being. There are also nutrition and health books on conquering stress and fatigue, exercise for senior citizens, and specific healing medicines, among other topics.

WHITAKER'S

Telephone: 800-924-5438
Fax No: 914-423-4243

1 Odell Plaza; P.O. Box 1061
Yonkers , NY 10701

Free Brochure

Return policy: Money-Back Guarantee

Accessibility experts since 1937, Whitakers has offered the most complete range of transport devices to aid the disabled. Their Stair-O-Lators, Stair-Tracs, Incline Lifts, Carrier Lifts and Vertical Lifts have helped thousands of handicapped individuals lead more independent and productive lives. Their products are built of solid, sturdy materials to last for years, yet provide superior comfort. Whitakers also offers a line of chair lifts, bath lifts and adjustable beds for total independent accessiblity. What's more, they can install and service all their own products.

ABC VACUUM WAREHOUSE

6720 Burnet Road - SM
Austin, TX 78757

Free Brochure

Telephone: 512-459-7943

DISCOUNT

Return policy: Returns accepted within 15 days

Clean up your act with a new vacuum at a great price. ABC carries New Rainbow, Kirby, Filter Queen, Tri-Star, Panasonic, Oreck, Royal, Riccar, Thermax, Princess, Sharp, the Sanyo Mite Hunter and even built-in vacuum sytems. It's simple to take advantage of these savings. Just call or write for a free brochure, which comes with full details on their ordering policies. Merchandise is discounted up to 50% off the national retail prices. Shipping is via parcel post or UPS in 3 weeks or less.

FOTO ELECTRIC SUPPLY

31 Essex Street
New York, NY 10002

Free Information

Telephone: 212-673-5222

DISCOUNT

Return policy: Returns accepted on damaged merchandise only

Foto Electric Supply Company offers you major brand appliances at low, low prices. Just call them with the name and model number of the appliance you're looking for. Their customer service representatives will give you discounted price quotes right over the phone. What's more, they ship abywhere in the U.S. in under a week.

HOME SALES DIAL-A-DISCOUNT

23-27 East 65th Street
Brooklyn, NY 11234

No Catalog

Telephone: 212-513-1513
or 718-241-3272

DISCOUNT

Certified Checks

Return policy: Money Back Guarantee

Major appliances are their specialty. Call for price quotes on name brand major appliances; they specialize in condos and co-ops. Call Monday-Friday 9am-5pm EST and speak with a knowledgeable salesperson. Items are shipped via trucking company in just a few days. Discounts vary - call for the best price.

SELECTRONICS KITCHEN APPLIANCES

1166 Hamburg Turnpike
Wayne, NJ 07470

Free Information

Telephone: 800-444-6300
Fax No: 201-628-8069

DISCOUNT

Return policy: Money-Back Guarantee

Selectronics has the lowest prices on high quality brands like Maytag, Jenn-Air, Thermador, Miele, Kitchen Aid, Amana and Snaidero. Ovens, cook tops, washers, dryers, refrigerators and dishwashers - Selectronics has what your home needs! Bathroom fixtures, kitchen cabinets, appliances and other home supplies are available, too. Selectronics also carries home entertainment items, like TVs, camcorders, CD players and more. Shop around. They have no competition. Call for unbeatable prices and enjoy it now - most merchandise can be shipped within 24 hours.

THE ORECK CORPORATION

100 Plantation Road
New Orleans, LA 70123-9989

Free Catalog

Telephone: 504-733-8761

DISCOUNT

Return policy: Money-Back Guarantee if returned within 30 days

Super sales, special savings and superb product selections are guaranteed in every issue of Oreck's catalog of discount home appliances. In addition to a limited supply of Sanyo products, they've put their own label on a line of high-tech vaccum cleaners for a variety of surfaces. Uprights, canisters, industrials, minivans and car vacs - they're all built to last and come with a variety of convenient attachments so that every crack and crevice will be dirt-free.

HOME APPLIANCES

ARCTIC GLASS AND WINDOW OUTLET
565 Country Road T
Hammond, WI 54015
Free Brochures
Return policy: Money Back Guarantee

Telephone: 800-428-9276
Fax No: 715-796-WARM
DISCOUNT

Originally from Alaska, the Wisconsin-based Arctic Glass and Window Outlet offers tempered glass windows and skylights by Velux and Kolbe & Kolbe at tremendously low prices. These insulated windows will keep you warm in the winter and cool in the summer. Should you have any questions, Arctic Glass and Window Outlet prides itself on being a large company with an accessible president. You can pay half your bill when you order and half when it arrives. Shipments to New York City must be prepaid, however.

CRAWFORD'S OLD HOUSE STORE
550 Elizabeth Street
Waukeshia, WI 53186
Free Information
Return policy: Money-Back Guarantee within 30 days (30% restocking fee)

Telephone: 414-542-0685

If you're planning full-scale remodeling or hoping to add finishing touches to complement your existing decor, Crawford's Old House Store has solid hardwood fixtures that lend an elegant, Victorian feel. Corner beads protect plaster, wallpaper and paint at the 'turn of the corner' where the wall is most often damaged by everyday traffic. They can also be used as decorative touches in archways, on pillars, and under stairwells. Crawford's also carries hard-to-find trims including post caps, corner blocks, hardwood doorstops and decorative finials.

DRIWOOD MOULDING COMPANY
P.O. Box 1729
Florence, SC 29503
2 Volume Catalog, $3.00 Each
Return policy: 15% Restocking Charge

Telephone: 803-662-0541
Fax No: 803-669-4874
COD

Driwood Moulding Company offers authentic period-style mouldings and millwork for professional architects and amateur home owners. Lavishly illustrated with color photos, their two-volume catalog provides decorative ideas while displaying Driwood mouldings in actual room settings. Delivery can usually be made within 2 to 3 days after the receipt of your order. While there is a charge for assembled samples, unassembled samples are available free of charge.

GRAND ERA REPRODUCTIONS, INC.
P.O. Box 1026
Lapeer, MI 48446
Free Catalog
Return policy: Require Prior Authorization. 15% Restocking Charge

Telephone: 313-664-1756
Fax No: 313-664-8957

Capture the charm of Victorian days gone by with one of the notable items available from Grand Era Reproductions. Oak moulding, fencing and doors provide a Victorian accent, while tiffany lamps, window seats and brass doorbell plates provide finishing touches to an authentic look your grandmother would be proud of. They even sell brass polish to keep your old-style items looking like new.

HORTON BRASSES

Nooks Hill Rd., P.O. Box 95
Cromwell, CT 06416

Telephone: 203-635-4400
Fax No: 203-635-6473

Free Catalog

Return policy: 15% Handling Charge

For the finishing touch to a Victorian poster bed or colonial desk, contact Horton Brasses. Makers of authentic reproduction furniture hardware, they can supply the accessories you require for period furniture of the 1680s to the 1920s. With over 45 types of plate-pulls alone, finding a missing accessory for that otherwise immaculate antique is easy. They are happy to answer any hardware question you might have; just mail it with a self-addressed stamped envelope.

KRUP'S KITCHENS & BATH LTD.

11 West 18th Street
New York, NY 10011

Telephone: 212-243-KRUP
Fax No: 212-243-3205
DISCOUNT

No Catalog

Return policy: Money Back Guarantee

Krup's is the ultimate and complete source for your bath and kitchen, offering over 30 years of experience and the best prices on home appliances, built-ins, air conditioners, VCRs and TVs. Huge selection of faucets and sinks form American Standard, Grohe, Hansa, Dornbracht, Franke, Elkay, Kohler and Delta, as well as decorative hardware including Baldwin, Hewi, and Jado at up to 35% off retail. For price quotes, call with the styles you're looking for.

LONG ISLAND BATH WHOLESALERS

717 East Jericho Turnpike, Suite 294
Huntington Station, NY 11746

Telephone: 800-553-0663

DISCOUNT

Free Brochures

Return policy: 25% Restocking Charge. Custom orders not returnable

Looking to beautify your bath without draining your bank account? Long Island Bath Wholesalers offers discounts on faucets, sinks, cabinets and accessories for kitchen and bath, plus a whole lot more. American Standard, Kohler, Eurotec, Raphael and Moen are only a few of the more than 30 faucet manufacturers carried by this terrific source of discounted bath supplies. Whirlpools by Jacuzzi and Pearl, as well as sinks and pedestals by Hastings and St. Thomas. If you need an item they don't carry, find out the manufacturer's name, model, style and color from your local store, and LIBW will get it for you at discounted prices.

MOULTRIE MANUFACTURING COMPANY

P.O. Box 1179
Moultrie, GA 31776-1179

Telephone: 800-841-8674
Fax No: 912-890-7245

Free Catalog

Return policy: Returns with written authorization. 20% Restocking Fee

Designs with distinction. The Old South collection by Moultrie Manufacturing can add a touch of charm to your home. Cast aluminum furniture will beautify your living room or patio while fountains can make your yard a place to behold. Primed for painting, easy-to-install metal columns offer a durable and practical alternative to costly wooden ones as weather-resistant decorative elements.

SILVERTON VICTORIAN MILLWORKS
P.O. Box 2987
Durango, CO 81302
Free Catalog
Telephone: 303-259-5915
Fax No: 303-259-5919

COD

Return policy: Up To 20% Restocking Fee

How much wood could a woodchuck chuck? Not as much as Silverton Victorian Millworks. Makers of high-quality wood ornamentation, they offer an extensive array of base mouldings, crown mouldings and arch mouldings with a distinctively Victorian accent. Woodwork is available in premium oak and pine, as well as standard grades of wood. If you are restoring a Victorian house, or adding a distinctive flare to a spare bedroom, you'll find the wall accessories you need

SOUTH BOUND MILLWORKS
P.O. Box 349
Sandwich, MA 02563
Free Catalog
Telephone: 508-477-9355

Return policy: Money-Back Guarantee if returned within 14 days

Sprucing up around the house? Check out the South Bound Millworks catalog of wood and wrought iron curtain accessories, linen bars, and decorative accents for your home. Curtain rods, 'cranes' and hold backs come in a variety of styles to turn even the plainest window treatment into a beautiful vision. They also have charming wooden telephone directories fashioned like antique shudders, plus an assortment of little wooden boxes for all your personal treasures and trinkets.

THE ANTIQUE HARDWARE STORE
9718 Easton Road; Route 611
Kintnersville, PA 18930
Catalog $3.00
Telephone: 215-847-2447
Fax No: 215-847-5628

Return policy: Money-Back Guarantee within 60 days (except custom orders)

Add a striking touch of yesteryear to your home with exquisite antique fixtures and accents by The Antique Hardware Store. These charming additions will add interest to old-fashioned decor and unexpected charm to more modern interiors. They have claw-foot bathtubs, pedestal sinks, pillbox toilets, high-tank toilets, marble doorknobs and lots of other lovely accents for indoors and out. They have a wealth of wooden brass fixtures for doors, bedrooms, bathrooms and kitchens, too. You don't want to miss the wonderful outdoor grouping, including Adirondack furniture, Victorian "Towne Center" clocks, mailboxes, and more.

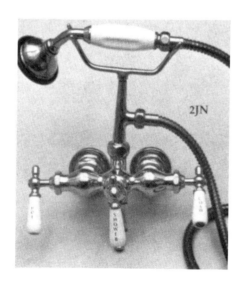

THE FAUCET OUTLET
Box 565
Monroe , NY 10950

Telephone: 800-444-5783

DISCOUNT

Catalog $5.00, refunded with 1st order
Return policy: Money-Back Guarantee

Buy decorator faucets from a wholesale leader and save! The Faucet Outlet's catalog offers top quality bathroom and kitchen faucets at 35% off suggested retail. Name brands including Kohler, American Standard, Grohe and Delta are available in all the popular styles, metals and colors. Related products such as hot water dispensers, food waste disposers and water filters are also at great savings.

THE OLD WAGON FACTORY
103 Russell Street, P.O. Box 1427
Clarksville, VA 23927-1427

Telephone: 800-874-9358
Fax No: 804-374-4646

Catalog $2.00
Return policy: 30-Day Money Back Guarantee, except Custom orders.

Bavarian bird houses, Chippendale-style porch swings and timeless brass door knockers are only a few of the unique home design touches available from The Old Wagon Factory. Suitable for restored Victorian manors and Cape Cod homes, these handcrafted items will add charm in your house or on your patio. With their Easy Payment Plan you are charged one third of your order when it is processed, another third in 30 days, and the balance on the day of shipment.

VALUE-TIQUE, INC.
P.O. Box 67
Leonia, NJ 07605

Telephone: 201-461-6500

Free Information
Return policy: Money-Back Guarantee

If you think you're not wealthy enough to warrant buying a safe, just ask yourself, "Am I wealthy enough to be robbed?" Burglars don't discriminate and neither do disasters like fires and floods. Value-tique offers a wide assortment of decorative home safes by Sentry, America's favorite name in secure storage. Store important documents, cash, jewelry and other valuables in a shallow or full-depth safes and fire-resistant file cabinets. Also, they have decorative enclosures for your safe, which look as inconspicuous as a fine wooden end table.

VAN DYKE'S RESTORERS
P.O. Box 278
Woonsocket, SD 57385-0278

Telephone: 605-769-4425
Fax No: 605-769-4085

Free Catalog

COD

Return policy: 30 Day Money-Back Guarantee. 10% Restocking Charge.

If you're a professional carpenter or a home hobbiest, Van Dyke's Restorers is acomplete source for carpentry tools and supplies. Their catalog is loaded with all types of hardware goodies. There are drawer knobs, chair components and roll-top desk kits, trunk parts, and zebrawood lumber, as well as historic nail reproductions for restoring with complete authenticity.

VERMONT CASTINGS
Prince Street
Randolph , VT 05060
Free Brochure
Return policy: Individual to Dealer

Telephone: 802-728-3181

Individual to Dealer

With hundreds of authorized dealers nationwide, Vermont Castings
gives you fuel-efficient, high-
quality, not to mention beautifully
crafted and designed fireplaces
and wood stoves. Their information booklet, The Fireside
Advisor, gives facts and figures
on cost, installation, authorized
dealers and maintenance.
Fireplaces and stoves are stylishly
self-sufficient, offering clean
burning, low-level smoke emis-
sion, solid cast iron construction
and attractive, "fire-viewing"
clear glass doors.

VINTAGE WOOD WORKS
513 S. Adams
Fredericksburg, TX 78624
Free Catalog

Telephone: 512-997-9513
Fax No: 512-997-4804

Return policy: Money-Back Guarantee if returned before installation.

Give your home an elegant, old world flair with beautiful wood accents and detail-
ing by Vermont Wood Works. Whether you're renovating or building anew, they
can sell handcrafted stair parts to create a breathtaking masterpiece. Newel posts,
balusters, railings, fittings and riser caps are made of solid oak and sized to your
specifications. They also carry decorative corbels, spandrels and brackets for dramatic effects over doors, windows or to incorporate into a stairway design.

GREATWOOD LOG HOMES, INC.
P.O. Box 707
Elkhart Lake, WI 53020
Plan Book $5.00

Telephone: 800-558-5812
Fax No: 414-876-2873

Why give up the dream of an old-fashioned log home when you can both live it and live in it! A Greatwood log home makes available the natural energy efficiency and traditional beauty of handcrafted cedar or pine logs at prices much lower than you'd expect. With 100 different designs, there is a style that is perfect for you. Their money-saving incentives make these attractive homes affordable to almost everyone. Contemporary cedar home designs are also available.

HISTORICAL REPLICATIONS, INC.
2629 Ridgewood Road
Jackson, MS 39236
Plans: 1/$12, 2/$20, 3/$30, 4/$38

Telephone: 800-426-5628

If you love old houses, then Historical Replications has the house plans for you. All of their designs incorporate modern technology and convenience into exteriors modeled after actual past-period houses. Own an old-style home without the hassle. There are over 150 stock plans in any of their unique house plan portfolios that highlight Victorian, Colonial, Southern and Classic styles. A custom design service is also available.

HOME PLANNERS, INC.
Dept. DM-9202, 3275 West Ina Rd.
Tucson, AZ 85741
Free Catalog

Telephone: 800-322-6797
Fax No: 602-297-6219

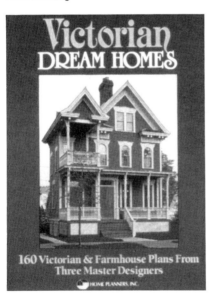

With over 3,650 designs to choose from, Home Planners has a house plan for everyone. Tudors, Colonials and Western ranches are only a sample of the wide variety of styles available from this house plan warehouse. There are even designs for earth-sheltered homes, landscaping and wooden decks. All orders are shipped within 48 hours.

INTERNATIONAL HOMES OF CEDAR, INC.
P.O. Box 886
Woodinville, WA 98072
Plan Book $8.00

Telephone: 206-668-8511
Fax No: 206-668-5562

While the prices of new homes are seemingly out of reach, International Homes of Cedar offers an attractive solution; custom-styled homes at bargain basement prices. All of the available homes feature cedar or pine walls with an optional layer of insulating material for the ultimate in energy efficiency. Each kit includes floor beams, exterior trim, windows, stopped-in glass, factory-hung doors and everything else you need to build it yourself (except tools)! If you haven't considered prefabricated housing and are looking for a new home, it might be worth your while to get some information on this affordable alternative.

LINDAL CEDAR HOMES
P.O. Box 24426
Seattle, WA 98124
Planbook $15.00, Videotape $19.95

Telephone: 800-426-0536

Western red cedar may be the source of Lindal Cedar Homes enduring beauty, but quality is the source of their 45 year reputation for excellence. With the capability to provide custom modifications to any of their over 100 floorplans, it's easy to create a dream home that is truly one-of-a-kind. Whether you would like a traditional log or clapboard home, or a more modern styled cedar house, Lindal Cedar Homes has the place you've been looking for.

ASF ENTERPRISES, INC.

Telephone: 616-429-3352

1588 Cardinal Drive
St Joseph, MI 49085

DISCOUNT

Free Catalog

Return policy: Money-Back Guarantee

For the top-quality goods you want and need for yourself, your family and your home, look to the ASF Enterprises catalog for the best values. From hi-tech stainless-steel cookware to genuine blue fox furs, they have a diversified selection of merchandise. It's like having an upscale discount department store at your fingertips. Fine china by Nikita, silver serving trays by Sterlingcraft, tools and cutlery by Maxam and cameras by Lexus are just some fine items available. Great values on selected luggage and genuine leather briefcases, as well.

BALLARDS DESIGNS

Telephone: 404-351-5099
Fax No: 404-352-1660

1670 DeFoor Avenue, NW
Atlanta, GA 30318-7528

Catalog $3.00

Return policy: 30-Day Money Back Guarantee, except special orders.

What do French provincial, American folk, and Italian renaissance have in common? Ballard Designs offers terrific interior design items in these styles. No matter what the scheme of your home, you can easily find items to complement your decor. Where else can you find folk art cupboards along with french canopy beds? Glass-topped tables can be customized with unique plaster table bases.

CASUAL LIVING

Telephone: 800-843-1881
Fax No: 813-882-4605

5401 Hangar Court; P.O. Box 31273
Tampa, FL 33631-3273

Free Catalog

Return policy: Money-Back Guarantee (excluding personalized items)

Since 1953, Casual Living has been redefining "R & R" with a clever assortment of indoor and outdoor home accents that add a new level of enjoyment to relaxing at home. Holiday decorating is a cinch with whimsical items for Easter, Christmas, Thanksgiving and other special days. They have great outdoor extras like charming birdhouses, birdbaths, pool toys and unique garden clothing. You'll also find funky jewelry treasures, decorative kitchen aids, and wonderful ethnic art.

FULLER BRUSH COMPANY

Telephone: 315-677-9161
Fax No: 315-476-3756

P.O. Box 6316
Syracuse, NY 13217

Free Catalog

Return policy: Satisfaction Guaranteed

Fuller Brush Company expands into mail order with a beautiful full color catalog. 36 pages of time-tested quality products that are "built to last & guaranteed no matter what"! Products cover laundry, kitchen, floor care, bath and much more. Fuller's commitment to manufacturing environmentally responsible products is evident throughout the catalog, and especially noticable in their new "Nature's Choice" line of home cleaning products. Catalogs are supplied by independent distributors, but the products are ordered directly from Fuller.

HOLD EVERYTHING
P.O. Box 7807
San Francisco, CA 94120-7807
Free Catalog
Return policy: Satisfaction Guaranteed

Telephone: 800-421-2285
Fax No: 415-421-5153

Is your space cluttered because you just don't have enough of it? Well, Hold Everything, help is on the way! These ingenius, great looking items are specifically designed to organize and store almost anything. Make the most of your space with wine racks, recycling bins, piggy banks, even a wall safe! After you organize your home you might not know what to do with all of your new found space.

LEMBICK
2559 Scott Blvd.
Santa Clara, CA 95050-2508
Catalog $2.00
Return policy: 30-Day Money Back Guarantee

Telephone: 800-825-1237
Fax No: 408-727-6757

Whimsical and wonderful, Lembick provides you with practical and pretty items for any room in the house. Decorative kimonos and porcelain pigs will brighten up the darkest corners of your home. Other items include an earthenware pheasant that doubles as a teapot, and a pewter whale that opens up to become an ice bucket that even Jonah would approve of.

MILES KIMBALL OF OSHKOSH
41 West Eighth Avenue
Oshkosk, WI 54906
Free Catalog
Return policy: Money-Back Guarantee

Telephone: Mail only

Homemakers take note! Just when you thought you had the most efficient household on the block, along comes Miles Kimball to make things run smoother. For those annoying problems around the house and in the garden that you never thought you'd solve, this catalog has the answers. They've got attractive covers for unsightly bare light fixtures in hallways and basements, chain-link escape ladders for added fire safety, double-length extension cords, and floor protector pads for furniture that normally mars your floors. There's a whimsical selection of toys and crafts for the kids, plus clever gift ideas at unbeatable prices.

MILLS RIVER INDUSTRIES INC.
713 Old Orchard Road
Hendersonville, NC 28739
Free Catalog
Return policy: 10% Service Charge

Telephone: 704-697-9778
Fax No: 704-693-1873

Wholesale America! Mills River provides you with a source of home accents that have a unique "down-home" American feel. The decorative churns will butter up your decor while the tin Christmas ornaments will add a coun-tree look to your home during the holiday season. The wholesale prices will prevent you from running up a trade deficit of your own. All of the items available make great gifts, especially for yourself.

H O U S E W A R E S

NEW ENGLAND BASKET COMPANY   Telephone: 800-524-4484
Box 1335
North Falmouth, MA 02556
Catalog $2.00   COD
Return policy: Prior Authorization Required. 15% Restocking Fee

They're not just for Easter anymore! With hundreds of wicker baskets to choose from in a multitude of sizes and colors, the New England Basket Company makes it easy to give gift baskets all year long. They also offer the cellophane, tissue paper, ribbons and bows that will let create your own unique gift baskets. Specialty items such as wicker bird cages, baby carriages, artifical fruit and wine baskets make it impossible to run out of gift ideas. Quantity discounts available.

OBJECTS BY DESIGN   Telephone: 800-872-7501
P.O. Box 11825   **Fax No:**   703-342-7393
Roanoke, VA 24022
Free Catalog
Return policy: Money-Back Guarantee

If you're hot for a few unusual pieces to give a traditional decorating scheme a little pizzazz, look no further! Objects By Design features the funkiest in decorating accessories including indoor/outdoor furniture, cleverly designed light fixtures, wall art, rugs and kitchenware. Once you've perked up your interior spaces, check out the equally groovy clothing and accessories for the whole family. They've got jewelry, ties, belts and other neat stuff.

POTTERY BARN   Telephone: 800-922-9934
P.O. Box 7044   **Fax No:**   415-421-5153
San Francisco, CA 94120-7044
Free Catalog
Return policy: Satisfaction Guaranteed

What's in a name? While the Pottery Barn offers colorfully-styled and exquisitely crafted glassware and stoneware of the highest quality, you would never believe what else they have in store for you. Maple bar stools and marble salt and pepper shakers are just the tip of the iceberg. They have tons of wonderful home accents and unique items. Iron-clad money back guarantee.

RING MY BELL
Telephone: 800-877-1920

500 South Douglas St.
El Segundo, CA 90245

Catalog $3.00

Return policy: 30-day Satisfaction Guarantee

We've all seen Garfield and Snoopy phones, but where can you get the gorgeous phones like the ones we used to have? Ring My Bell offers lovingly restored vintage phones from the 1920s to the 1960s. In addition to their 30-day money back guarantee, all phones come with a one year warranty. After a year, all you pay for is parts, they will repair any phone without charging service fees. Get on that phone and get that phone!

ROWE POTTERY WORKS
Telephone: 800-356-5003
Fax No: 608-423-4273

404 England Street
Cambridge, WI 53523-9116

Free Catalog

Return policy: Satisfaction Guaranteed (with authorization for returns)

Discover the individual beauty of handmade salt-glaze stoneware. Craftsmen create museum-quality respresentations of this 19th-century folk art form. Salt is placed in the flames of the kiln when the pottery is being fired. Salt explodes into vapor, forming a durable and unique glaze onto the pottery. The authentic design pattern from the 1800s is added, and a microwave- and dishwasher-safe heirloom has been created. These are uniquely functional pieces of America's heritage.

SPORTY'S PREFERRED LIVING CATALOG
Telephone: 513-732-2411
Fax No: 513-732-6560

Clermont County Airport
Batavia, OH 45103-9747

Free Catalog

Return policy: Money-Back Guarantee if returned within 1 year

Sporty's Preferred Living Catalog is brimming with the most opulent selections in fine indoor/outdoor furnishings, electronics, recreational products and household gadgetry. The good life means an outdoor grill that's like having a gourmet kitchen right there on your patio; a garden hose that's electronically programmed to water your lawn so you don't have to; and a car waxing/polishing machine that eliminates hours of back-breaking work.

TAYLOR GIFTS
Telephone: 215-293-3613

355 East Conestoga Road; P.O. Box 206
Wayne , PA 19087-0206

Free Catalog

Return policy: Money-Back Guarantee

Since 1952, Taylor Gifts has offered the most interesting household timesavers and whimsical gift ideas. You'll recognize many of the items from those television ads for products "not available in stores" like the Be Dazzler for applying rhinestones to fabric; the Emson mini sewing machine; and The Doctor's Book of Home Remedies by the editors of Prevention Magazine. There are tons of other products from the clever to the unusual; space-saving closet organizers, stovetop convection ovens, brass Oriental wall ornaments and crystal glassware.

WALTER DRAKE

52 Drake Building
Colorado Springs, CO 80940
Free Catalog
Return policy: Money-Back Guarantee

Telephone: 719-596-3853
Fax No: 719-637-4984
DISCOUNT

Here's another well known mail-order company, supplying America with the unusual items in gifts and household gadgetry for over 45 years. Walter Drake has a wide range of indoor and outdoor home helpers like vaccum extension hoses, backyard furniture covers, retractable garden hoses, extendable ceiling fan cleaners, mini-blind dusters, and more. No homemaker should be without this valuable resource for some of effecient, money-saving products.

YIELD HOUSE

Dept. 4750; P.O. Box 5000
North Conway, NH 03860-5000
Catalog $3.00
Return policy: Money-Back Guarantee

Telephone: 800-258-0376
Fax No: 603-356-8942

The relaxed spirit of country living is reflected in every object in the Yield House catalog. If you favor country looks, you'll love their assortment of genuine pine Shaker furnishings, wooden sculptures, woven rugs, handwoven quilts, porcelain tableware, brass accents, and other country treasures. Wood furniture is available in a variety of finishes like Antique, Honey Pine, Beachwood and Heirloom.

ZIMMERMAN HANDICRAFTS

254 East Main Street
Leola, PA 17540
Free Brochure
Return policy: Exchanges For Credit Only

Telephone: 800-732-0157

Fresh from the farm! Zimmerman Handicrafts offers you butterchurns and buckets, apple stackers and hay rakes, wooden apples and corn driers. Items come stained, laquered or unfinished, so they are easily adaptable to any decor. Make a purchase with your friend or coworkers and take advantage of the wholesale price list included with your catalog which offers extensive savings on goods in quantity.

ADCO JEWELRY & ACCESSORIES
P.O. Box 10949
Chicago, IL 60610-0949
Free Catalog
Return policy: Money-Back Guarantee

Telephone: 312-337-1637

Just about anything your little heart desires in fashion jewelry and accessories can be found in the exciting Adco catalog. In addition to classic styles in gold and silver plate, you'll find African, Native American, Old World, French, and Tropical themes among the assortment of casual styles available. They also have distinctive designer looks for occasions that call for added sophistication. Don't miss the grouping of faux favorites, as well as the humorous theme selections like "Rock 'N Roll" and "Viva Las Vegas."

ALL EARS
114 Fifth Avenue
New York, NY 10011
Free Catalog
Return policy: Satisfaction Guaranteed

Telephone: 212-675-1273

DISCOUNT

Each of the hundreds of costume jewelry items available from this terrific source are the same pieces you've seen in department stores at much higher prices. Priced as attractive as they look, no one will believe how little you paid for the earings, bracelets, necklaces, pins and button covers available here unless you show them the catalog. You'll save up to 50% on orders of 7 items or more, so you might want to share this source with your friends

BOSTON GEM CONNECTION, INC.
63 Domino Drive
Concord, MA 01742
Free Catalog
Return policy: Money-Back Guarantee

Telephone: 800-388-1414
Fax No: 508-369-0329

They've got the genuine articles and the fabulous fakes, but the only difference is in the price. Boston Gem Connection offers you up-to-the-minute styles in costume and genuine gems at fabulous prices. Rings, bracelets, necklaces, earrings and pins are available in brilliant cubic zirconia, silver and gold plate, faux pearl; plus genuine diamonds, cultured pearls, sapphires, emeralds and other precious stones. Men, don't miss the selection of handsome jewelry for you, as well.

DIAMOND ESSENCE
6 Saddle Road
Ceder Knolls, NJ 07927
Catalog $5.00
Return policy: Satisfaction Guaranteed

Telephone: 800-642-4367
Fax No: 201-267-4385

Nothing shimmers or sparkles like a real diamond, except for the best simulated diamonds ever created. Diamond Essence captures the fiery brilliance of a real diamond at a fraction of the cost. So flawless that even experts cannot distinguish between Diamond Essence simulated stones and actual mined gems, show off your rings, bracelets and necklaces fearlessly and bathe in the jealousy of your friends when they see the rock you've got. Simulated birthstones are available, too.

J
E
W
E
L
R
Y

&

A
C
C
E
S
S
O
R
I
E
S

145

DIAMONDS BY RENNIE ELLEN

Telephone: 212-869-5525

Rockefeller Sta., P.O. Box 1745
New York, NY 10185

Free Brochure

Return policy: 7-Day Money Back Guarantee.

In an industry where value and price hinges upon quirks visible only to the jeweler's eye, the title of "most honest diamond merchant" is one to be proud of. Widely acknowledged as the most reputable jeweler in the toughest town for diamond sellers, Rennie Ellen offers the lustrous glow of genuine, high-quality diamond jewelry at a fragment of what some merchants charge for inferior stones.

LEWIS & ROBERTS

Telephone: 800-879-5336
Fax No: 800-933-2420

Scienta Park; P.O. Box 6527
Chelmsford, MA 01824-0927

Free Catalog

Return policy: Money-Back Guarantee

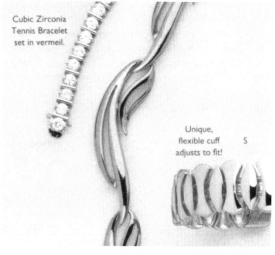

Cubic Zirconia Tennis Bracelet set in vermeil.

Unique, flexible cuff adjusts to fit!

As close to the genuine article as you can get without the costly price - Lewis & Roberts gives you the best of both worlds. Is that the correct price on the lovely diamond tennis bracelet or is it a typo? The price is right, but those aren't diamonds. The bracelet is set in cubic zirconia. It's just as lovely though, as the many fine jewelry styles you'll find in this catalog. Luminous synthetic and semi-precious stones set off bracelets, earrings, rings and pins in beautiful designs. Flattering quartz watches areattractive in design and function.

LINDAM

Telephone: 800-487-8027
Fax No: 510-540-1057

1442A Walnut Street, Suite 314
Berkeley, CA 94709

Free Information

Return policy: Money-Back Guarantee

Lindam's beautifully crafted sterling silver business card case is the elegant executive accessory, reflecting taste, style and sophistication. Masterful design details are evident even inside the case, a true mark of quality. Packaged in a burgundy felt pouch and boxed, the case is sized to fit credit cards and identification cards, too. Priced at $85.00, it makes a distinctive gift for the style-conscious executive in your social or business circle.

NATURE'S JEWELRY

27 Industrial Avenue
Chelmsford, MA 01824-3692
Catalog $5.00
Return policy: Satisfaction Guaranteed

Telephone: 800-333-3235
Fax No: 800-866-3235

Here's a unique collection of earrings, bracelets, necklaces and pins that has something for everyone. Environmentally sensitive, Nature's Jewelry offers stunning, one-of-a-kind items that make great gifts for everyone on your gift list. From simple stud earrings to golfbag pins, you'll want to get almost everything. Whimsical and fashionable, these appealing accessories include tiger eye watches and onyx pendants.

PALM BEACH INT'L. JEWELRY COLLECTION

6400 East Rogers Circle
Boca Raton, FL 33499
Free Catalog
Return policy: Money-Back Guarantee

Telephone: 407-994-2211

DISCOUNT

If you like fine jewelry and rock-bottom wholesale prices, you'll love this catalog. They have lovely genuine and costume jewelry priced way below what you'd normally pay for merchandise of such quality. A genuine diamond pendant for $9.50? Genuine onyx pierced earrings for $2.50? These are just two examples of the 67% savings you'll find on your favorite jewelry in the full-color catalog. There's also a wide assortment of cubic zirconia, simulated stone, faux pearl, and gold and silver plate jewelry, plus many great designs for men.

RAINY'S

1317 N. San Fernando Blvd., Suite 318
Burbank, CA 91504
Catalog $3.00, refunded with 1st order
Return policy: Money-Back Guarantee if returned within 10 days

Telephone: 818-244-6814

DISCOUNT

Here's a jewel of an offer! In Rainy's full-color catalog, you'll find over 1,300 items, all discounted 25-75%. It features jewelry for women and men, including14K gold, sterling silver, genuine stones and a selection of beautiful costume jewelry. You'll find rings, chains, pendants, earrings and more at great prices.

RICHARD PHILLIP DESIGNS

5 West 36th Street
New York, NY 10018
Free Catalog
Return policy: Money-Back Guarantee

Telephone: 800-235-2042
Fax No: 212-714-1032

Stylish elegance and high value combine in sterling silver jewelry by Richard Phillip Designs. Exquisitely crafted earrings, necklaces, rings, bracelets, charms and pins are offered in sculptured and traditional designs. Each silver piece is a true work of art, joined with precious and semiprecious gems like cubic zirconia, onyx, marcasite, citrine, amethyst, peridot and other stones. Earrings are available in French post, clip-on styles, in addition to traditional pierced-ear varieties.

JEWELRY & ACCESSORIES

147

ROSS-SIMONS

9 Ross Simons Drive
Cranston, RI 02920

Telephone: 800-521-7677
Fax No: 401-463-8599

Free Catalog

Return policy: 30-Day Money-Back Guarantee (except personalized items)

For over 40 years, Ross-Simons has been highly recognized for beautiful collection of precious and semi-precious gems. Diamonds, rubies, sapphires, emeralds, pearls, jade, coral and other jewels are available in the most sophisticated designs imaginable. But jewels are not their only forte. You'll also find famous-maker home accents and gifts. China by Mikasa, Royal Doulton, and Noritake; Lenox crystal; and Lladro porcelain pieces exemplify the collection of upscale goods.

SIMPLY WHISPERS EARRINGS

33 Riverside Drive
Pembroke, MA 02359-1910

Telephone: 800-451-5700

Free Catalog

Return policy: Money-Back Guarantee

Here's an attractive alternative to giving up the earring styles you love the most because of an allergic reaction to some metals. Simply Whispers offers fashionable, non-irritating earrings made of 100% surgical stainless steel. Medically proven hypoallergenic, the jewelry is plated in 24k gold using a nickel-free process and assembled without irritating solders. This way, you needn't worry about swelling, rashes or itching. Clip-ons are back and they've got them! The styles range from sophisticated day looks for work and play to sleek simulated stones, faux pearls and other bewitching varieties for night. Simply Whispers also offers a grouping of replacement backs and posts for all your earrings.

GARDENER'S EDEN
P.O. Box 7307
San Francisco, CA 94120-7307

Telephone: 800-822-1214
Fax No: 415-421-5153

Free Catalog

Return policy: Money Back Guarantee

It might seem odd that a catolog with 5 hand tools caters to the gardening enthu-saist, but Gardener's Eden is paradise for anyone who enjoys floral pleasures. Lapel flower vases and botanical notepads allow you to indulge yourself at the office while the exquisitely crafted willow furniture will surround you in natural luxury. Other unique exclusives include the Months of Flowering Bulbs. This pro-gram delivers bright colors and sweet scents to your door during winter and spring.

GARDENS FOR GROWING PEOPLE
P.O. Box 630
Point Reyes Station, CA 94956-0630

Telephone: 415-663-9433

Free Catalog

Return policy: Money-Back Guarantee

We were kids once and know they want the same stuff adults have. The people at Gardens For Growing People believe that this holds true for gardening supplies as well. It's never too early to start kids on a lasting, respectful relationship with nature and the environment. This catalog features rakes, shovels, wheel barrels, hoes and a range of accessories, all sized to fit little green thumbs. There are easy-to-read books and games on the virtues of conserving the environment, as well.

GOOD DIRECTIONS, INC.
24 Ardmore Road
Stamford, CT 06902

Telephone: 800-346-7678
Fax No: 203-357-0092

Free Brochure

Return policy: 30-Day Money Back Guarantee

You'll always know which way the wind blows with a Good Directions weather-vane. Designs range from the traditional arrow to the unconventional wind-surfer, but each adds a warm touch to any home. A limited supply of blemished or dented weathervanes are available for 50% off. Since these imperfections aren't visible from the ground, only you and the four winds will be the wiser.

PLOW & HEARTH
301 Madison Road; P.O. Box 830
Orange , VA 22960-0492

Telephone: 800-866-6072
Fax No: 703-672-3612

Free Catalog

Return policy: Money-Back Guarantee

No matter what the size, Plow and Hearth can help turn your exterior space into a relaxing outdoor retreat with their selection of country lawn furnishings and dec-orative home accessories. Then bring the outdoors indoors with their country wood interior furniture including Adirondack Cedar. While away the hours on solid oak, maple, teak and wrought iron furniture. Wooden arbors, fabric ham-mocks, cast iron birdbaths, Oriental windchimes and decorative iron weather-vanes round out the assortment of outdoorsy touches. Keep your paradise look-ing great with their generous assortment of lawn and gardening supplies, too.

RINGER CORP.
9959 Valley View Road
Eden Prairie, MN 55344-3585
Free Catalog
Return policy: Money Back Guarantee

Telephone: 800-654-1047
Fax No: 612-941-5036

30 years before manufacturers jumped on the "environmentally-safe" bandwagon, Ringer was developing natural lawn and garden care products, as well as pesticides, that offered an alternative to "quick-fix" chemical products. Ringer provides homeowners and gardeners with the highest quality products for growing healthy plants the natural way. With a wide selection of plant foods, bug killers and tools, there is no better source for a sound garden and a safe environment.

SMITH & HAWKEN TOOLS OF THE TRADE
25 Corte Madera
Mill Valley , CA 94941
Free Catalog
Return policy: Money-Back Guarantee

Telephone: 415-383-6399
Fax No: 415-383-7030

Smith & Hawken was originally founded to supply gardeners with long-lasting, quality tools to support and simplify their efforts - tools for cultivating, composting, cutting, digging, containing, carrying, maintenance, irrigation management, pest control, planting and harvesting. Strong advocates of organic gardening, they carry a variety of tools for this practice including compost worms, leaf composters and other specialized tools. There's also a unique selection of sturdy gardening clothes that are as comfortable as they are classic.

WALT NICKE COMPANY
36 McLeod Lane, P.O. Box 433
Topsfield, MA 01983
Catalog $.50
Return policy: Money Back Guarantee

Telephone: 508-887-3388

Published twice a year, Walt Nicke's Garden Talk is the ultimate source for gardening tips, tools and supplies. You'll never know how you tended your garden without these sensible items that you never knew existed. Ergonomically designed trowels and ratchet-cut pruning shears are only a sample of the wealth of goods available in this 64 page horticulturist's dream book.

WORTHINGTON GROUP LTD.
P.O. Box 53101
Atlanta, GA 30355
Catalog $3.00

Telephone: 800-872-1608
Fax No: 404-872-8501

COD

Return policy: 30-Day Return Policy, except glass doors, gates & custom orders.

Wothington Group, Ltd., offers incredible interior accents that can truly transform your home into a masterpiece. Hand carved entryways of solid mahogany greet your visitors with warmth and elegance. Breathtaking glass domes and classic fireplace mantels will dominate the rooms of your choice, without distracting from the refined style you seek. The catalogs are artful works in and of themselves. The decorating ideas they'll inspire is worth the cost, alone!

AUTHENTIC DESIGNS
Telephone: 802-394-7713

The Mill Road
West Rupert, VT 05776

Catalog $3.00

Return policy: 60-Day Money Back Guarantee

Authentic Designs delivers just what the name says; authentically designed re-creations of Early American lighting fixtures. Like the original items, every sconce and chandelier is painstakingly crafted by hand. Only the finest materials available are used to ensure the high standard of quality authentic designs is famous for. All of these brass lights are burnished by hand to bring out the lusterous glow of these historical and practical works of American art.

HERITAGE LANTERNS
Telephone: 800-544-6070

70A Main Street
Yarmouth, ME 04096

Free Catalog, Video Cassette $7.50

Return policy: 30-Day Money Back Guarantee

How many homeowners can claim that their houselights actually beautify their home? Can you? With a Heritage Lanterns reproduction, you are guaranteed to own one the finest Colonial-style lamps, sconces, lanterns or chandeliers available in the world today. Made of brass, copper or RoyalPewter, these lights are so close to the actual ones used 200 years ago that some fixtures are candle or oil-based instead of running on electricity!

LIGHTING BY GREGORY, INC.
Telephone: 212-226-1276
Fax No: 212-226-2705

158 Bowery
New York, NY 10012

DISCOUNT

Free Catalog

Return policy: Money Back Guarantee. Special Orders are not returnable

The Lord said "Let There Be Light" and there was light. It's almost that easy to obtain contemporary fixtures of exceptional quality from Lighting By Gregory, Inc. Their attractive 144-page catalog is jammed with chandeliers, wall brackets, accent lighting, outdoor lighting and downlighting. With over 50 recessed reflecting ceiling light styles to choose from, the selection is immense. It's worth getting the catalog for the tips in the "Lighting By Design" section.

REJUVENATION LAMP & FIXTURE COMPANY
Telephone: 503-249-0774
Fax No: 503-281-7948

901 North Skidmore
Portland, OR 97217

Free Catalog

Return policy: 30 Day Money Back Guarantee

In a time of cold, modern fixture styling, the Rejuvenation Lamp and Fixture Company will return you to the days when interior lighting was still a luxury. Reproductions of period-style light fixtures and bulbs give a warm glow to any room and will add the perfect touch to your restored Victorian abode. Authentic in design, these wonderful light fixtures replicate all the major styles from the late 1800s to 1930s including gas-style fixtures and the recently introduced art deco line. Enjoy classic style with modern convenience.

CHOCK CATALOG

74 Orchard Street
New York, NY 10022

Telephone: 800-222-0020
Fax No: 212-473-6273

DISCOUNT

Catalog $1.00

Return policy: Satisfaction Guarantee

The Chock Catalog is your one-stop resource for underwear, sleepware and hosiery for the entire family. Once you see the large selection of women's, girl's, boy's and infant's clothing and you'll understand why Louis Chock has been in business since 1921. BVD, Hanes, Calvin Klein, Munsingwear, Jockey, and Duofold is a partial list of the brand names available for Men's Underwear alone. The Chock Catalog makes it easy to fill all your family's needs "down under."

FREDERICK'S OF HOLLYWOOD

P.O. Box 229
Holywood, CA 90078-0229

Telephone: 310-637-7770

Catalog $2.00

Return policy: Money-Back Guarantee

This name and the look are synonymous with sexy and provocative in sportswear, swimwear, eveningwear and lingerie. Body conscious casual looks in denim, cotton, lace and leather are far from timid. The swimwear collection includes maillots and bikinis in prints and designs that are hotter than the California sun! Look for the most tempting evening styles including sequins, satin and lots of lace. The lingerie leaves little to the imagination in delicate confections of satin, silk, lycra and lace. Men's looks are equally brazen in intriguing sportswear, swimwear and underwear looks that give new meaning to the word "unique."

HIDDEN ASSETS

Dept. P, P.O. Box 20056, Cherokee Sta.
New York, NY 10028

Telephone: 212-439-0693
Fax No: 212-439-0694

Free Postcard And Flyers

Return policy: Unworn Merchandise Exchangeable

Fashion enhanced by security. Hidden Assets offers attractive half-slips with zippered pockets concealed in the hem. You can carry keys, cash, credit cards and other valuable or important items without the risk of having your purse snatched. A reinforced waistband provides comfort and prevents the weight of the pocket contents from pulling the slip downward. A Mini-Assets slip is available for girls age 7-14 so they can be as safe and secure as their mothers are.

LADY GRACE STORES

P.O. Box 128
Malden , MA 02148

Telephone: 800-922-0504

Free Catalog

Return policy: Satisfaction Guaranteed

For over 55 years, millions of women have turned to Lady Grace Stores for their superior selection of fine intimate apparel. Every major manufacturer is represented in a complete style and size range. Bra sizes go as high as 52, while cup sizes go as high as H. Lady Grace experts will answers all your questions on intimate apparel. Most orders are shipped promptly within one week.

NATIONAL WHOLESALE COMPANY, INC.
400 National Blvd.
Lexington, NC 27294

Telephone: 704-249-0211

DISCOUNT

Free Catalog

Return policy: Satisfaction Guaranteed

After 40 years, National Wholesale Company, Inc. really knows hose. Page after page of pantyhose, stockings and knee-highs at tremendous discounts. Bras and panties by manufacturers like Playtex, Glamorise, Lily of France and Exquisite Form are available at substantial savings because of National's purchasing power. With slippers and house dresses also available, you can completely revise your "at home" wardrobe at an affordable price.

ROBY'S INTIMATES BRAS BY MAIL
121 South 18th Street
Philadelphia, PA 19103

Telephone: 800-878-8BRA
In PA 215-751-1730

DISCOUNT

Catalog $1.00

Return policy: Exchanges allowed, no returns on special orders

Ladies, shop for your "bras-by-mail" in the privacy of your home 25% discounts. Over 50 brand names are represented, including Bali, Vanity Fair, Olga, Maidenform, Christian Dior, Warners, Smoothie, Lili of France and more. Girdles, lingerie and hosiery, too. Shipping is by UPS in 2-4 weeks. Returns are not encouraged, so be sure you know yur preference before you order, particularly if its a special order.

SHOWCASE OF SAVINGS
P.O. Box 748
Rural Hall, NC 27098-0843

Telephone: 919-744-1170
Fax No: 919-744-1485

DISCOUNT

Free Catalog

Return policy: Satisfaction Guaranteed

Showcase of Savings is a business built on customer satisfaction. Discounts of up to 55% off name brand apparel from manufacturers like Bali, Isotoner and Underalls, and on L'eggs and Hanes slightly imperfect hosiery, make it hard to be dissatisfied. Even if you aren't happy with your purchase, Showcase of Savings will replace the item or give you a full refund quickly and easily.

THE PETTICOAT EXPRESS
315 West 39th Street
New York, NY 10018

Telephone: 212-594-1276

DISCOUNT

Free Catalog

Return policy: Returns accepted for exchange only

Ladies, the Petticoat Express offers the right net and tafetta slips for formal ensembles in different styles at 40% discounts. Perfect for brides and bridesmaids, too. These slips are perfect for full-skirted bridal gowns, A-line dresses, tea-lengths, and flounced styles. Underneath it all, a petticoat is a must for that picture-perfect look.

THE SMART SAVER
P.O. Box 105
Wasco, IL 60183
Free Catalog
Return policy: Satisfaction Guarantee.

Telephone: Mail Only

With more Playtex styles and sizes than the largest retail store discounted up to 25% off of typical retail prices, what smart shopper wouldn't buy from The Smart Shopper. Intimate apparel by Vanity Fair, Exquisite Form and Lollipop is here at a 20% savings. With one low price for shipping, regardless of the amount of items in your order, do you need another reason to get your hands on this catalog? Mail order only.

THE SOCK SHOP
818 North Main Street; P.O. Box 390
Sweetwater, TN 37874
Free Catalog
Return policy: Money-Back Guarantee

Telephone: 615-337-9203

COD

Nothing's more comforting to tired, aching feet than a soft, absorbent pair of cotton socks. But even if you prefer woolens or thermal varieties, the Sock Shop can cover your feet without emptying your wallet. They have turn-down crew, roll-up sport, slouch and men's casual varieties in a full range of popular colors, all in cool 100% cotton. For winter sports and other cold-weather activities, they've got wool dress and casual socks, and thermal socks in wintery solid shades and two-tone combinations.

THE SOCK SOURCE
P.O. Box 1680
Burlington, NC 27216
Free Catalog
Return policy: Money-Back Guarantee

Telephone: 800-637-SOCK

Formerly Jefferies Socks, The Sock Source has virtually every hosiery style on the market for men, women and children. Anklets, knee-highs, tights, argyles, woolens, sport socks, dress socks and non-skid slipper socks are some of the best-selling varieties. Many of the women's and children's socks are accented with lace, hand-painted designs, bows and other details. All styles can be found in a range of fashion colors - from fun brights to conservative neutrals and dark shades.

VICTORIA'S SECRET CATALOG
P.O. Box 16589
Columbus, OH 43216
Free Catalog
Return policy: Unconditional Satisfaction Guarantee.

Telephone: 800-477-9977
Fax No: 800-577-6005

Enjoy the luxury of shopping directly from home with Victoria's Secret Catalog. Their International collection encompasses lingerie and fashion for the most discerning tastes. Receive a coupon for up to $50.00 off your first purchase. Shipping is via UPS or Federal Express.

A TO Z LUGGAGE
4627 New Utrecht Avenue
Brooklyn, NY 11219

Telephone: 800-342-5011
Fax No: 718-435-6317

DISCOUNT

Free Catalog

Return policy: 30-Day Money Back Guarantee.

For 20-50% savings on famous name luggage including Hartmann, American Tourister, Samsonite, and Le Club, call or write for a free catalog from A to Z Luggage. They have an enormous selection to choose from including attaché cases, wallets, backpacks and gift items. Expert repairing, too.

ACE LEATHER PRODUCTS
2211 Avenue U
Brooklyn, NY 11229

Telephone: 800-DIAL-AC E
In NY 718-891-0998

Free Catalog

Return policy: Store credit and exchanges allowed only

Ace is the place for fulfilling all your luggage needs. They feature leather attache cases, luggage, wallets, handbags and a wide assortment of gift items. They also offer great service, selection and prices on major must-have name brands like Boyt, Delsey, Samsonite, Tumi, Andiamo, Lark, Lodis, Schlesinger and Hartman & Finch. All orders are usually shipped the same day via UPS.

AL'S LUGGAGE
2134 Larimer Street
Denver, CO 80205

Telephone: 303-295-9009

DISCOUNT

Free Catalog

Return policy: Money-Back Guarantee

Samsonite lovers, pay special attention! Al's Luggage offers 30-50% savings on Samsonite luggage. Choose from over 100 models, including carry-ons, beauty cases, valets, duffles, piggybacks, garment bags, attaches, camera cases and nested sets. Hardside and softside cases combine premium quality and style with proven versatility. All manufacturers warranties apply on merchandise damages, but returns are accepted based on style/color preferences (less shipping charges).

AMERICAN TOURISTER, INC. FACTORY OUTLET
3301 Outlet Boulevard; Suite #156
Myrtle Beach, SC 29577

Telephone: 803-236-7787

DISCOUNT

Free Information

Return policy: Money-Back Guarantee

Whether you plan to travel around the world, visit Grandma for the weekend, or pack important papers for that 9a.m. meeting with the boss, American Tourister's Factory Outlet can fill your luggage needs at 40-70% savings! Long-lasting, hard-sided luggage; stylish, lightweight soft-sided luggage; attaches and portfolios that mean business; totes to go anywhere in style; and accessories that keep you organized are just a few of the premium-quality examples. Shop first, then call the outlet store with the color and 4-digit series number. Orders are usually shipped the same dayand no sales tax is issued on out-of-state purchases.

USED RUBBER, USA

Telephone: 415-616-7855

597 Haight Street
San Francisco, CA 94117-3406

Free Catalog

MasterCard VISA [icon] COD

Return policy: Money-Back Guarantee

Leave it to the fashion world to come up with a clever idea for recycled rubber from old tires. Used Rubber USA has replaced the leather you'd normally expect to find in briefcases, handbags, wallets, datebooks and other accessories with high-grade, recycled rubber. Yes, you read right - rubber! And the incredible thing is it looks absolutely fantastic. All of the items are handcrafted with post consumer inner-tube rubber and accented with aluminum, brass, bronze or nickel plated hardware. They also have the coolest canvas sail jackets, trenches and accessories with rubber accents for women and men. Finally, fashion saves the world!

BOSOM BUDDIES

Telephone: 914-338-2038

P.O. Box 6138
Kingston, NY 12401

Free Brochure

Return policy: Money Back Guarantee

Finally, a source of fashions and accessories exclusively for nursing mothers and their babies. At Bosom Buddies you will find Leading Lady nursing gowns and underwire nursing bras in all cup and bust sizes. A short guide for determining the right size makes a perfect fit a sure thing. Even so, if you are dissatisfied with your Bosom Buddies purchase they will be happy to give you a full refund (postage not included).

MOTHERS WORK MATERNITY

Telephone: 215-625-9259
Fax No: 215-440-9845

1309 Noble St., 5th Floor
Philadelphia, PA 19123

Free Catalog

Return policy: 10-Day Money Back Guarantee

Where can today's woman find reasonably-priced maternity suits, dresses and sportswear for lounging at home or working at the office. Mothers Work provides expectant women with an impressive array of colors, styles and fabrics suitable for all business and social occasions. Colorful and bright, Mothers Work fashions help put the style back into maternity clothing. Delivery is fast because they know your schedule is tight and rather inflexible.

MATERNITY CLOTHING

HUNTINGTON CLOTHIERS & SHIRTMAKERS   Telephone: 800-848-6203
1285 Alum Creek Drive
Columbus, OH 43209-2797

Free Catalog

Return policy: Satisfaction Guaranteed. Monogrammed Items Not Returnable.

Pure quality is the best way to describe the merchandise available from Huntington Clothiers. Clothes for every aspect of your life are available. Browse through this catalog of exceptional men's attire and you'll find beautiful wool suits, comfortable cotton oxfords, and easy-to-live-in khaki twills.

INTERNATIONAL MALE   Telephone: 717-633-3300
741 "F" Street
San Diego, CA 92112-9027

Catalog $2.00

Return policy: Money-Back Guarantee

For the gentleman who's daring enough, International Male offers the latest in fashion-forward, west coast-inspired clothing in designs and colorations that are anything but timid. There are a few conservative dress casuals, but the catalog is packed with racy, street and beach-wise looks in unique swimwear, funky sportswear and slick dress looks that are perfect for nightlife action. There's also a generous assortment of workout gear, underwear and fashion accessories, too.

J. PETERMAN COMPANY   Telephone: 800-231-7341
2444 Palumbo Drive
Lexington, KY 40509

Free Catalog

Return policy: Satisfaction Guaranteed

People love clothes inspired by romance. This is the premise upon which J. Peterman offers wonderful clothing and accessories in his clever catalog. Classic pieces that you'll wear and wear. Wool fisherman sweaters, roomy trenchcoats, leather bombers, 'Gatsby' shirts, boot cut jeans, and full-cut cotton canvas pants are just some of the timeless items. They are displayed in the catalog with charming sketches and witty descriptions. You can also find a number of unique, top-quality accessories, like leather satchels, fisherman's caps, and vintage boots.

PAUL FREDRICK SHIRT COMPANY
Telephone: 800-247-1417

140 West Main Street
Fleetwood, PA 19522

Catalog $1.00

Return policy: Money-Back Guarantee

Here's the best-kept secret in men's apparel. For weel over 35 years, Paul Fredrick Shirt Company has been manufacturing the finest private-label shirts for men's specialty stores nationwide. A glance through their catalog will quickly convince you of their exceptional quality, yet purchasing direct from the manufacturer will save you up to 50%. Choose from a variety of matching Italian silk ties in rich patterns and colors, as well as cuff links, belts and other fine furnishings accessories.

M
E
N'
S

C
L
O
T
H
I
N
G

SHORT SIZES INC.
Telephone: 216-475-2515
Fax No: 216-475-7440

5385 Warrensville Center Road
Cleveland, OH 44137

Catalog $1.00

Return policy: 30-Day Money Back Guarantee

If you are under 5'8" shopping can be difficult. Finding those elusive sizes can make buying clothes a huge ordeal. Bob Stern's Short Sizes has a huge inventory of suits and sportswear tailored to fit the needs of shorter gentleman, in sizes usually unavailable in retail stores. Hart Schaffner & Marx, John Weitz and Oleg Cassini are only a few of the designers available. Bob Stern is the best source of distinctive apparel for the shorter man.

THE KING SIZE COMPANY
Telephone: 800-846-1600
Fax No: 617-982-8766

P.O. Box 9115
Hingham, MA 02042-9115

Free Catalog

Return policy: Money Back Guarantee

Arrow. Izod. Dockers. Bill Blass. Now tall and large men can enjoy these name brand clothes, as well as Members Only, Greenline and Sergio Tacchini. The King Size Co. caters to men who usually have problems getting the styles they want because their size isn't stocked. Buy with confidence. These are the fashions and quality you have been shopping for, but with the convenience of mail order.

UNDERGEAR
Telephone: 717-633-3300

Building 77
Hanover, PA 17333-0077

Free Catalog

Return policy: 15-Day Money Back Guarantee

Here's a catalog that uncovers the basic and bold elements of a man's wardrobe in styles that many merchants keep under wraps. Not for the faint of heart, this exotic register of personal men's clothing gets to the bare essentials as boxers, briefs, shorts and tops are all exquisitely displayed by sultry male models. This catalog is guaranteed to be a conversation piece for men and women alike.

AMERICAN PIE

P.O. Box 66455
Los Angeles, CA 90066

Telephone: 310-821-4005
Fax No: 310-823-3389

Catalog $2.00

Return policy: Satisfaction Guaranteed

Thousands of your favorite oldies are available on compact discs, cassettes, 45's and even video at American Pie. Their huge catalog features hard-to-find hits from your favorite artists from the 40's to the 90's; plus books and other memorabilia. Their prompt, reliable service includes speedy shipping by UPS or mail.

BOSE EXPRESS MUSIC

The Mountain
Framingham, MA 01701-9168

Telephone: 800-451-BOSE

Catalog $6.00; refunded with 1st order

Return policy: Money-Back Guarantee

They call themselves "The First Complete Record Store In A Catalog." Now you can shop from your home for virtually any CD, Tape or Video in print today. You will find over 50,000 Rock, Jazz and Classical titles in the world's largest music catalog. Bose subscribers get the 320-page 1992 catalog; one free year of updates covering new releases, recommendations and music specials; plus a whopping $50.00 in merchandise credits.

MOSAIC RECORDS

35 Melrose Place
Stamford, CT 06902

Telephone: 203-327-7111
Fax No: 203-323-3526

Free Catalog

Return policy: Satisfaction Guarantee

Acclaimed by music critics and jazz aficionados, Mosaic Records presents complete, definitive collections of history's most important jazz musicians. Artists like Grant Green, T-Bone Walker, Fredie Redd, Herbie Nichols, Thelonious Monk and many others, are available for a whole new generation to appreciate. All of the music sets are offered as both Compact Discs and LPs, making Mosaic one of the few true record companies.

PATTI MUSIC CORPORATION

414 State Street, P.O. Box 1514
Madison, WI 53701-1514

Telephone: 608-257-8829
Fax No: 608-257-5847

`DISCOUNT`

Catalog $2.00

Return policy: Returns only on defective merchandise

Opening a Patti Music Corporation Mail Order Catalog is like stepping into a sheet music library. Thousands of classical, instructional and new age works are at your fingertips with discounts of up to 25%. Giants like Bach, Beethoven, Brahms and Mozart are available, as is the music of lesser known artists, such as Franck, Diemer, Gretchaninoff and Vorisek. Music for your eyes.

TRUE BLUE MUSIC

35 Melrose Place
Stamford, CT 06902

Free Catalog

Return policy: Satisfaction Guaranteed

Telephone: 203-327-7111
Fax No: 203-323-3526

True Blue Music has been offering the finest in jazz since 1939. The sounds of Miles Davis, Dexter Gordon, Nancy Wilson, Ella Fitzgerald and Cole Porter are right at your disposal. True Blue Music readily accepts returns if you are dissatisfied with your purchase. All musical selections are available on compact disc, and many are on cassette. It's never been so easy to shop for that's music so hot it's cool.

M
U
S
I
C

A.L.A.S. ACCORDION-O-RAMA

16 West 19th Street
New York, NY 10011

Telephone: 212-675-9089

DISCOUNT

Free Flyers, Videotapes $25.00

Return policy: Satisfaction Guaranteed

At one point or another everyone has wanted to play the accordian. Well, almost everyone. Portable and unique, an accordian is a lively departure from the over-crowded world of guitars and guitarists. Models at Accordian-O-Rama range from inexpensive student models, to full-featured professional instruments. New music technologies, such as MIDI, rhythm boxes and electric pick-ups, are available on many models at prices of 40% off list and more! Ask about rebuilt models for additional savings.

CARVIN

1155 Industrial Avenue
Escondido, CA 92029

Telephone: 800-854-2235
Fax No: 619-747-0743

DISCOUNT

Free Catalog

Return policy: 10-Day Money Back Guarantee

Here is the best friend a guitarist could ask for. With a catalog crammed full of American-made guitars, basses, amps and professional sound gear, Carvin instruments are timeless classics that won't make you bite the bullet. By ordering directly from the warehouse you can save up to 50% off of retail prices on everything they sell, from guitar picks to 16 channel multi-track stereo mixers. Find out why they have been the guitarist's buddy for nearly 50 years.

DISCOUNT MUSIC SUPPLY

41 Vreeland Avenue
Totowa, NJ 07512-1120

Telephone: 201-942-9411
Fax No: 201-890-7922

DISCOUNT

Free Catalog

Return policy: 14-Day Money Back Guarantee

It might be difficult to believe that Discount Music Supply can fulfill all of your guitar needs while boasting only 7 electric guitars in their catalog, but after looking through this no-frills compilation of effects processors, rhythm machines, amps, microphones and multi-track recorders by Boss, Dunlop, Gorilla and Vestax, you'll know they're for real. All the accessories your guitar will ever need are right here, from strings to cases. Gift certificates are available.

DISCOUNT REED COMPANY

P.O. Box 6010, Suite 496
Sherman Oaks, CA 91403

Telephone: 800-428-5993
Fax No: 818-990-7962

DISCOUNT

Free Brochure

Return policy: Unopened Boxes Only

Here's the place to meet all of your reed needs. No matter what you play, the Discount Reed Company stocks single and double reeds from all the manufacturers you can think of at prices up to 50% below retail. Rico, Mitchell Lurie, Vandoren and Lamode are among the fine cane reeds available. Accessories, such as reedguards, reed cases and cork grease sell at the same low prices.

FREEPORT MUSIC

Telephone: 516-549-4108

41 Shore Drive
Huntington Bay, NY 11743
Catalog $1.00
Return policy: 7-Day Money Back Guarantee

The Freeport Music catalog might be slim, but it has as varied and complete a selection of merchandise as you'll find anywhere. The entire band is listed! Guitars, drums, keyboads and synthesizers are offered alone with musical saws, electric autoharps and US regulation bugles. With lighting effects, fog machines and mirror balls, you're ready to take your show on stage, while the travel cases let you take it on the road. Coupon specials are included in every catalog.

INTERSTATE MUSIC SUPPLY

Telephone: 800-982-BAND
Fax No: 414-786-6840

P.O. Box 315, 13819 W. National Ave.
New Berlin, WI 53151
DISCOUNT
Free Catalog
Return policy: 10-Day Money Back Guarantee, with authorization

Where can you pick up a timpani, maracas and professional temple blocks? Right on the interstate! Interstate Music Supply can help you start your own orchestra with everything you need; instruments, music stands, orchestra risers, even the conductor's baton. While Interstate Music Supply provides schools with additional discounts, anyone can take advantage of their huge inventory.

LONE STAR PERCUSSION

Telephone: 214-340-0835
Fax No: 214-340-0861

10611 Control Place
Dallas, TX 75238
DISCOUNT
Free Price List
Return policy: Returns accepted with 2 weeks. 20% Restocking Fee

Bang the drum or pound the tam-tam. Lone Star Percussion is the only source of strictly percussion supplies you will ever need. The price list is 47 pages long (this is a price list, not a catalog!). Any orchestral item is available at discounts of up to 50% off list prices. Mallets, metronomes, tamborines and timpanis are all here. More items than you can shake a drumstick at!

MANDOLIN BROTHERS LTD.

Telephone: 718-981-3226
Fax No: 718-816-4416

629 Forest Avenue
Staten Island, NY 10310-2576
Free Catalog

Return policy: 3-Day Money Back Guarantee

Mandolin Brothers has been called "The Smithsonian Institution of Fretted Instrument Dealers" for good reason. Stocking one of the largest inventories of acoustic and electric guitars, mandolins and banjos, as well as collectable instruments from all eras and by all manufacturers, if they don't have what you're looking for it probably doesn't exist. Clevinger, Hohner, Rickenbacker, Fender and Gibson are only a few licks from their emense inventory. Mandolin Brothers publishes The Vintage News, a monthly newsletter full of rare instruments for sale. A collector's dream, they offer gift certificates.

METROPOLITAN MUSIC COMPANY

Mountain Road, P.O. Box 1415
Stowe, VT 05672

Telephone: 802-253-4814
Fax No: 802-253-9834

Free Catalog

COD With Deposit

Return policy: Subject To Service Charge

As manufacturers and craftsmen of quality string instruments and accessories become farther and fewer between, exemplary merchants are increasingly difficult to locate. Nestled in the mountains of Vermont is the sole distributing agency for Famous "John Juzek" violins, violas, cellos and bassess. In addition to these superbly-crafted imported instruments, Metropolitan Music Company offers parts and tools for repairs, as well as texts for instrument making and violin playing.

PHILIP H. WEINKRANTZ MUSIC SUPPLY

870 Market Street, Suite 1265
San Francisco, CA 94102-9955

Telephone: 800-73-MUSIC

DISCOUNT

Free Catalog

Return policy: 14-Day Money Back Guarantee 5% Restocking Fee

Philip H. Weinkrantz provides the finest in classical string instruments and accessories at discounted prices of up to and over 40% off. Quality craftsmanship from the workshops of Ernst Heinrich Roth, Benker, Andreas Morelli and Roman Teller for professionals and students are available for a song. There are music stands and metronomes for the home conservatory or classroom. If the instrument you are seeking isn't in their catalog, it's only because there wasn't any room for it! Call for special orders.

WEST MANOR MUSIC

831 East Gunhill Road
Bronx, NY 10467

Telephone: 212-655-5400

DISCOUNT

Free Catalog

Return policy: No Returns Accepted

Don't expect high gloss paper with color photos when requesting this moneysaving price list. The West Manor Music catalog is short on glitz but long on value. You can buy any instrument in the orchestra from this super music supplier, woodwinds, brasses, strings and percussion. There are special school discounts for orders of three or more, and free gifts or additional discounts with purchases over $200.00. How can you go wrong with discounts of over 50% off list price. Be sure you know what you want, as returns are not accepted.

BUSINESS ENVELOPE MANUFACTURERS, INC.
900 Grand Blvd.
Deer Park, NY 11729

Telephone: 800-275-4400
Fax No: 516-586-5988

Free Catalog

Return policy: Satisfaction Guaranteed

Business Envelope Manufacturers isn't the most imaginative name, but it certainly describes this printer and supplier of custom produced envelopes, forms, and flyers. They offer over 40 styles of envelopes in a multitude of colors, at prices lower than typical mail-order houses. No matter what image you want your business to present, the first impression people get is made by the envelope you send your letters in. Office supplies, such as, packing tape and time clocks, are yours for the asking, as well.

FAX CITY
2711-B Pinedale Road
Greensboro, NC 27408

Telephone: 800-426-6499
Fax No: 919-288-1735
DISCOUNT

Free Flyers

Return policy: All Sales Final.

Just the fax, at discount prices. Fax City, the country's fastest growing wholesale distributor of fax paper, machines and supplies, can save you up to 50% off office supply store prices on everything they sell. All of the latest equipment, from plain paper machines to machines that let you send and receive at the same time. Why pay more for machines by Sharp, Canon, Savin, Brother, Murata and Ricoh when you can pay less!

FRANK EASTERN CO.
599 Broadway, Dept. SBM
New York, NY 10012

Telephone: 800-221-4914
Fax No: 212-219-0722
DISCOUNT

Free Catalog

Return policy: 20% Restocking Charge For Undamaged Merchandise

For savings up to 60% on office and computer furniture, check out the Frank Eastern catalog. A large selection of office chairs, desks, bookcases, file cabinets, conference tables, computer work stations. Also, lease plans to furnish your entire office. Orders shipped UPS or truck-freight.

NATIONAL BUSINESS FURNITURE
905 Mateao St.
Los Angeles, CA 90021

Telephone: 800-558-1010

DISCOUNT

Free Catalog Corporate Accts.

Return policy: Authorized Returns Only.

Furnishing an office is a hassle most business people can do without. National Business Furniture makes this chore a pleasure. Workstations, conference tables, desks and chairs are listed on page after page of this intelligently laid out catalog. Styles to furnish every room of your workplace and prices to fit every budget. National Business Furniture stands by their products with a 15-year guarantee. With low prices and guaranteed quality how can you go wrong!

RAPID FORMS
301 Grove Rd.
Thorofare, NJ 08086-9499
Free Catalog
Return policy: Satisfaction Guaranteed

Telephone: 800-257-5287
Fax No: 800-451-8113

Rapid Forms allows you to truly take advantage of your computer in your business with convenient forms designed to work specifically with the specific software packages you use. The software compatablity index allows you to order forms for use with the particular programs you use with confidence. Don't waste time and money trying to adapt your existing forms. Instead, make life easier for your accounting department, order department or billing department.

READY MADE
480 Fillmore Avenue
Tonawanda, NY 14150
Free Catalog
Return policy: Returns must be authorized. Custom orders not returnable

Telephone: 800-346-1375
Fax No: 800-222-1934

Looking for a sign? Well, aren't we all. Ready Made can end your search for a sign. You can have a custom sign produced, or you may purchase a sign with your choice of available warnings. These signs are intended for industrial use, but who can resist the temptation of a "Caution: Watch Out for Fork Lifts" or "Warning: HOT" sign? Seriously, there is a solution to your business sign needs here, and there are volume discounts!

RELIABLE HOME OFFICE
P.O. Box 804117
Chicago, IL 60680-9968
Catalog $2.00
Return policy: Money-Back Guarantee

Telephone: 800-326-6230
Fax No: 800-326-3233

Finally, a shop-by-mail furniture and supply resource for the home office. The difference is clearly in design. You won't find and stodgy, office-y looks here. We're talking designer craftsmanship in work stations, desks, bookcases, file cabinets, chairs, and other furnishings that accent your existing household decor. Ever heard of a Queen Anne File Cabinet? But there's more. You'll also find computer systems, software, home copiers, electronic organizers and all-in-one home fax/phone/answering machines.

STAPLES, INC.
Phone Orders Only

Telephone: 800-333-3330
or 508-370-8958

Corp. Accts.

Return policy: Satisfaction Guaranteed

From laptop computers to no. 2 pencils, Staples offers anything and everything to keep your business running smoothly. With the lowest prices around, you can stock up on red pens while staying in the black! Everything for the office like coffee, printers, phone systems, cash registers and erasers available at Staples at discounted prices. Stock up on items for the home like pens, pencils, tape and envelopes. It's a great place for school supplies, too.

THE BUSINESS BOOK
One East Eighth Avenue
Oshkosh, WI 54906
Free Catalog
Return policy: Money-Back Guarantee

Telephone: 800-558-0220
Fax No: 414-426-1132
DISCOUNT

The Business Book offers today's finest stationery and office supply products at unbeatable savings. Just compare their prices with those advertised in other mail-order office supply catalogs and you'll see the difference. You can buy pressure-sensitive printer labels, stationery, envelopes, order forms, memo pads, greeting cards and a wide assortment of other paper products at considerable savings. The Business Book can even customize these items for you at an additional charge. They also carry a variety of office essentials including personal paper shredders, computer and printer covers, signs, desk-top laminators and a lot more. Their commitment to offering recycled paper products saves you even more money while helping to protect the environment.

VIKING OFFICE PRODUCTS
13809 S. Figeroa St., P.O. Box 61144
Los Angeles, CA 90061-0144
Free Catalog
Return policy: 30-Day Money Back Guarantee

Telephone: 800-248-6111
Fax No: 800-SNAPFAX
DISCOUNT
House Accounts

Save up to 70% off list prices on computer equipment, accessories and software, as well as free shipping! Viking Office Product offers everything and anything related to computers in the workplace. IBM compatable PC's, printer ribbons, dust covers and computer workstations are available to fit the needs of every home and business. With their risk-free policy, try any item for 30 days. If you're not satisfied, just return it and pay nothing. You can't lose.

VULCAN BINDER & COVER
P.O. Box 29
Vincent , AL 35178
Free Catalog
Return policy: Money-Back Guarantee if returned within 15 days

Telephone: 800-634-5923
Fax No: 800-344-8939
COD

A notebook is a notebook is a notebook - right? Well, Vulcan Binder & Cover says "wrong," and they have the high-quality binders and other indispensible office supplies to prove it. Use your imagination and their expert capabilities to get custom binders, folders, displays, easels and holders made to your specifica-tions. Do you prefer regular or D-ring binders? Would you like the company logo screen-printed on the cover or would you prefer a clear overlay for inserting your own design? How about zippers or sturdy handles for easy carrying? The sky isn't even a limit to the possibilities. What's more, their range of other sup-plies runs the gamut - from notebook dividers to business card files to do-it-your-self binding systems.

DIAL A CONTACT LENS, INC.
P.O. Box 91219
San Diego, CA 92169
Telephone: 800-233-LENS
Fax No: 619-459-5014
DISCOUNT
Free Brochure
Return policy: Free Replacements For 30 Days

With your contact lens prescription, you can enjoy the combined benefits and convenience of ordering your contact lenses by mail with delivery to your door and save money, too! Dial A Contact Lens offers an easy way to get eye prescriptions filled at discount prices. Once you've ordered from them your replacement lenses are as close as your phone. They have both clear and colored contact lenses. (See coupon at back of book.)

LENS DIRECT
P.O. Box 147
Hewlett, NY 11557
Telephone: 800-772-LENS
DISCOUNT
Free Brochure
COD
Return policy: 15-Day Money Back Guarantee

Save up to 75% on all major brands of contact lenses including Johnson & Johnson, Barnes-Hind, CibaVision, Bausch&Lomb and Cooper Vision. Order with confidence; they have over 40 years of optical experience and offer excellent service. Over 50,000 lenses in stock at all times! You can call with your prescription or they'll get it for you. Most orders are shipped within 24 hours, which is a great plus when you lose or damage a lens. They do have a $15 membership fee, but they send you coupons worth up to $45.

LENSFIRST
400 Galleria; #400
Southfield , MI 48034
Telephone: 800-388-2400
DISCOUNT
Free Brochure
Return policy: Money-Back Guarantee if returned within 30 days

Lensfirst guarantees the most affordable and convenient alternative for refilling your contact lens prescription. They provide the exact same contact lenses prescribed by your doctor, in factory sealed vials, at a savings of up to 70% off! Plus, they offer the convenience of delivery right to your home or office. Call the toll-free number to get the free-color brochure.

OPTICAL OUTLET
P.O. Box 225, Bay Ridge Station
Brooklyn, NY 11220
Telephone: 800-275-3338
Fax No: 800-275-3338
DISCOUNT
Free Flyer
Return policy: 14 Day Satisfaction Guarantee

To get a great deal on your contact lenses choose Optical Outlet. Once you find out how convenient it is to phone in or fax your prescription instead of taking a trip to the store you'll wonder why you didn't order your lenses this way earlier. With prompt delivery and personalized service, you'll feel like you had contacts when buying your contacts at the Optical Outlet. Two-week money back guarantee.

PRISM OPTICAL, INC.
10992 NW Seventh Ave., Dept. SBM92
North Miami, FL 33168

Telephone: 305-754-5894
Fax No: 305-754-7352

DISCOUNT

Free Catalog

MasterCard VISA 💳 📋 COD

Return policy: Satisfaction Guaranteed

Can you clearly read this? Prism Optical carries a full line of frames, lenses, coatings and sport and dress style prescription eyeglases. Shop directly by mail with 100% satisfaction guaranteed, try them for 30 days. Call or write for a catalog. Free delivery and prices 30% to 50% below retail.

SUNGLASS AMERICA
P.O. Box 147
Hewlett, NY 11557

Telephone: 800-424-LENS

DISCOUNT

Free Catalog

MasterCard VISA 💳 📋 COD

Return policy: 30-Day Money Back Guarantee. 15% Restocking Fee For Non-Defective Returns

Looking for a new pair of shades? Serving the sunglass industry for over 40 years, Sunglass America, the largest wholesale distributor in the Northeast, now brings these whole sales prices direct to consumers. Save up to 75% off retail prices. Brand names include Revo, Porsche, Donna Karan, Serengeti, Vuarnet, Ray-Ban, Laura Biagiotti & more. Their huge inventory, fast delivery and big discounts are too great to miss. For your holiday shopping, remember sunglasses make the perfect gift.

O
P
T
I
C
A
L

CRATE & BARREL

P.O. Box 3057
Northbrook, IL 60065-3057

Telephone: 800-323-5461
Fax No: 708-272-0517

Free Catalog

Return policy: Money-Back Guarantee

Turn your patio, deck or terrace into one of the most enjoyable living spaces in or out of the house with handsome furniture, decorator accents and other accessories by Crate & Barrel. Leave the stodgy old picnic table and benches in the basement and opt for tropical hardwood tables, chairs, 'sunbrellas', rockers, hammocks, outdoor sofas; plus metal beach-bound varieties with fabric accents. The selection of terra cotta planters, lanterns, and candle holders is impeccable, as are the handwoven rugs from India. Not to be missed is the exquisite dinnerware collection and the select grouping of innovative barbecue gadgets.

DAVID KAY

One Jenni Lane
Peoria, IL 61614-3198

Telephone: 800-348-6483
Fax No: 309-691-9357

Catalog $2.00

Return policy: Money-Back Guarantee, excluding customized items

Imagine relaxing in your own private Eden and you're probably thinking of many of the lovely items found in the David Kay catalog. Exquisite floral furniture with wrought-iron frames, authentic Adirondack furniture, beautiful stone sculptures and fountains, garden planters and a wealth of other treasures abound in the full-color catalog. Your garden or patio will be perfect for summertime parties and barbecues given their portable party lights from the Netherlands and handy rool-away counter carts, among other essentials. You'll also find the right storage accessories and furniture covers to protect all your garden accents from damaging weather conditions.

JOHN DEERE

1400 Third Avenue
Moline, IL 61265

Telephone: 800-544-2122
Fax No: 800-626-1462

Free Catalog

Return policy: Money-Back Guarantee

For home and garden furnishings that reflect your adventurous, outdoorsy nature, look to John Deere, "purveyors of plows and other fine things since 1837." They've come a long way in 155 years. Consult your local hardware store for John Deere Plows. Here, you'll find gorgeous wicker furniture, charming 18th Century cast aluminum furniture, marble sculptures and decorative fountains for the garden, durable outdoor toys for kids, sturdy hammocks and lots of other items that are just as timeless as they are handsome. Don't miss the selection of genuine hardwood furniture for indoors or out. Want a quality guarantee? Try one that's good for 150 years!

OUTDOOR FURNITURE

SMITH & HAWKEN GARDEN FURNITURE

25 Corte Madera
Mill Valley, CA 94941

Telephone: 415-383-6399
Fax No: 415-383-7030

Free Catalog

Return policy: Money-Back Guarantee

Well-known for their beautiful selection of flowers and bulbs, Smith & Hawken also offers mail-order wonders in sturdy garden furniture - from the simple to the ornate. Rich teak wood heightens the character of handcrafted tables, chairs, benches, stools, rockers, planters and other furniture. They also have charming French "courtyard" furniture in sturdy steel and cast aluminum that reflect the charm of a Parisian cafe. Stay cool and avoid the harsh rays of the sun with their colorful selection of free-standing Piazza umbrellas, too.

UNIQUE SIMPLICITIES

P.O. Box 1185
New Paltz, NY 12561

Telephone: 914-895-2549

DISCOUNT

Free Catalog

Return policy: Money-Back Guarantee if returned within 30 days

If you've dreamed of whiling away those lazy, warm-weather evenings in your backyard, do it in the comfort of sturdy outdoor furnishings by Unique Simplicities. They carry hammocks crafted into chairs, swings and the traditional lounge style; plus fine hardwood Adirondack chairs, tables and lounges. They also offer classic metal patio furniture reminiscent of the kind Grandma had in her back yard. What's more, Unique Simplicities will match or beat any other advertised priced on the same high-quality merchandise.

WOOD CLASSICS, INC.

Osprey Lane
Gardiner , NY 12525

Telephone: 914-255-7871
Fax No: 914-255-7881

Free Catalog

Return policy: Money-Back Guarantee

The garden should be an invitation to rest and reflect, not to complain about how uncomfortable your outdoor furniture is. Rest and reflect assured that Wood Classics furnishings are made to fit you comfortably with wider back and seat slats, higher seat elevation and contoured backs, among other pluses. In style, you can choose from a large stock of chairs, tables, benches and swings in Chippendale, British, Carved Art, Adirondack and Sante Fe modes. They also offer comfy cushioning and classic market umbrellas in great outdoor shades. The furniture is available partially or fully assembled and comes in your choice of teak or mahogany hardwoods.

CHISWICK TRADING INC.

33 Union Avenue
Sudbury, MA 01776

Free Catalog

Telephone: 800-225-8708
Fax No: 508-443-8091

COD

Return policy: 30-Day Satisfaction Guarantee

Chiswick offers everythingfor your business packaging needs, whether you're a small company or mega-giant corporation. Plastic bags of all shapes and sizes, including zipper storage bags, heat-sealed bags, furniture bags/covers, anti-static electronics bags, bubble-cushioned bags, as well as mylar paper totes. Add to this mailing labels, postal scales, cushioned manila envelopes and tape dispensers, and you've got a complete mailroom!

CONSOLIDATED PLASTICS COMPANY

1864 Enterprise Parkway
Twinsburg, OH 44087

Free Catalog

Telephone: 800-362-1000
Fax No: 216-425-3333

House Acct.

Return policy: Returns accepted with written authorization only

Consolidated Plastics Company has made a commitment to excellence in serving business and industry for over 60 years. They bring you same-day shipping and a knowledgeable staff, in addition to providing an extensive range of products. From the strongest, most durable trash containers and utility carts to wall protection systems and all-weather protective floor matting, you'll be amazed at the selection. Don't miss the Rubbermaid products including the exclusive recycling system

FREUND CAN COMPANY

197 West 84th Street
Chicago, IL 60620

Free Catalog

Telephone: 312-224-4230

COD

Return policy: Returns accepted with written authorization only

Contain yourself!...and everything you own with innovative, hard-to-find containers by Freund. Metal, glass, plastic, and paper take shape in sturdy bottles, jars, jugs, cans, drums, boxes, bags, and closures for packing, mailing or storing just about anything. For home or business, you'll find the perfect container for hazardous chemicals, paints, cleaning aids, food, garbage or whatever. Save big bucks with quantity discounts when buying in bulk. For serious containment, don't miss the selection of Freud closing tools, can sealers and cap tighteners.

NATIONAL BAG COMPANY, INC.

2233 Old Mill Road
Hudson, OH 44236

Free Catalog

Telephone: 800-247-6000
Fax No: 216-425-9800

Return policy: Money-Back Guarantee if returned within 90 days

No matter how small or large the object, National Bag Co. has thousands of plastic bags in a range of sizes to fit any need. Resealable plastic bags, tie-on protective bags, bags with drawstrings and super-strong garbage bags, discounted when you buy in bulk. They also carry corrugated shipping boxes, wrapping paper, mailing boxes, envelopes and labels. Mailing scales, sealing tools, and storage bins make a most efficient mail-room. They maintain a commitment to environmental protection, too. Most products, paper or plastic, are made from recycled materials.

THAT'S A WRAP, INC.

120 West Madison Street, #14A
Chicago, IL 60602

Free Brochure

Return policy: All Sales Final

Telephone: 800-354-0512
Fax No: 708-475-0477

 COD

That's a Wrap presents the finishing touch to any gift; ribbons and bows. Every color, size, shape and style of decorative ribbons are available, including custom designs. Ribbons can transform almost anything from dull to delightful! Add a bow to brighten table-settings, picture frames, even your lapel! With wholesale savings for bulk orders, you can tie a yellow ribbon 'round the old oak tree, young elm tree, or just about any other tree, without spending a lot of green.

P
A
C
K
A
G
I
N
G

CHADSWORTH INCORPORATED
P.O. Box 53268
Atlanta, GA 30355

Telephone: 404-876-5410

Catalog $3.00

Return policy: 20% Restocking Fee. Custom Orders Are Not Returnable.

Simply put, Chadsworth columns are elegant accents for your home's interior or exterior. Quality craftsmanship with modern technology recreates designs true to the specifications laid down in 1563 by major archetect Giacomo Barozzi da Vignola. The importance of customer service has not been overlooked. With free consultation, Chadsworth treats every client with personal service that has made them famous in America and abroad.

DESIGN TOSCANO
7 East Campbell St.
Arlington Heights, IL 60005

Telephone: 800-525-0733

Catalog $6.00, refunded with 1st order

Return policy: 30-Day Money Back Guarantee.

Gargoyles and griffons are invading America and if you're lucky enough to get one you will no doubt be one of the first on your block to provide a perch for a gothic styling element that looks great indoors or out. In the middle ages these creatures were used to ward evil away from cathedrals and the congregation. Today they can protect your home from the mundane and the ordinary. Whimsically, sometimes frighteningly styled, some are authentic reproductions from European structures. Given as gifts, they will be treasured always.

CRAZY CAT LADY

P.O. Box 691920
Los Angeles, CA 90069
Catalog $1.00
Return policy: Money Back Guarantee

Telephone: 800-282-MEOW
Fax No: 818-843-5328

Here's a pet product supplier with a difference. Crazy Cat Lady, as the name implies, caters only to the owners of felines. This is one fun catalog, and it's full of interesting products that wil make your kitty's life more enjoyable. Shampoos, combs and powders for grooming are available, as are games and toys to keep tabby healthy and fit. An additional publication, Crazy Cat Chat, is published a few times a year, and is full of tips, hints and products all written in a sharp, witty style.

ECHO DISCOUNT AQUARIUM SUPPLIES

Box 850145
Westland, MI 48185
Catalog $1.00
Return policy: 15% Restocking Fee

Telephone: 800-262-4818
Fax No: 313-453-0306
DISCOUNT

Something Fishy's going on here! All the supplies and accessories for beginning and experienced keepers of tropical fish are available here. Anyone can enjoy the hypnotic beauty of the undersea world with low prices on tanks, filters, food and fertilizer. There are toys and decorations by all major manufacturers. Medium sized fish tanks in all shapes are available. If fish could talk (Echo sells an underwater tank microphone if you'd like to find out!) they'd ask for Echo.

J-B WHOLESALE PET SUPPLIES, INC.

289 Wargaraw Road
Hawthorne, NJ 07506
Free Catalog and Handbook
Return policy: 28-Day Money Back Guarantee, except videos, vaccines, books

Telephone: 201-423-2222
Fax No: 201-423-1181
DISCOUNT

What?! You don't have a copy of the J-B Wholesale Catalog & Handbook?! They have a more complete selection of professional dog products & equipment available anywhere-at low, low prices! They have everything in stock; vaccines, supplements, combs and brushes, shampoos and grooming products. Their sale flyers are terrific. J-B cannot ship vaccines to addresses in New Jersey.

MASTER ANIMAL CARE

Lake Road; P.O. Box 3333
Mountaintop, PA 18707-0330
Catalog $2.00
Return policy: Money-Back Guarantee

Telephone: 800-346-0749

Your pet will be assured of its rightful place with essential supplies and clever care items for felines and canines. Kitty will appreciate its own designer furniture, car seats, ID collars, feeding dishes, climbing trees and toys. Doggy dudes will love designer beds, kennel doors, generously sized feeding dishes, toy bones and other items. What you'll appreciate are the security gates, furniture protectors, pet repellents and effective cleaning supplies to keep your home from looking and smelling like a kennel. Don't skip the lightweight pet carriers and travel accessories for your furry friends.

PATIO PACIFIC, INC.
Worldport Center,1931-C N. Gaffey St.
San Pedro, CA 90731-1265

Telephone: 800-826-2871

Free Flyers

MasterCard VISA PERSONAL CHECKS COD

Return policy: 30-Day Money Back Guarantee

The most practical and economical entrance you can provide for your pet is an Instant Pet Door by Patio Pacific. The flap door is built into an aluminum and glass panel that easily slides into the door or screen track of your sliding patio door. Other manufacturers and styles are available to suit specific needs, such as for installation in a french door. When they can come and go as they please, your pet will be happier and better behaved.

PEDIGREES
1989 Transit Way, Box 905
Brockport, NY 14420-0905

Telephone: 716-637-1434
Fax No: 716-352-1272

Free Catalog

MasterCard VISA PERSONAL CHECKS

Return policy: Satisfaction Guaranteed

Finally, a mail order house to make the special member of your family more than just a pet. Special feeding bowls for larger or smaller pets make dining a pleasure while heated pet beds are cozy on even the coldest nights. There are even seat belts for safer travel. Hundreds of other ways to let your dog or cat know that they're special. There are even halloween costumes to let your pet join in on holiday celebrations.

PET DOORS USA
4523 30th Street West
Bradenton, FL 34207

Telephone: 813-753-7492

Catalog $.50

MasterCard VISA PERSONAL CHECKS

Return policy: 30-Day Money Back Guarantee

Pet Doors USA offers freedom for you and your pet. An easy-to-install pet door will end your days of being on duty 24 hours a day, and it will enable your dog or cat to come and go as they please. You'll never have to worry about letting the cat out, or wondering if you walked the dog. Unlike old style pet doors, the Plexidor pet doors offered here automatically close with a concealed mechanism. Designed for installation on metal doors, wood paneled doors, windows and walls, the "Rolls Royce of Pet Doors" locks to keep your pet in and intruders out. There are electronically opening doors for the ultimate in pet convenience.

R. C. STEELE
1989 Transit Way, Box 910
Brockport, NY 14420-0910

Telephone: 800-872-4506
Fax No: 716-352-1272

DISCOUNT

Free Catalog

MasterCard VISA PERSONAL CHECKS

Return policy: Two-Week Satisfaction Guarantee

Attention, dogs. Products for you at incredible low prices. R.C. Steele stylish collars are all the rage, but the standard leather strap is here too. Anything and everything you need for your escape from the dog-eat dog world (no offense!). Houses, gates, doors, even the latest in fashion raincoats and sweats. They even have toys for the kitties! Get in style while saving your pet's valuable money!

RANGER KENNELS

Telephone: 501-443-2041

P.O. Box AA
Fayetteville, AR 72702

DISCOUNT

Free Catalog

Return policy: Money-Back Guarantee

Keep your canine friends "Safe From Danger, in a Ranger!" This company offers quality kennels in three levels of security and they're portable, too. But the best part is their 30% savings off the market prices. Choose the economical, the commercial or the maximum security kennel that offers the level of security you want for your pet, be it light, heavy or extra-heavy. All the kennels are made of welded, galvanized steel tubing, finished in aluminum paint, and have dog-proof latches. A wrench is all you'll need to assemble the kennel in less than an hour.

SIR MAXWELL'S

Telephone: 407-394-8814

7979 La Mirada Dr.
Boca Raton, FL 33433

Free Brochure

Return policy: Freshness Guaranteed

Treat your pooch to homemade classic cookies from Sir Maxwell. Dogs of all shapes and sizes will love these all-natural treats. Baked fresh, these nutritional cookies contain no artificial flavors, colors or preservatives and are a natural and healthy supplement to your dog's daily diet. Choose from over 10 shapes, including Valentine's Day hearts, Halloween pumpkins, Chanukah dreidels and menorahs, and even birthday ice cream cones!

THE CANINE FENCE COMPANY

Telephone: 800-628-2264

493 Danbury Road
Wilton, CT 06897

Free Brochure

Return policy: 30-Day Satisfaction Guarantee

The typical exercise we give our pooches is a walk on a leash. This prevents them from running away, but it also prevents them from running at all! Make your dog happy as a clam by giving it the entire yard! Invisible Fencing offers an attractive alternative to chainlink fences. Your dog is humanely conditioned to respect the boundaries of your property. And you'll save money you save on fence repairs and maintenance.

UPCO

Telephone: 816-233-8800
Fax No: 816-233-9696

3705 Pear Street; P.O. Box 969
St. Joseph, MO 64502

DISCOUNT

Free Catalog

COD

Return policy: Money-Back Guarantee

Celebrating their 40th year, UPCO offers affordable pet care. The full-color catalog is brimming with the best, most practical, most unusual, and most innovative products available for animals of all sorts. Grooming aids, vaccines, odor removers, kennel equipment and first aid kits are just a few items from the diverse product selection. Oster, Lambert Kay, Ring 5, Gerard-Pellham, and Best 'N Show are some of the well-known name-brands. Quantity discounts available.

AMERICAN FRAME CORPORATION
1340 Tomahawk Dr., Arrowhead Park
Maumee, OH 43537-1695

Telephone: 800-537-0944
Fax No: 419-893-3553

Free Catalog

Return policy: Damaged Merchandise Exchanged

Top quality and custom cut, the American Frame Corporation has a large selection of premium wood and metal picture frames. With 18 enameled colors and 10 anodized colors in 8 different styles for metal frames alone, you will be able to get the perfect style for the room you want to hang your frame in. There are dozens of wood frame styles in a multitude of additional colors. You'll want to hang onto this catalog for a while.

COS-TOM PICTURE FRAMES
5401 Linda Vista Road; #405
San Diego, CA 92121

Telephone: 800-854-6606

DISCOUNT

Free Catalog

Return policy: Exchanges Only With Authorization

Picture this: picture frames at factory direct prices. Call for a catalog, which features many types of frames, including metal sections, wood sections and ready-made frames. You'll save 25% on frames and receive even bigger discounts on quantity purchases. Frames are shippped UPS in about 2 weeks.

EXPOSURES
2800 Hoover Road
Stevens Point, WI 54481

Telephone: 800-222-4947

Free Catalog

Return policy: Satisfaction Guaranteed

An album or frame is more than just a place to put your photos. Exposures is well aware of this. Using glass, wood, leather and metal, they offer items that actual enhance your pictures with their simple, yet tasteful design ideas. Silver-plated renaissance styles dress up your formal shots while contemporary wood fames can understate your dramatic portaits. Playful colors are great for photos of the kids. With a generous assortment of bindings, colors and styles there is a photo album and frame waiting for you and your pictures.

FRAME FIT COMPANY
P.O. Box 8926
Philadelphia, PA 19135
Free Flyers
Return policy: Satisfaction Guaranteed

Telephone: 800-523-3693
Fax No: 800-344-7010

DISCOUNT

COD

Frame Fit Company offers quality aluminum frames at low prices in 100 colors and styles. These frames do not arrive assembled, but the few minutes it takes to put them together is worth the amount of money you've saved for yourself. Although there is a large selection of options available with Frame Fit, if you know basically what you're looking for you will have no problem finding it. Free shipping in most cases.

GRAPHIK DIMENSIONS, LTD.
41-23 Haight Street
Flushing, NY 11355-4247
Free Catalog
Return policy: 15% Restocking Charge; Customer Orders Not Returnable

Telephone: 800-221-0262
Fax No: 718-463-2470

Each frame is like a work of art. Beautifully textured patterns and marvelous colors set Graphik Dimensions frames apart from all the rest. How many places offer lacquered frames in almost two dozen colors. Museum quality custommade frames are available in many styles and colors, and will add the finishing touch on that special piece. Oval frames and preassembled contemporary wood pieces made to exacting standards are here for less than you'd expect. Mat cutting tools are here, too. This is the choice for the amateur, professional, or amateur professional.

P
I
C
T
U
R
E

F
R
A
M
E
S

ALLEN-EDMONDS SHOE CORP.

201 East Seven Hills Road; P.O. Box 998
Port Washington, WI 53074-0998

Telephone: 414-284-7158
Fax No: 414-284-7499

Free Catalog

Return policy: Money-Back Guarantee (provided shoes do not show wear)

Describing Allen-Edmond shoes as "top-quality" is not enough. Perhaps "tip-top-quality" more befits their beautiful collection of fine men's shoes of timeless, style and superior craftsmanship. They carry conservative styles for business executivse including wing-tips, loafers, monk-straps and oxfords; plus classic casuals with saddle, moccasin or woven details. Qualilty materials include calfskin, leather, suede, lizard and crocodile.Prices are a little higher, butworth it for such impeccable quality. Shoes are guaranteed to withstand the roughest wear, and they have a unique repair service that'll get themback into "tip-top" condition.

BOOT TOWN

10838 North Central
Dallas, TX 75231

Telephone: 800-222-6687

DISCOUNT

Free Catalog

Return policy: Money-Back Guarantee

If you love boots and Western wear, Boot Town has all your favorite styles at savings of up to 70%. Tony Lama, Lucchese, Justin, Nocona and many other well-known names are available in boots, leather accessories and more. Call them for a free, full-color catalog.

G.H. BASS AND CO. BY MAIL

301 U.S. Route 1
Scarborough, ME 04074-8380

Telephone: 800-333-2258
Fax No: 207-883-7701

Free Catalog

Return policy: Satisfaction Guarantee

Over a hundred years ago G.H. Bass started producing long-lasting, quality shoes. They wore so well that George's namesake company is still going strong. Mens, Ladies and Childrens shoes with a unique touch of comfort has long been a Bass trademark in all styles. Rugged and casual, walking shoes and hiking boots are for sale right alongside dress shoes. Usually sold through exclusive stores and outlets, you can buy them convenience of mail order.

GOTHAM SHOE COMPANY

P.O. Box 409
Kirkwood, NY 13795

Telephone: 607-775-1332
Fax No: 607-775-0539

Free Catalog

Return policy: Exchanges on unused merchandise

Students who march to the beat of a drum will find a great selection of shoes specially designed for marching bands and cheerleading. They have classic black or white oxford models; plus saddle oxfords in colors to match virtually any uniform. There are corp-style, drill team and majorette boots with stretch gores for better fit around the calf, among other comfort details. Oxford soles are made for marching with extra padding, foam cushion insoles and genuine leather uppers.

HANOVER SHOES
440 North Madison St. P.O. Box 340
Hanover, PA 17331-0340
Free Catalog
Return policy: Satisfaction Guaranteed

Telephone: 800-426-3708
Fax No: 800-832-8058
DISCOUNT

What happens when America's finest men's shoemaker sells their footwear directly to you instead of to a middleman? You save about 30% off retail prices. Hanover has been making highest quality shoes for almost 100 years. Their world famous loafers, oxfords and wingtips are available from this catalog in all sizes. Since man does not live by dress shoes alone, incredibly comfortable slippers and casuals of the same quality are here, too. Gift certificates available.

JUSTIN DISCOUNT BOOTS & COWBOY OUTFITTERS
101 Highway 156, P.O. Box 67
Justin, TX 76247
Free Catalog
Return policy: Returns accepted on unworn items only

Telephone: 800-677-BOOT

DISCOUNT

World-famous Justin Boots of Texas features styles for men, women and children at discount prices. The original Justin Roper Boot for men is priced at $79.97. Other authentic styles include Justin Straw Hats, Wrangler Jeans, Charhartt coats and overalls and much more.

JUST JUSTIN
1505 Wycliff Avenue
Dallas , TX 75207
Free Catalog
Return policy: Satisfaction Guaranteed

Telephone: 800-BYA-BOOT

DISCOUNT

Buy direct from a Texas favorite and save big bucks on boots! Get men's and ladies genuine leather and lizard boots at fantastic prices. All their cowboy boots are always 50-70% off the retail prices. Just give them a toll-free holler with the size and style number. They'll ship anywhere by UPS and satisfaction is guaranteed or your money back!

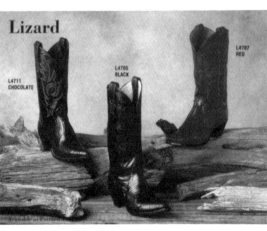

LEE'S COMFORT SHOES

Telephone: 800-753-4736

P.O. Box 728, 126 South Sandusky Ave.
Bucyrus, OH 44820

Free Catalog

Return policy: 60-Day Money Back Guarantee

Have you been good to your feet recently? Lee's Comfort Shoes will let you take care of them, without putting a strain on your wallet. Brand names like New Balance, Easy Spirit, Extra Depth and Clinic will offer casual style and comfort for your aching toes. Pumps, sandels and dress shoes that feel so good you'll never want to take them off. Free shipping on all orders. This, along with their low prices, saves you a bundle.

MASON SHOE MANUFACTURING COMPANY

Telephone: 800-826-7030

Chippewa Falls, WI 54774

DISCOUNT

Free Catalog

Return policy: One-Year Money Back Guarantee

If you're looking for a complete selection of shoes for every facet of your lifestyle at factory direct prices, then look no further than Mason Shoes. Men's and ladies casual, dress and sport shoes in all colors are offered at ridiculous prices. From patent leather wingtips to the walking shoes of the U.S. Post Office, it's all here. No matter what shoe you are specifically seeking, you'll find it here. Ladies handbags are also available.

MASSEYS

Telephone: 800-4MASSEY
Fax No: 800-446-2329

601 Twelfth Street, P.O. Box 10088
Lynchburg, VA 24506-0088

DISCOUNT

Free Catalog

Return policy: Satisfaction Guaranteed

Where can you get great brand name ladies footwear for less than you'd pay in stores for inferior quality shoes? Masseys is a direct footwear merchant who uses their tremendous buying power to get outrageous deals on name brand shoes by Liz Claiborne, Evan Picone, Nina and Bass. Hiking boots, walking shoes, clogs, pumps and more. A shoe for every aspect of your life, and a shoe for every budget.

MINNETONKA BY MAIL

Telephone: 212-365-7033

P.O. Box 444B
Bronx, NY 10458

DISCOUNT

Free Catalog

Return policy: Satisfaction Guaranteed

Put some savings in your step. Buy 2 pairs and save $10 on those famous Minnetonka moccasins, shoes and boots for men, women, and children. Call or write to receive a full-color catalog featuring hundreds of styles, including beaded, buttoned, fringed, zippered, soft and hard soles, deerskin, pile-lined and other varieties. All styles are in stock for immediate shipment.

OKUN BROTHERS SHOES

356 East South Street
Kalamazoo, MI 49007

Telephone: 800-433-6344
Fax No: 616-383-3401

DISCOUNT

Free Catalog

Return policy: Money-Back Guarantee

The Okun Brothers shoe concept is "Famous Brands For Less...That's Why We're Famous". Their latest catalog helps you take advantage of this concept's success by offering remarkable savings on famous-maker shoes for men and women. Rockport, Soft Spots, Dexter and Easy Spirit are a few of the names you trust in walking and dress varieties. Reebook, Nike, Avia and New Balance round out the athletic category. Okun Bros. also offers a selection of high quality dress and athletic hosiery, plus a few indispensible shoe care products.

SHOECRAFT CORPORATION

P.O. Box 129
Accord, MA 02018

Telephone: 800-225-5848
Fax No: 617-871-1976

Free Catalog

Return policy: Money-Back Guarantee, if returned within 60 days

For larger sized women's footwear, you could scan the retail selections (good luck!), or shop easily and inexpensively by mail with the Tall Gals catalog from the Shoecraft Corporation. You'll find gorgeous, up-to-the-minute fashion styles on casuals, dressy heels, boots and athletic shoes. They carry sizes from 10 to 14 only, with selected styles available in wide widths. Suede and leather are the textures of choice; plus they carry dyable shoes for special occasions that call for head-to-toe perfection.

S
H
O
E
S
&
B
O
O
T
S

ATHLETES WEAR COMPANY
145 Market Avenue
Winnipeg, MB CANADA R3B 9Z9
Free Catalog

Telephone: 204-949-1885
Fax No: 204-943-3866

💳 VISA 💳 📧 COD

Return policy: 30-Day Returns With Authorization, except Custom Orders

Whatever your game, Athletes Wear has for every sport under the sun or under a roof. For organized teams there are custom rings and uniforms, as well as trophies awaiting to be engraved with your award-winning player. For sports equipment, this is a treasure trove of supplies, from the usual—baseball, basketball, football, lacrosse, track and field—to the exotic like wallyball, squash & curling.

EXPLORAWEAR
420 N. Fifth Street; Suit #520
Minneapolis , MN 55401-1318
Free Information

Telephone: 612-340-9870
Fax No: 612-340-9921

💳 VISA 📧

Return policy: Money-Back Guarantee

Finally, someone has invented a line of travel and active clothing that's not only great-looking, but it'll stay that way. Be it climbing, flying, camping, hiking, fishing or whatever your adventure, you'll notice the difference quality travel clothes can make. The no-iron, tight-packing clothing collection features pants that transform into shorts; tailored shirts that keep you cool in the hottest sun; and safari jackets that have more compartments than your suitcase. They laugh at wrinkles and each contains a hidden security pocke.

JAZZERTOGS
1050 Joshua Way
Vista, CA 92083-7807
Free Catalog

Telephone: 800-FIT-IS-IT
Fax No: 800-2-FAX-TOG

💳 VISA 💳 📧

Return policy: Exchanges Only

From the popular Jazzercise exercise video series comes Jazzertogs mail-order workout gear, sportswear and accessories. Fashionable designs take shape in leotards, leggings and sweats. There's a full range of accessories to choose from, including headgear, jewelry, Avia athletic shoes, and support lingerie. They also carry fun-colored exercise mats, dumbbells, and water bottles to keep you sweating in style! And, of course, every Jazzercise workout video ever made.

ROAD RUNNER SPORTS
6310 Nancy Ridge Road
San Diego, CA 92121
Free Catalog

Telephone: 800-551-5558

DISCOUNT

💳 VISA 💳 📧

Return policy: Satisfaction Guarantee

Stop running around long enough to order this catalog and you'll be pleasantly surprised at the money you'll save on brand-name fitness clothing. For men and women, there are tights, jogging sets, bike shorts, t-shirts, and bathing suits from Dolfin, Movin Comfort, Asics, Tinley, Gore-Tex, Hind and Tri-Fit. There's are running, walking, hiking and sport shoes from Brooks, Nike, Tiger, Saucony, Hi-Tec, Adidas, Avia, Etonic, Reebok and New Balance. Save up to 35% on these famous names and take advantage of the "Runner's Hotline" 800-662-8896.

BIKE NASHBAR

4111 Simon Road
Youngstown, OH 44512-1343

Free Catalog

Return policy: 30 Day Money Back Guarantee

Telephone: 800-NASHBAR
Fax No: 800-456-1223

DISCOUNT

Here's where cyclists save! Bike Nashbar offers brand name bike apparel, equipment and accessories at prices that will make your wheels spin. Derailleurs by Shimano, Suntour and Campagnolo make for easy shifting while the custom pedals will get you locked and loaded. Indoor bicycle trainers let you keep your form all year long. You can even get wheels with disk brakes for extra stopping power.

COLORADO CYCLIST, INC.

2455 Executive Circle
Colorado Springs, CO 80906

Free Catalog

Return policy: 30-Day Money Back Guarantee

Telephone: 800-688-8600
Fax No: 719-576-3598

COD

No matter what kind of bicycle you've got, if you're serious about it you'd better get the Colorado Cyclist Catalog, if you don't already have it! For helmets to shoes and everything in between, you're covered. Completed bicycles or get any of the derailleurs, pedals, frames or forks to customize your own bike. All of the products offered here are of the highest quality and are in use by professional cyclists worldwide. Why not join them?

CYCLE GOODS

2801 Hennepin Avenue South
Minneapolis, MN 55408

Catalog $2.00

Return policy: 20-Day Satisfaction Guarantee. Bikes and Frames Excluded

Telephone: 800-328-5213

Here's where the serious cyclist will find what they're looking for. Cycle Goods caters to true bicycling enthusiasts, as opposed to the casual rider. All of the high quality parts and accessories you need to build a competition bike are offered. There's more to this great mail order source, though. Eyewear, helmets, shoes and attire are also available, as are more "consumer-oriented" products, like child seats and training wheels.

BICYCLES

FIRST CLASS BMX

P.O. Box 66290, Department B
Portland , OR 97290-6290

Free Catalog

Return policy: Money-Back Guarantee, less restocking fee

Telephone: 503-253-8688

DISCOUNT

Voted #1 in discount mail order bicycle sales, First Class BMX offers serious cyclists the very best in high performance bikes and biking accoutrements at discount prices. Mountain bikes, road bikes, all-terrain models and racers are available in addition to every part imaginable; except of course, your part. Mongoose, GT, Powerlite and Redline are just some of the well-known names to choose from. Buy the bikes complete, or custom build your own model. You choose!

PERFORMANCE BICYCLE SHOP

One Performance Way; P.O. Box 2741
Chapel Hill, NC 27514

Free Catalog

Return policy: Money-Back Guarantee

Telephone: 800-727-2453
Fax No: 800-727-FAX-1

DISCOUNT

The nation's largest catalog retailer of cycling products offers a full-color catalog of merchandise for all aspects of the popular sport. Thay have a full line of biking apparel, helmets, shoes, cyclometers, components and packs. Prices are below normal retail. Airborne Overnight and UPS shipping are available.

BASS PRO SHOPS OUTDOOR WORLD
1935 South Campbell
Springfield, MO 65898-0200
Free Catalog

Telephone: 800-227-7776
Fax No: 417-887-2531

Return policy: 30-Day Satisfaction Guarantee

You won't have to go fishing for values when seeking camping supplies if you get the catalog from Bass Pro Shops. Tents large enough to fit the whole outdoors inside at prices that will raise the roof. Accessories include portable showers, lanterns, even a portable fish cooker. Rods and reels by Quantum, Daiwa and Shimano help to make your casting call smooth and easy, while the lures spell trouble for the locals! Fishing boats and speed boats by Nitro and Tracker are available in all sizes. The largest selection of outdoor supplies at greatprices.

CAMPING WORLD
Three Springs Rd., P.O. Box 90017
Bowling Green, KY 42102-9017
Free Catalog

Telephone: 800-626-5944
Fax No: 502-781-2775

Return policy: 30-Day Money Back Guarantee

Make the most of your RV by browsing through the Camping World catalog. Neat necessities and nifty novelties can increase the enjoyment you get out of your camper. TV antennas, fans, exterior awnings, gas-powered generators, easy chairs and propane ovens all make your home away from home a little homier. All of the major manufacturers of recreational gear are included in this huge 140 page catalog. There's so much great stuff here that you may end up moving out of your house and into your home (motor home, that is).

GANDER MOUNTAIN, INC.
Box 248, Highway W
Wilmot, WI 53192
Free Catalog

Telephone: 800-558-9410
Fax No: 800-553-2828

Return policy: Satisfaction Guaranteed

Outfitters of sportsman for generations, Gander Mountain provides clothes and equipment catering to hunters, campers and fisherman. Insulated camouflage clothing will keep you warm and cozy while waiting to bag the trophy of a lifetime. Elk, moose and duck calls are here, as are supplies for bow and rifle hunters. Compound bows and crossbows provide the ultimate hunting challenge.

CAMPING OUTDOOR

ORVIS OUTDOOR CATALOG

1711 Blue Hills Dr. Box 12000
Roanoke, VA 24022-8001

Free Catalog

Return policy: Satisfaction Guaranteed

Telephone: 800-653-7635
Fax No: 703-343-7053

The highest quality rods and reels any angler could ask for are available from America's oldest mail order company. This merchandise is meant for the serious fisherman, don't expect to find cheap plastic poles and flimsy spinning reels, these rods are made of graphite, composites and bamboo. They also offer clothing, waders and accessories.

SEARS OUTDOORS CATALOG

1630 Cleveland Avenue
Kansas City, MO 64127-2246

Free Catalog

Return policy: Money-Back Guarantee

Telephone: 800-366-3000

DISCOUNT

Sears,

Another great catalog from a great American retailer, featuring brand name boating and camping equipment by Hodgman, Sevylor, Apelco, Bottom Line, Taylor, Fulton, Superwich, Hydra, Impulse, Teleflex and more. Fishing boats, canoes, mini boats and kayaks are all priced within reach and can be purchased using the Sears monthly payment plan. You'll also find a plethora of boat motors, water ski equipment, fishing gear, safety supplies and accessories for the aquatic sportsman. Take the rough out of "roughing it" with top-quality camping gear like tents, sleeping bags, cooking tools, clothing and hunting accessories.

SIERRA TRADING POST

1625 Crane Way
Sparks, NV 89431

Free Catalog

Return policy: Money-Back Guarantee

Telephone: 702-355-3355
Fax No: 702-355-3366

DISCOUNT

Buzzwords like "overstock," "closeouts," and "irregulars" are terms that symbolize big savings to the consumer. The Sierra Trading Post uses such terminlogy on 35-70% savings on name-brand outdoor clothing and equipment. Names like Patagonia, Marmot, Sportif USA, Caribou & The North Face are just the beginning. There's down outerwear, polarized sunglasses, sleeping bags, luggage, tents, backpacks, hiking shoes, and a full range of clothing for the adventurer in you.

CHICK'S

P.O. Drawer 59
Harrington , DE 19952
Free Catalog

Telephone: 302-398-4630

DISCOUNT

MasterCard VISA PERSONAL CHECKS COD

Return policy: Money-Back Guarantee if returned within 30 days

Equestrians will appreciate the superior quality products andgreat savings on a complete line of riding and stabling needs from Chick's. Hand-tooled leather saddles, breast collars, leather harnesses, woven western blankets and a huge array of stabling and horse grooming products. There are traditional equestrian items including boots, riding breeches, riding jackets, gloves, and helmets. Chick's also has charming novelty items and informative books for the equine set.

COLORADO SADDLERY COMPANY

1631 15th Street
Denver, CO 80202-1391
Catalog $8.50

Telephone: 800-521-2465
Fax No: 303-825-0643

MasterCard VISA PERSONAL CHECKS

Return policy: Money-Back Guarantee with authorization, except custom orders

Professional horseback riders know what a difference the right saddle can make. Colorado Saddlery Company has been a major supplier to stables across the country for nearly 50 years. Their unique catalog offers a huge assortment of beautiful, hand-tooled leather saddles, from stock or made to your exact specifications. They also have a variety of other essential riding equipment including stirrups, cinchas, headstalls, reins, training equipment and saddle blankets. Horseshoes, hoof care items and veterinary products are also featured.

LIBERTYVILLE SADDLE SHOP

P.O. Box M
Libertyville, IL 60048-4913
Free Catalog

Telephone: 800-872-3353
Fax No: 708-680-2491

MasterCard VISA ¢ PERSONAL CHECKS

Return policy: 15-Day Money Back Guarantee

Hold your horses! The Libertyville Saddle Shop is the horse source for everyone. Western, English or Ranch catalogs are available on a rotating basis throughout the year, so you will be able to get a lavishly illustrated catalog tailored to your specific interest. Products in these catalogs will provide you with the highest quality riding saddles available, as well as brushes, shampoos, conditioners, saddle racks, shelves, ice boots and medicines. No matter where your equine styles lay, what you need is at the Libertyville Saddle Shop.

PHELAN'S EQUESTRIAN CATALOG

P.O. Box 37
Sausilito, CA 94965
Free Catalog

Telephone: 415-332-6001
Fax No: 415-332-4638

MasterCard VISA ¢ PERSONAL CHECKS

Return policy: Satisfaction Guaranteed

If you love horses, you'll love Phelan's Catalog, jammed with riding gear that is both fashionable and functional. Vests and breeches not only hold up to the rigors of riding, but will keep you looking smart even when a horse isn't under you. Saddles from the Frank Baines Saddlery will let your horse look sharp, too. Bridles and stirrups are also available.

E
Q
U
E
S
T
R
I
A
N

CONCEPT II, INC.
RR1 Box 1100
Morrisville, VT 05661-9727

Telephone: 802-888-7971
Fax No: 802-888-4791

Free Brochure

Return policy: 1-Year Full Manufacturer's Warranty

They say that the vast majority of their customers have never rowed on water and yet The Concept II Ergometer rowing machine has maintained and broadened its clientele of non-professional rowers. The exercise trainer, which was developed in 1981 as an off-water training device for pro rowers, has been shipped to homes, health clubs, pro football teams and even NASA. The technological advances that have been made in the original design have further increased its effectiveness in working the muscles of your legs, back, shoulders, buttocks, arms, stomach; not to mention the benefits to the heart and lungs. The machine is available with a video performance monitor that actually regulates your performance.

NORDICTRACK
141 Jonathan Boulevard North
Chaska, MN 55318

Telephone: 800-328-5888

Free Brochure

Return policy: Money-Back Guarantee if returned with 30 days

Undoubtedly, the most widely publicized 'aerobiciser' on the market today is NordicTrack. For those of you who tend to be a little leery of all the exercise gadgetry advertised on TV, they invite you to send for this free brochure which explains exactly how the product works. Simulating the motion of cross-country skiing (supposedly the best workout since the decathlon), the machine exercises every major muscle group. The are 7 different models to choose from, each designed for varying degrees of advanced training. The Nordic Track label now also appears on the new Back & Stomach Machine and the Fitness Chair: two new products worth investigating.

AUSTAD'S

4500 East 10th St., P.O. Box 5428
Sioux Falls, SD 57196-0001

Telephone: 800-444-1234
Fax No: 605-339-0362

Free Catalog

Return policy: Satisfaction Guaranteed

FORE! You can't miss with Austad's golf equipment. Practice driving nets and slice-inhibiting woods will improve your distance game, the surlyn putters and chippers will help out your short game while the sharp golf attire will improve you all over. Accessories include a score card keeper and beverage holder in one, personalized golfballs and distance finders so there's never any guessing as to how far from the hole you are. Everything a golfer wants or needs is here for the asking.

GOLFSMITH INTERNATIONAL, INC.

10206 North IH-35
Austin, TX 78753-9982

Telephone: 512-837-4810
Fax No: 512-837-1245

DISCOUNT

Free Catalog

COD

Return policy: No Returns Without Valid Cause. 10% Restocking Charge

If you had your choice of standard golf clubs or a set built to your own specifications, which would you take? Although it's actually aimed at golf shop owners, the Golfsmith International catalog is full of all the supplies necessary for you to build your own set of clubs. Choose the grip you want, the type of clubhead your game is tailored for and the shaft length. Then put it together. Kits are available for different clubs, but if you don't want to be bothered with it, buy the materials and get a shop to assemble it for you. What a great way to get terrific clubs at tremendous discounts.

BERRY SCUBA COMPANY

6674 North Northwest Highway
Chicago, IL 60631

Telephone: 800-621-6019
Fax No: 312-775-1815

DISCOUNT

Free Catalog

Return policy: 30 Day-Return Policy. 15% Restocking Fee On Returns only

Go under water and stay under budget! Berry Scuba offers wet suits and dry suits, tanks and regulators, fins and masks and every other diving accessory available at prices of up to 50% off list. By purchasing a complete diving packages you can save even more! Underwater spear guns, hunting supplies and cameras let you capture your undersea prey, by hook or by film. A wet suit repair service is available even if you bought your wet suit elsewhere. If you've ever wanted to explore this hobby, they even offer classes.

IN THE SWIM DISCOUNT POOL SUPPLIES

902 Paramount Parkway
Batavia, IL 60510

Telephone: 800-374-1500
Fax No: 800-POOL FAX

DISCOUNT

Free Catalog

Return policy: Money-Back Guarantee

Dive into a pool of great savings on all the equipment, maintenance supplies and accessories for your swimming pool from In The Swim. They carry quality water balancing chemicals, chlorine additives, bromine tablets, algae fighters, stain fighters and other chemicals to keep the water true-blue and sparkling clean. Liners, covers, vacuums, and fun aquatic accessories round out the stock of products.

PERFORMANCE DIVER

P.O. Box 2741
Chapel Hill, NC 27514

Telephone: 800-727-2453
Fax No: 800-727-FAX-1

DISCOUNT

Free Brochure

Return policy: Money-Back Guarantee

Performance Diver offers a full line of the latest scuba gear available, as well as diving apparel. The prices are discounted well below the regular prices found in your local diving gear shops. Airborne Overnight and UPS shipping is also available.

SKIN DIVER WET SUITS

1632 South 250th Street
Des Moines, WA 98198

Telephone: 206-878-1613
Fax No: 206-824-3323

Free Catalog

Return policy: 30-Day Money Back Guarantee

Although the name is Skin Diver Wet Suits, they cater to surfers, water skiers, kayakers, or enthusaists of just about any water sport. Although they are suitable for any water activity, two specific styles of suits are offered—Skin Diver and Water Skier. Coordinating accessories such as gloves, "wet socks" and boots are also available. Quality crafted, every seam is glued and blindstitched for added security and optimum wear. Satisfaction guaranteed.

HOLABIRD SPORTS DISCOUNTERS
9008 Yellow Brick Road
Baltimore, MD 21237
Free Information

Telephone: 410-687-6400
Fax No: 410-687-7311
DISCOUNT

Return policy: Returns accepted for exchange or store credit only

Holabird offers top-quality sports equipment, including athletic shoes, tennis gear, and a plethora of other products and accessories at great discounts. They combine unbeatable service and quality with discounted pricing to serve the serious athlete - be s/he novice or professional. They can ship your order anywhere in the country within 48 hours, usually at no cost to you.

SAMUELS TENNISPORT
7796 Montgomery Road
Cincinnati, OH 45236
Free Price List

Telephone: 800-543-1153
Fax No: 513-791-4036
DISCOUNT

Return policy: 15% Restocking Fee

Any one for tennis? Here's one of the best sources in the country for racquets, gloves, shoes and balls for all types of racquet sports. Get great prices on equipment by brand name manufacturers like Prince, Yonex, Head, Wilson, Head, Reebok, Avia, Leader and Penn. There is only one low charge for shipping, regardless of how much merchandise you order. On top of the low prices, you will be hard pressed to find a better deal.

SPORTLINE OF HILTON HEAD, LTD.
3720-C Alliance Drive
Greensboro, NC 27407
Free Catalog

Telephone: 800-438-6021

DISCOUNT

Return policy: Money-Back Guarantee

Sportline of Hilton Head, Ltd. products are backed by more than just a money-back guarantee. Every product reflects a sheer commitment to excellence, quality and discount value. They specialize in affordable golf and tennis gear including activewear by the Multi-Sport Club Collection. They have tennis rackets by Head, Prince, Pro Kennex, Wilson and Rossignol among other famous makers; plus Prince ball machines. The Sportline logo adorns athletic bags, golf bags, tees, sweats, soccer balls, basketballs and volleybals. What's more, they carry a full line of athletic shoes by Adidas, Converse, New Balance and Prince.

Sports

T
E
N
N
I
S

GODDARD MANUFACTURING COMPANY   Telephone: 800-437-1986

P.O. Box 502
Logan, KS 67646

Free Brochure   MasterCard VISA PERSONAL CHECKS COD

Return policy: No Returns, All Orders Custom Made

Add a touch of beauty that will be the focal point of your home. Spiral staircases by Goddard provide space-saving access to a basement or upper level in your choice of long-lasting steel or natural oak. Either way you go, an attractive and easy to install staircase will be the result. It takes less than an hour to put one up and they can be made to suit all building codes. Custom built and installed curved stairways are also available.

THE IRON SHOP   Telephone: 800-523-7427

400 Red Road; P.O. Box 547
Broomall, PA 19008   [DISCOUNT]

Free Brochure   MasterCard VISA e PERSONAL CHECKS

Return policy: Satisfaction Guaranteed

For spiral stair kits that offer the best value to be found in the home improvement marketplace, shop direct from The Iron Shop, the leading manufacturer of spiral stair kits for more than 60 years. Choose from contemporary metal, rich oak, or high strength aluminum Victorian spiral stair kits. All kits have been designed so that no special skills or experience are necessary for installation. They have a wide range of accessories available, as well as floating stair kits. Call or write for the free brochure.

YORK SPIRAL STAIR   Telephone: 207-872-5558
                              Fax No: 207-872-6731

Route 32
North Vassalboro, ME 04962

Free Brochure   MasterCard VISA PERSONAL CHECKS COD

Return policy: No Returns, All Orders Are Custom Made

The simple elegance of a York Spiral Stair is an economical alternative to straight stairways without the unsightly centerpost of an ordinary spiral staircase. Oak or Mahogany is individually crafted into a gracefully curved staircase with both an inner and outer handrail. Available in diameters of 5', 6', 8' 6" and 18', there is one perfect for your home. All stairways are easily installed in less than a day. If you pay up front there is a 3% discount off the final price.

AMERICAN STATIONERY COMPANY, INC.
Telephone: 800-822-2577

100 Park Avenue
Peru , IN 46970

DISCOUNT

Free Catalog

Return policy: Money-Back Guarantee

Here you'll find a wide variety of stationery needs, including embossed and calligraphy notes, shells notes, invitations and more. They also have address labels, hostess letters, mini-letter pads and even children's stationery sets. The best part is the savings of up to 50%. In business since 1919, all orders are backed by a 70-year guarantee.

BIRTH WRITES
Telephone: 301-363-0872

6 Gwynns Mill Court; P.O. Box 684
Owings Mills, MD 21117

Free Information

Return policy: Money-Back Guarantee

Celebrate the arrival of your new family addition with Birth Writes formal, printed, custom designed birth announcements and thank-you cards. Their special thermographic engraving process is comparable to the finest quality engraving, yet they can produce your announcements and thank-you cards much faster than local printers, department stores or even so-called 'quick print' shops. All Birth Writes paper stock is formal white heavy vellum with optional embossed panels and colored borders, as well as five interchangeable typestyles to choose from.

CHECKS IN THE MAIL
Telephone: 800-733-4443

P.O. Box 7802
Irwindale, CA 91706

DISCOUNT

Free Brochure

Return policy: Money-Back Guarantee

For over 60 years, Checks In The Mail has been printing checks in a wide of assortment of designs and styles from the whimsical to the most traditional. Take your mind off the money you're signing away with their Bubbles, Dream Machines, Wildlife and Country Cats designs. If you're looking for something a little more conservative, they've got standard designs like Currency, Antique and Blue Safety. What's more, they can print your name and your financial institution directly on the check in your choice of typestyles.

CROMPOND CALLIGRAPHY & STATIONERY
Telephone: 914-528-0645

Townsend Road; P.O. Box 72
Crompond, NY 10517

Free Information

Return policy: Satisfaction Guaranteed

Announcing a special occasion and need distinctive, personalized invitations in a flash? Crompond is the answer! They feature an outstanding collection of wedding invitations; plus all the accessories, like toasting glasses, aisle runners and guest books. You can also choose from an enormous selection of personalized stationery, holiday greeting cards, birth announcements, thank-you notes, napkins, matches and more.

S T A T I O N E R Y

CURRENT, INC.
Express Order Porcessing
Colorado Springs, CO 80941
Catalog $1.00

Telephone: 800-525-7170
Fax No: 719-531-6510
DISCOUNT

Return policy: 30-Day Money Back Guarantee

Save up to 70% on cards, stationery and gifts. They carry hundreds of quality products; greeting cards, stationery, gift wrap and much more. You'll find lower-than-card-shop prices and huge selections. Free shipping; quantity discounts. Full money back guarantee on every product they sell, even custom imprints. Orders are shipped UPS in 7-10 days.

ENFIELD STATIONERS
215 Moody Road, P.O. Box 1800
Enfield, CT 06083
Free Catalog

Telephone: 203-763-3980
Fax No: 203-749-1892
DISCOUNT

Return policy: Satisfaction Guaranteed

Cards for all of your custom holiday needs are available from Enfield Stationers. The many available designs include beautiful winter scenes, humorous illustrations and bold colors. There are many additional special effects that can can be ordered, including foil stamping and calendar cards for businesses. Personalized envelopes are also available for true distinction. While they offer cards for Thanksgiving, if you order holiday cards early you are eligible for a 25% discount.

H & F ANNOUNCEMENTS
3734 West 95th Street
Leawood, KS 66206
Free Catalog

Telephone: 800-338-4001
Fax No: 913-649-6312

Return policy: Satisfaction Guaranteed.

Birth announcements and invitations by H & F Announcements help make a special occasion just a little more special. Colorful and fun, there are many different kinds of invitation styles that are suitable for any special event, be it Christmas, Halloween, Graduation or a child's birthday. Save time and effort by getting your thank-you cards printed, instead of writing them out by hand. Any of the fun designs will give your notes a touch of whimsy. They even offer diapers printed with your choice of a college or baseball team logo.

HEART THOUGHTS BIRTH ANNOUNCEMENTS
6200 East Central; Suite 100
Wichita , KS 67208
Free Catalog

Telephone: 800-524-BABY
Fax No: 316-687-2846

Return policy: Money-Back Guarantee

Tell the world about the arrival your new bundle of joy with adorable birth announcements by Heart Thoughts. Their full-color brochure gives you a complete listing of the styles available including holiday themes, thank-you cards, and their exclusive Ribbons & Lace collection. They also carry a special grouping of informative books and videos on pregnancy, childbirth, fitness for the mom-to-be, and post-natal care.

S
T
A
T
I
O
N
E
R
Y

L & D PRESS
Box 641, 78 Randall Street
Rockville Center, NY 11570
Free Flyers
Return policy: Exchanges Only

Telephone: 516-593-5058

If you're worried about first impressions then call L & D Press and ask for their flyer today. Envelopes and letterhead with raised printing instantly give your correspondence a distinctive look. The raised letter business cards can provide you with the feel of embossing and the appearance of fine engraving. Rubber stamps of your return address and signature will save you time and trouble at home or at the office. L & D Press also offers a hand embosser with exchangeable plates. It converts plain paper and envelopes into personalized stationery.

NEBS
500 Main Street
Groton, MA 01471-0009
Free Catalog
Return policy: Satisfaction Guaranteed

Telephone: 800-323-2580
Fax No: 800-234-4324

NEBS provides peronalize holiday greeting cards for business & personal use. From the serious, to the sentimental, to the humorous, you will be able to find the perfect card to suit your needs. They offer winter holiday cards specifically designed for pet stores, lumber yards, video stores, florists, and many others. You can choose from 12 selections to be printed inside you cards, or you may write your own for an additional fee.

PAPERDIRECT
P.O. Box 618205 Chubb Avenue
Lyndhurst, NJ 07071-0618
Free Catalog
Return policy: Satisfaction Guaranteed

Telephone: 800-A-PAPERS
Fax No: 201-507-0817

PaperDirect has the largest selection of unique papers available. From certificate borders to graduation-shaded paper, there is a bright look awaiting your written word. Brochures are easy to make with the pre-designed mailer. Just print what you want on the paper and you have an instant mailer. With PaperDirect Desktop ColorFoil, adding eye-catching color to laser printed paper is easy and convenient. Corporate accounts are available.

POSH PAPERS
532 Elmgrove Avenue
Providence, RI 02906
Free Catalog
Return policy: Satisfaction Guaranteed

Telephone: 401-331-9873

Whimsical and elegant, Posh Papers offers greetings with style. Artistic cards with personalized calligraphy give your stationery the mark of true distinction. Adornments of Victorian couples, oriental lamps, cats and sport scenes will make the recipients of your notes ohh, ahh and smile. Each box of notes comes with matching envelopes and is attractively priced.

PRATT & AUSTIN COMPANY

P.O. Box 587
Holyoke, MA 01041-0587

Telephone: 413-532-1491
Fax No: 413-536-2741

Free Catalog

Return policy: Money-Back Guarantee with proper authorization

There's more to effective correspondence than the words you use. The right stationery can make a huge difference in the way those words are perceived. If you're sending informal business correspondence, invitations to a social affair or just reminding Junior to take out the trash, Pratt & Austin has the right products to underscore your message. Personal and informal messages will gain a distinctive edge on colorful boxed thank-you notes, postcards and printed stationery. There are many styles to chose from including new designer series and embossed boxed note cards. There's even a floral collection entirely on recycled paper.

PRUDENT PUBLISHING COMPANY

P.O. Box 500
Ridgefield Park, NJ 07660-9970

Telephone: 201-641-0070
Fax No: 800-772-1144

Free Catalog

Return policy: Satisfaction Guaranteed

The Gallery Christmas Card Collection has been recognized throughout the world for its unique and exquisite designs. Gold foil and gorgeous high quality color printing make these cards the ones to beat. The cards are custom imprinted with your choice of 9 greetings, envelope imprinting is also available. Say thank your business patrons, or say "Happy Holidays" to your friends.

THE GRAYARC GREENWOODS COLLECTION

P.O. Box 660429
Dallas, TX 75266-0429

Telephone: 800-533-1572
Fax No: 800-447-8938

DISCOUNT

Free Catalog

Return policy: Money-Back Guarantee

Send memorable, heart-warming holiday greetings from your family or business with customized cards by The Grayarc Greenwoods Collection. Unsurpassed quality and fine craftsmanship go into each exclusive design. You can personalize your cards to further reflect your appreciation, best wishes or professional image. Use your own logo or choose from their extensive selection of alternatives. Outstanding savings include 'early order' discounts of up to 45%.

THE STATIONERY HOUSE, INC.

1000 Florida Avenue, P.O. Box 1393
Hagerstown, MD 21741-9893

Telephone: 800-638-3033
Fax No: 800-55-HURRAY

Free Catalog

Return policy: Satisfaction Guaranteed

For all seasons and special occasions, The Stationery House offers high quality holiday cards with custom printing available. Business and personal card needs, here's a source that truly delivers. Whether you're thanking patrons for their fine service, or sending out birthday party invitations, you can choose from a myriad of styles, colors and options, including calendars. All orders are returnable, including custom printing.

THE WRITEWELL COMPANY
Telephone: 800-968-5850

5850 West 80th St., P.O. Box 68186
Indianapolis, IN 46268-0186

Free Catalog

Return policy: Satisfaction Guaranteed

For home, office, or even for the home office! Self-sticking address labels, and embossed personalized stationery and envelopes are available, but The Writewell Co. also offers office goods. Personalized memo forms, Post-It notes and post cards are available, as are unusual goods like pocket postal scales, household inventory books, they even offer a Shop-By-Mail Diary to help keep track of all your mail order purchase. Pretty handy, hmm?

TRUMBLE GREETINGS
Telephone: 800-525-0656
Fax No: 303-530-5124

P.O. Box 9800
Boulder, CO 80301

DISCOUNT

Catalog $1.00

Return policy: Satisfaction Guaranteed. Custom Orders Not Returnable

Shop by mail and save up to 1/3 on Leanin' Tree Christmas and all-occasion greeting cards. Fine art greeting cards feature America's heritage in country, mountain, western, coastal & southwestern themes from sea to shining sea. Over 200 cards and gifts are available to choose from.

UNICEF CARDS & GIFTS
Telephone: 800-553-1200

1 Children's Boulevard; P.O. Box 182233
Chattanooga, TN 37422

Free Catalog

Return policy: Money-Back Guarantee

Since 1946, UNICEF, the United States Children's Fund, has worked to protect children around the world, helping them realize fuller, richer, healthier lives. The organization depends entirely on voluntary contributions, including proceeds from it's exclusive UNICEF Greeting Card and Gift collection. It features a super assortment of corporate and family greeting cards including lavish holiday varieties that promote peace, international good will, and the joy of the season. Unless otherwise noted, all cards are printed in red ink in five of the official U.N. languages - English, French, Spanish, Russian and Chinese.

VISIBLE
Telephone: 800-323-0628
Fax No: 800-233-2016

1750 Wallace Avenue
St. Charles, IL 60174

Free Catalog

Return policy: Money-Back Guarantee if returned within 30 days

For problem-solving products, as well as the everyday items that keep your home or office computer running smoothly, you can have complete confidence when buying from Visible. They have a full line of computer and office supplies such as copier toner cartridges, space-saving office machine stands, labels, stationery, ribbons and special vaccum cleaners that reduce the risk of malfunctions that can result in costly repairs. You'll also find competitive prices on storage modules and office furniture. Don't pass up the special Bonus Gift offer.

A. B. LAMBDIN
US Highway 19N
Americus, GA 31710
Free Catalog
Return policy: 30-Day Money Back Guarantee

Telephone: 800-554-9231
Fax No: 800-221-9231
DISCOUNT

Bright colors, low cuts, cool fabrics and flirtatious styles make A. B. Lambdin the choice for your summertime wardrobe. All shapes, sizes and motifs are featured Hot bikinis splashed with color are great for catching rays or catching stares. After the beach, dresses, shorts and tops will keep you the center of attention, but the prices will be your best-kept secret. There are some men's swimsuits, but the merchandise is primarily for women, including the summer footwear.

THE FINALS
21 Minisink Avenue
Port Jarvis, NY 12771
Free Catalog
Return policy: Satisfaction Guaranteed

Telephone: 800-431-9111
Fax No: 914-858-8645

Performance swimwear and sportswear for the competitive swimmer. The Finals offers serious swimwear, not bathing suits, but of course, non-competitive swimmers can wear these goods. All of their swimwear is made of the finest quality materials and designed with a sense of style that will let you look cool, even when the competition is hot. Swimming caps, time clocks, goggles, and custom printing are available for teams or individuals.

UJENA INTERNATIONAL
1400 North Shoreline Boulevard
Mountain View, CA 94043
Free Catalog
Return policy: Only Defective Merchandise Is Returnable

Telephone: 415-965-7850

Top quality bargains on ladies swimwear. Colorful and stylish, Ujena International offers spectacular one- and two-piece suits and bikinis designed to make you look your best. In addition to swimwear, their summer activewear and eveningwear will turn heads, while the lingerie will turn the only head that matters in your life! The only thing hotter than summer are the fashions available from Ujena.

WILLIAM B. HUGG SWIMMING ACCESSORIES
1721 Kirks Lane
Dresher , PA 19025
Free Catalog
Return policy: Money-Back Guarantee

Telephone: 800-255-SWIM
Fax No: 215-646-1280

Serious swimmers, this one's for you! Take advantage of this quality selection of high-tech swimming gear for the whole family. William B. Hugg carries performance swimwear by Speedo, Tyr and Arena, many styles endorsed by world-famous Olympic swimmers. They also specialize in accessories like goggles, swim caps and aquatic shoes, plus specialized groomers for the swimmer including anti-fog eyedrops, swimmer's ear drops, waterproof suntan products and anti-chlorine shampoos and conditioners.

FACTORY DIRECT TABLE PAD COMPANY

Telephone: 800-428-4567

959 North Holmes Avenue
Indianapolis, IN 46222

DISCOUNT

Free Information

Return policy: Custom Made Pads Are Not Returnable

Did you know that 60% of the price of a custom-fitted table pad goes to the measurer? While this service isn't easily available throughout most of the country, the Factory Direct Table Company can make a custom-fitted table pad for you based on measurements you take at home in 5 minutes? While some tables require specific measurements, Factory Direct has saved the pattern of every pad they have made so they can usually make one for you with simple measurements. Add to this the guaranteed lowest prices and you have an unbeatable combination.

PIONEER TABLE PAD COMPANY

Telephone: 800-541-0271

P.O. Box 449
Gates Mills, OH 44040-9901

DISCOUNT

Free Information

Return policy: 30-Day Money Back Guarantee

In these days of robotics and mass production, Pioneer table pads are handcrafted, as they have been for over 75 years. The experience they have acquired over that time period enables them to manufacture the highest quality pads your table will ever know. Their vinyl tops have a fabric backing, as opposed to paper backings, for added stability they still reinforce their pads with stitching which helps them last longer than other table pads. Free information comes with table pad samples.

SENTRY TABLE PAD COMPANY

Telephone: 800-328-1595

1170 Stella Street
St. Paul, MN 55108

DISCOUNT

Free Flyers

Return policy: 30-Day Satisfaction Guarantee

For piece of mind and protection a custom Sentry table pad offer the highest quality and the guaranteed lowest prices. America's oldest and largest table pad company, Sentry offers pads are individual made to match the pattern of your tabletop. Since their pads are direct from the factory, Sentry guarantees to beat any price. With their computerized manufacturing process, if your table was made in the last five years they will have the table specifications and you won't have to measure it. Ordering tablepads has never been easier.

T
A
B
L
E

P
A
D
S

ANHEUSER-BUSCH, INC.
P.O. Box 503015
St. Louis , MO 63150-3015
Free Catalog
Return policy: Money-Back Guarantee

Telephone: 800-325-9665
Fax No: 314-577-7430

Budweiser lovers, take heart! The quintessential American brew now brings you all the fun gadgets and memorabilia you ever imagined possible - and you don't even have to be of legal age to enjoy them! Legendary in all its red, white and blue splendor, the Bud label appears on selected sportswear, swimwear, home accents and recreational accessories. You must see the heirloom Budweiser, Civil War and U.S. Olympic commemorative plates and steins they carry for gift-giving or home collecting.

CHEERS
155 West Street
Wilmington, MA 01887
Free Catalog
Return policy: Money-Back Guaranteed

Telephone: 800-962-3333

As a result of the widespread popularity of the "Cheers" television show and the Bull & Finch Pub in Boston (the inspiration for the show's set), you can now choose from a complete line of official, licensed "Cheers" merchandise. The collection includes t-shirts, sweats, tank tops and accessories emblazoned with the famous logo and Victorian pub designs. Choose from "Cheers" beer mugs, bags, towels, hats and other novelties. They offer an exclusive gift service, as well as free membership to their "Cheers Pub Club" with any purchase.

SEVENTH GENERATION
Colchester, VT 05446-1672
Free Catalog
Return policy: Satisfaction Guaranteed

Telephone: 800-456-1197
Fax No: 800-456-1139

Introduce yourself to the greenest catalog of them all. Seventh Generation is the ultimate source of environmentally sound housewares, sundries and clothes under the sun. Organic skin and hair care products are available, as well as non-toxic animal and insect repellent. Paper towels, picture frames and disposable plates are all made from recycled paper. Tons of neat stuff that helps us make the world a better place for the future.

THE COMPLETE COLLEGIATE
490 Route 46 East
Fairfield, NJ 07004
DISCOUNT
Free Catalog
Return policy: Satisfaction Guaranteed

Telephone: 201-808-9249

This company specializes in necessities for the college-bound. Two-sided laundry bags, backpacks, crates, fanny-packs, and lamps are discounted 35-50%. Unique graduation gifts such as lucite lap desks, hot pots, and leather-bound dictionaries and thesauruses can be personalized at no additional charge. A fun and informative booklet is availble on "How to Survive Freshman Year", free with each purchase of $25 or more.

THE WARNER BROTHERS CATALOG

Telephone: 800-223-6524

P.O. Box 60048
Tampa, FL 33660-0048

Free Catalog

Return policy: Money-Back Guarantee

Show your cinematic appreciation for your favorite Warner Brothers feature films with merchandise from their catalog of collectibles, gift items and clothing. Each item is a work of merchandising genius including posters, t-shirts, watches, drinking mugs, toys, ties and great looking

Hip headgear for summer! The BATMAN RETURNS leather cap.

The Caped Crusader is back and he's a force to be reckoned with – and you will be too, in this handsome Batman Returns cap made of soft black leather. Adjustable back band. One size fits most adults. #9928 Batman Returns Leather Cap **$24.00**

jackets. Enjoy them as simple objects of nostalgia from box office hits like Bat Man, Lethal Weapon and JFK. Looney Tune fans, take note! They've got a fun assortment of items featuring all your favorite characters, including that "wascally wabbit", Bugs Bunny.

FAMOUS SMOKE SHOP
55 West 39th Street
New York, NY 10018
Free Catalog
Return policy: Money-Back Guarantee

Telephone: 800-672-5544
Fax No: 212-921-5458
DISCOUNT
COD

When the great news calls for a round of cigars, win smiles of approval when you purchase them from the Famous Smoke Shop catalog. It features the world's finest brands including Dunhill, Olor, Upmann, Henry Clay, Arturo Fuente, Baccarat and Flamenco, among others. The best feature is the pricing, set at up to 67% off retail prices. The cigars are sold in bundles of up to 100, in a variety of sizes and colors. With some brands, you even get a handsome wooden box for storing cigars and other smoking essentials.

FRED STOKER & SONS, INC.
P.O. Box 707
Dresden, TN 38225-0707
Free Flyers
Return policy: Returns For Exchange Or Credit Only

Telephone: 800-243-9377
DISCOUNT

Fred Stoker & Sons has chaw for yer jaw 'n snuff with stuff, all at prices that will lower your tobacco bill! Chewing tobacco for those who enjoy smokeless pleasure is available in favors like Apple, Peach, Coffee and Black Wild Cherry. This is one of the few sources of dry and moist snuff left in the US, and definitely one of the few who offer it through mail order. Pipe and cigarette tobaccos are also for sale.

THOMPSON & CO., INC.
P.O. Box 31274
Tampa, FL 33633-0537
Free Catalog
Return policy: Satisfaction Guaranteed

Telephone: 800-237-2559
Fax No: 813-882-4605

A treasure trove for connoisseurs of fine tobacco, Thompson & Company, Inc. offers the finest in smokes and gifts for real American men. In addition to name brands like Dutch Masters, Garcia Vega and Backwoods, hand-rolled imported cigars are available from countries all over the world, including Honduras, Nicaragua, the Dominican Republic, Mexico and the Philippines. Dozens of pipes and pipe tobaccos of international origin are for sale, too. Unique gift items like Porsche lighter replicas and beer steins round out this collection.

WALLY FRANK, LTD.
63-25 69th Street
Middle Village, NY 11379-1798
Free Catalog
Return policy: Satisfaction Guaranteed

Telephone: 718-326-2233
Fax No: 718-326-0453
DISCOUNT

Cuban seed leaf cigars are available from other smokes sources, but Wally Frank, Ltd. offers cigars with actual tobacco grown in Castro's country. This is only one possible selection from a major source of cigars, pipes and fine tobacco. Sample the delights of cigars from the east with Indonesian cigars, or try mild Brazilian tobacco. Bulk buying allows them to offer their quality smokes at savings of up to 50% off regular prices.

BAILEY'S
Telephone: 800-322-4539

Free Catalog

Return policy: Money Back Guarantee

TIMBER! Loggers are going to love this place. Everything from anvils to axes, log scales to log splitters and saws to suspenders. Offering materials by major chainsaw manufacturers like Homelite, McCulloch and Poulan, as well as parts and accessories, anyone interested in the woods is going to love this catalog. Boot dryers, hatchets, thermal socks all have universal appeal, as do the "how-to" video tapes. There are mail order addresses in California, New York and Tennessee, depending onwhere you live.

BRIDGE CITY TOOL WORKS, INC.
1104 N.E. 28th Avenue
Portland, OR 97232-2498

Telephone: 800-253-3332
Fax No: 503-287-1085

Catalog $2.00
Return policy: 90-Day Money Back Guarantee

Bridge City Tool Works creates perhaps the highest quality tools crafted in the world today. Should any tool fail you in the course of your lifetime, all you pay is five dollars to have it recalibrated, resquared or replaced. Plans for a tool chest that will soon be a family heirloom are available, as well as books on furniture making, wood finishing and chip carving. Any handyman, or handywoman, wants this catalog. A terrific source of Father's Day gifts.

BROOKSTONE
5 Vose Farm Road
Peterborough, NH 03458

Telephone: 800-846-3000
Fax No: 603-924-0093

Free Catalog
Return policy: Lifetime Satisfaction Guarantee

World famous Brookstone is the supplier of "hard-to-find" tools. You can't imagine all of the stuff available. Ingenious items like tangle resistant hose reels, a compound leverage pruner that increase cutting power, ergonomically designed super scissors and a drain clog gun to eliminate sink clogs with a pull of a trigger. There are also items for home enjoyment like a tree-free hammock and a no-pump unsinkable pool float. There are plenty of things in this catalog that can really make life easier. This just a plain old fun catalog to look through.

KITTS INDUSTRIAL TOOLS
22384 Grand River Avenue
Detroit, MI 48219

Telephone: 800-521-6579
Fax No: 313-538-6499

Catalog $2.00

Return policy: 30-Day Satisfaction Guarantee

With over 200 tons of tools in stock, you can only imagine how much buying leverage Kitts Industrial Tools has. As a result, the offer all types of tools and hardware at tremendously low prices. Power drills, saws, sanders and impact wrenches can be had for less than you'll find just about anywhere. Spray guns and accessories, electrical tools, automotive tools and carpentry tools to suit whatever need you have. 99% of all orders are shipped the same day.

T O O L S

LEHMAN'S HARDWARE AND APPLIANCES

4779 Kidron Road, P.O. Box 41
Kidron, OH 44636

Telephone: 216-857-5771
Fax No: 216-857-5785

Catalog $2.00

Return policy: 30-Day Money Back Guarantee

The Amish are famous for the tools and goods they make. Designed to last for a lifetime, this high standard of quality is built into everything offered in Lehman's Non-Electric "Good Neighbor" Heritage Catalog. Decorative and function, many of the items offered here are unavailable elsewhere. From hand tools to wood stoves, there is no end to the ways you can incorporate the Amish practice of living in harmony with nature into your own life. Home appliances, lights and tools, all of which run without electricity, will save both energy and your utility bill.

LEICHTUNG WORKSHOP

4944 Commerce Parkway
Cleveland, OH 44128

Telephone: 800-321-6840
Fax No: 216-464-6764

Free Catalog

Return policy: 90-Day Money Back Guarantee

Leigchtung furnishes tools and supplies for any job around the house you can think of. Drill bits for special jobs, such as drilling into metal or for cutting countersinks, as well as miniature drill bits and pliers are yours for the asking. There are handy adapters for transforming your power screwdriver into a power drill, and for drilling at a 90 degree angle. Plans for outdoor projects are available, too.

MODERN FARM

P.O. Box 1420
Cody, WY 82414-1420

Telephone: 800-443-4934

Free Catalog

Return policy: Satisfaction Guaranteed

The name of the game is tools. What kind of tools? All kinds of tools. Kitchen tools, gardening tools, auto tools and barbeque tools. Post drivers and electric branding irons are just a small sample of the varied merchandise that farmers will flip over. Overalls for the rancher and ear tags for the ranchee! Steam juicers and french fry cutters are tools for everyone, so don't feel like you need a farm for this great catalog of items you certainly won't see anywhere else.

NORTHERN

Dept. 95557, P.O. Box 1499
Burnsville, MN 55337

Telephone: 800-533-5545

DISCOUNT

Free Catalog

COD

Return policy: Money-Back Guarantee, if returned with 30 days

Northern saves you 20-50% on power tools, hand tools, gas engines, generators, welders, log splitters, jacks, air compressors, airtools, trailers, trailer parts and more. In-stock orders are shipped within 24 hours. Call or send for the 136-page discount catalog from the company where professionals and true handymen shop - Northern.

T
O
O
L
S

TOOLS ON SALE
216 West 7th Street
St. Paul, MN 55102-2599
Free Catalog

Telephone: 612-224-4859
Fax No: 612-224-8263
DISCOUNT

Return policy: Returns allowed with written authorization only

Tools On Sale is your guide to America's lowest prices on tools and tool accessories, including products by Panasonic, Bosch, Milwaukee, Black & Decker and Makita, among other famous makers. Demolition hammers, drills, sanders, saws, bench grinders, soldering guns, pneumatic nailers and tons of accessories - from drill bits and socket sets to utility knives and level instruments - are all featured. They also have how-to books on woodworking, toymaking and furniture building.

TREND-LINES
375 Beacham Street
Chelsea, MA 02150
Catalog $2.00

Telephone: 800-877-7899
Fax No: 617-889-2072
DISCOUNT

Return policy: Money-Back Guarantee if returned within 30 days

Trend-lines claims to have more discounted power and hand tools under one roof than you've ever seen. The full-color catalog features items by Reliant, Ryobi, Dremel, Delta and other brands.. But wait until you see the wide variety of woodworking equipment, including sanding supplies, woodbits, drills and dowelling, before you make up your mind. If you're building a house to live in or a dollhouse for your little girl, you'll find everything you need to do it right.

WHOLE EARTH ACCESS
822 Anthony Street
Berkeley, CA 94710
Free Catalog

Telephone: 800-829-6300
Fax No: 415-845-8846
DISCOUNT

Return policy: Money-Back Guarantee

From the simplistic to the hi-tech, Whole Earth Access brings you one of the largest and most unique assortments of woodworking tools and supplies Woodworkers and contractors will enjoy terrific values on a wide range of saws, drills, sanders, carving tools, work benches and other essentials. Skil, Incra, Bosch, Stanley, Ryobi and Delta are some of the well-known names. They've also got replacement parts and accessories for these tools, as well as a select grouping of protective clothing and safety products to keep your project moving.

WOODCRAFT
210 Wood County Industrial Park
Parkersburg, WV 26102-1686
Catalog $3.00

Telephone: 800-535-4482
Fax No: 304-428-8271

Return policy: Money-Back Guarantee if returned within 90 days

About the only thing you won't find in this catalog of top-quality woodworking tools and supplies is wood! So, you buy the wood. When you're ready to sand it, scrape it, bore it, carve it, finish it or whatever, look to Woodcraft. They have an extensive selection of hi-tech tools and machinery by Delta, Woodhaven, Leigh, Jacobs, Bosch, Conover and other top brands. Don't miss the vast grouping of brass hardware including knobs, hinges, shelf supports, latches and more.

T
O
O
L
S

WOODWORKER'S SUPPLIES, INC.
5604 Alameda Place, NE
Albuquerque, NM 87113-2100
Catalog $2.00
Return policy: Satisfaction Guaranteed

Telephone: 800-645-9292
Fax No: 505-821-7331

Where else wood a carpenter turn? Try to find a tool that Woodworker's Supply doesn't carry, and you'll be searching for a mighty long time. Professional power sanders, routers, drill presses and band saws, will make your next project a breeze. There are pages of drill bits, router heads, screws and dowels to fit every situation. They also offer kits and plans for carpenters of all skill levels. This 110-page catalog will quickly become your carpenter's best friend.

T
O
O
L
S

BITS AND PIECES

1 Puzzle Place, B8016
Stevens Point, WI 54481-7199

Telephone: 715-341-3521
Fax No: 715-341-5958

Free Catalog

Return policy: 60-Day Money Back Guarantee

Puzzled over where to find great gift items for friends and family? Bits and Pieces is the solution. This fun catalog is full of puzzles, mind games and models that everyone will enjoy playing around with. Everything from the perplexing Purple Passion (a solid purple jigsaw puzzle for the insane) to a cardboard Cathedral of Chartes. Three dimensional hardwood puzzles are available, as well as kaleidescopes and slot machines. There's even a puzzle that becomes a working clock

CEDAR WORKS

Route 1, Box 640
Rockport, ME 04856

Telephone: 800-244-7757
Fax No: 207-236-2574

Free Catalog

Return policy: Satisfaction Guaranteed

Strong enough to support elephants, CedarWorks playsets are also strong enough for kids. Made from natural cedar, these sets are as beautiful to look at as they are fun to play with. They arrive unassembled, but it takes less than a day to put them up. Accessories like clubhouses, steering wheels and hoists let these sets grow with your children. Let your kids' imaginations run wild, and their bodies will, too.

CHILDLIFE INC.

55 Whitney Street
Holliston, MA 01746

Telephone: 800-462-4445
Fax No: 508-429-3874

Free Catalog

Return policy: 30-Day Money Back Guarantee

Making fitness fun for children is exactly what a backyard playset does. Designs for safe play with quality construction is what sets ChildLife wooden playsystems apart. These modular systems can easily be expanded with new equipment, or you can incorporate smaller playsets with larger ones to create the ultimate jungle gym! Built to last, a 25 year warranty guarantees that these playsets will delight your children until they outgrow it.

CONSTRUCTIVE PLAYTHINGS

1227 East 119th Street
Grandview , MO 64030-1117

Telephone: 800-832-0572
In Mo 816-761-5900
Fax No: 816-761-9295

Free Catalog

Return policy: Money-Back Guarantee

Turn your kids on to many of the exciting toys and play accessories you enjoyed as a kid, as well as many new playthings that are thoroughly modern. The Constructive Playthings catalog contains classic kiddie favorites like Tic-Tac-Toss, Playmobil Sets, Duplo, Lego and Bristle blocks. New editions include Fantasy Gears Building Sets, Magnetooli and Maxi Hama Beads, among other fun stuff. They also carry a few non-toy necessities for parents including stroller shades, inflatable potties and baby linens.

HILL'S DOLLHOUSE WORKSHOP

Telephone: 201-226-3550

9 Mayhew Drive
Fairfield, NJ 07006

Free Information

COD

Return policy: Money-Back Guarantee

Tudors, Colonials, Victorians - no it's not a tour of the New England country-side. These are just a few of the lovely styles offered by Hill's Dollhouse Workshop. Your little one will enjoy hours of enchanted play with these sturdy, heirloom dollhouses in a choice of colors and style variations. You'll be pleased with the quality workmanship and easy assembly of a "Hill House."

INTO THE WIND

Telephone: 800-541-0314
Fax No: 303-449-7315

1408 Pearl Street
Boulder, CO 80302-5307

Free Catalog

Return policy: Satisfaction Guaranteed

When was the last time you flew a kite? Probably so long ago that you can't remember. I bet that the last time you saw a kite you wanted to fly one again. Well, what are you waiting for? Into The Wind offers an amazing variety of kites for beginners and experts. Dozens of stunters and high flyers are available, as well as whimsical creations and replicas of historic aircraft.

KEN-WIS, INC.

Telephone: 414-722-1400
Fax No: 414-727-4787

1180 American Drive
Neenah, WI 54956

Free Brochure

Return policy: Exchanges Only

How many different ways have you tried to get your kids reading, only to find books coming in second to G.I Joe, Barbie or the occasional Disney special? While toys and TV are a fun part of growing up, don't overlook the fundamental-sof reading. Well, the folks at Ken-Wis, Inc. have found a clever way to make reading more than just mere page-turning. They've coupled the magic of your child's favorite stories with the pride and joy of collecting trading cards. The result is a new series of Collector Story Cards, starting with The Berenstain Bears. Each set of cards is a complete story at just $5.95.

LITTLE COLORADO, INC.

Telephone: 303-278-2451
Fax No: 303-278-4245

15866 West 7th Avenue
Golden, CO 80401

Catalog $2.00

Return policy: Satisfaction Guaranteed

Western Furniture for little cowboys and cowgirls. Step on up to Little Colorado where solid pine furniture is easy to rustle up for your little cowpoke without spending a bunch of buckaroos. Beds, chests, lamps and accessories for toddlers and tots are available in your choice of any one of 6 finishes. They can also be shipped unfinished, so you can paint it to match your decor. All items come with a lifetime guarantee, so when your ranchhands get ranches of their own, their little cowpunchers can use these great pieces.

PLEASANT COMPANY
P.O. Box 497
Middleton, WI 53562-0190
Free Catalog
Return policy: Satisfaction Guarantee

Telephone: 800-845-0005
Fax No: 608-836-0761

The Pleasant Co. presents the American Girls Collection; a series of dolls based on characters of the successful book series of the same name. Each doll is an American girl from a different point in history. Felicity comes from pre-revolution America, the Victorian era is Samantha's home while Molly hails from the '40s. Your daughter will have a great time while learning about the country's past.

SENSATIONAL BEGINNINGS
300 Detroit; Suite E
Monroe, MI 48161
Free Catalog
Return policy: Money-Back Guarantee

Telephone: 800-444-6058
Fax No: 313-242-8278

At Sensational Beginnings, every product is tested and only those with the highest standards for safety, durability and educational/creative growth are chosen. Every parent knows a child can be a fireball of energy that needs constant exercise to work off steam. Fun outdoor toys, like scooters, trikes and wagons, help children develop skill-building, while giving hours of unlimited, unstructured fun. There's also cuddly stuffed animals, puzzles, books, games, kitchen play sets, toy trains and music. Don't miss the fantastic selection of Sesame Street toys and books, too.

THE ENCHANTED DOLL HOUSE
P.O. Box 1617
Manchester, CT 06045-1617
Catalog $3.00
Return policy: Money-Back Guarantee

Telephone: 800-243-9110
Fax No: 203-645-0504

Come to the Enchanted Doll House land of make-believe and pretend again with their catalog of heirloom-quality toys, dolls and dollhouses. Turn the pages, and you'll wish you were a kid again given their beautifully crafted Early American houses, furniture and other miniatures. Fairytale and historic doll collections include Gone with the Wind, Peter Pan & Farmer's Daughter dolls. There's also collector edition Barbies you won't find in stores. For boys, there are western, military and builder themes. Many dollhouses come partially assembled for safe shipping.

THE ENCHANTED FOREST
85 Mercer Street
New York, NY 10012
Free Catalog
Return policy: Money-Back Guarantee

Telephone: 212-925-6677

The Enchanted Forest explores the world of the wild with beautifully crafted and surprisingly life-like stuffed animals that are a far cry from mere toys. Made of luxurious pile fabrics and other quality materials, these animals are only the beginning. You'll find classic as well as modern fun items, like tops, jacks, pick-up sticks, Jacob's Ladder and The Ozark Dancing Man. Don't miss the charming collection of animal puppets by Naomi Machado.

THE LEARNING COMPANY

6493 Kaiser Avenue
Fremont, CA 94555

Free Brochure

Telephone: 800-852-2255

Return policy: Money-Back Guarantee if returned within 30 days

The Learning Company is dedicated to producing high-quality software products that enrich the education of young people ages three and up. Their line of software products is unique in that the focus is clearly on building the child's underlying thinking skills, while utilizing the adventurous video-game format today's kids seem to crave. Entertainment and ease of use are the premier qualities of The Learning Company's products. Intriguing characters, challenging situations, and rich game environments are the main ingredients in these captivating programs that your youngster will enjoy for hours. The full-color brochure outlines each program and the age groups for which they have been designed.

THE TOY WORKS

Fiddler's Elbow Road
Middle Falls, NY 12848

Free Catalog

Telephone: 518-692-9665
Fax No: 518-692-9186

COD

Return policy: Returns accepted with proper authorization (less 15% restocking fee); no cash refunds

The storybook friendships you cherished as a child are here for you to rekindle and share with your own children in this catalog by The Toy Works. The Velveteen Rabbit, Peter Rabbit, Babar, Mother Goose and Raggedy Ann & Andy are just a few of the old acquaintances that they've turned into huggable stuffed toys and home accents. These toys are available ready-made or in sew-it-yourself kits. You can even get the original storybooks by Jean De Brunhoff, Beatrix Potter and Margery Williams, among other authors. The Toy Works has also found a few new friends for you and your child to meet, like Squeak the Dinosaur, Kitty Cucumber, and Punch & Judy. You'll want to keep in touch this time.

THE WALT DISNEY CATALOG, INC.

One Disney Drive, P.O. Box 29144
Shawnee Mission, KS 66201-9144

Free Catalog

Telephone: 800-247-8996
Fax No: 913-752-1095

Return policy: Satisfaction Guaranteed

Thumper, Bambi, Winnie the Pooh and Tigger, too! All of your childhood friends are here, in one form or another. The Disney Catalog is loaded with the types of toys, collectables and clothes you can't go wrong with. Who doesn't want a Mickey Mouse watch (they have a dozen to choose from!). Dresses, shirts, pants and sleepwear are available, and not just for small girls and boys, but for the many Peter Pans out there who never grew up! The memories that the items in this catalog will spur on are worth on their own make this catalog worth your while.

WISCONSIN WAGON COMPANY

507 Laurel Avenue
Janesville, WI 53545

Telephone: 608-754-0026

Free Catalog

Return policy: Money-Back Guarantee

Wisconsin Wagon Company is dedicated to reviving the durability and utilitarian design of the childrens' toys enjoyed by past generations. Constructed of natural, strong and solid materials, these toys could be counted on to last a lifetime and even generations. The Janesville Ball Bearing Coaster Wagon was THE American standard back in the thirties. Sixty years later, some are still in use and many more are collectors' items. You'll find the solid oak Coaster, along with The Islander, The Tag-a-Long and their Stake-Sided wagon styles. They also have cleverly designed swings, sleds, see-saws, scooters, wheelbarrows and other vehicles - all in sturdy solid oak. Don't miss the heirloom baby and doll cradles available as well.

WOODPLAY, INC.

1108 New Hope Road Ext.
Raleigh, NC 27610-1016

Telephone: 800-982-1822
Fax No: 919-231-3074

Free Catalog

Return policy: 1-Year Satisfaction Guarantee

Oh, to be a kid again. When we were kids there was no Nintendo, mutant turtles or the like, but we certainly didn't miss them. Woodplay produces the same great playsets we loved as children, that are just as much fun today. Start with a basic set and add new equipment to make a truly unique play area that will not only make your child the envy of the neighborhood kids, it will give them a safe place to play; the backyard.

WORLD WIDE GAMES

P.O. Box 517
Colchester, CT 06415

Telephone: 800-937-3482
Fax No: 203-537-2866

Free Catalog

Return policy: 30-Day Satisfaction Guarantee

World Wide Games has been providing quality action games for recreation, therapy and education for a long time. While this catalog of long-lasting games is aimed primarily at therapists and urban centers, any parent will find terrific toys for their own children. Designed for years of use, all of the items offered build hand-eye coordination and confidence. Games cabinets with as many as 26 games are available, and will keep youngsters busy with stimulating fun. Toys for small children are also offered.

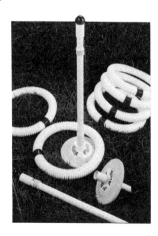

T
O
Y
S

&

G
A
M
E
S

MAGELLAN'S
P.O. Box 5485
Santa Barbara, CA 93150-5485

Telephone: 800-962-4943
Fax No: 805-565-6935

Free Catalog
Return policy: Money-Back Guarantee

A clever array of gadgets and essential supplies for the international traveler have been assembled for Magellan's mail-order catalog. These state-of-the-art products have been designed to eliminate some major barriers to international travel. There's a hand-held "interpreter" that actually translates five major European languages to English; a calculator that converts foreign currency; and a clock that takes the confusion out of foreign time zones. But these products only scratch the surface. Check out the assortment of electric converters and adapters for all your travel appliances, not to mention the grouping of luggage items, appliances and handy security products to keep your vacation from turning into a disaster. The prices are quite reasonable for such valuable merchandise and they ship within 24 hours so you can get your purchase quickly and be on your way!

ORVIS TRAVEL
Historic Route 7A, P.O. Box 798
Manchester, VA 05254-0798

Telephone: 800-541-3541

Free Catalog
Return policy: Satisfaction Guaranteed

Next time you're on vacation, the unique products available from the Orvis Travel catalog will enable you to make the most of your time and space. Items like a razor with shaving cream in the handle saves space by leaving the bulky toiletry items at home. Page after page of convenience items, like compact booster cables, zip off pants that convert to shorts, money belts and compact fishing reels and rods, will save you valuable luggage space and increase the amount of pleasure you get from your vacation. That's a good reason to get this catalog.

PERILLO TOURS
577 Chestnut Ridge Road
Woodcliff Lake, NJ 07675-9888

Telephone: 800-431-1515

Free Brochure

Enjoy magnificent cruises and vacations that you will remember forever, and that won't keep you in debt for the same amount of time. ClubPerillo offers all inclusive vacations to paradise. Caribbean Cruises with everything paid for in advance and Perillo trips to the Bahamas and Hawaii help make your getaway a great one. With package tours to Italy at discount rates, Perillo has the vacation you've been looking for at a terrific price.

TODD UNIFORMS FOR BUSINESS

P.O. Box 29107
St. Louis, MO 63126

Free Catalog

Return policy: Satisfaction Guaranteed

Telephone: 800-458-3402
Fax No: 314-984-5736

Whatever your uniform needs, Todd Uniforms for Business can easily fulfill them. Oxford or sport shirt uniforms are available in a multitude of color combinations. You can choose having your company or team logo as an emblem, screen printing or direct embroidering. Special items, such as caps, visors, raincoats, vests and aprons make it possible for you to uniform your employees, no matter what your business may be.

WASSERMAN UNIFORMS CO., INC.

1082 West Mound Street
Columbus, OH 43223-2296

Free Catalog

Return policy: Lifetime Money Back Guarantee

Telephone: 800-848-3576
Fax No: 614-464-0416

Here is a REAL mail order house! The Wasserman Uniforms Company will deliver official United States Postal Service attire right to your door. We've all seen those sexy postal shorts; who wouldn't want a pair? Seriously, once you get past the fact that these goods are emblazoned with the post office logo, you are left with comfortable and rugged clothes that make great gifts and conversation pieces. They also sell terrific walking shoes. Wasserman's only ships through the postal service, of course!

U
N
I
F
O
R
M
S

BLUE STAR CANVAS PRODUCTS
300 West Main
Missoula, MT 59802
Telephone: 800-752-8877
Fax No: 406-728-1757
Free Catalog
Return policy: Money-Back Guarantee within 14 days

Now here's a unique company - providing you with pack and trail gear, you'll find Dog Packs, Fanny Packs and collapsible waterbuckets. But the really unique stuff are actual tepees! Included with every tepee order is: cover, liner, pegs, poles, lacing pins, rope, door cover, canvas carrying bag, complete set-up instructions plus The Indian Tipi book by Gladys & Reginald Laubin. For that camping trip you've been planning they have a nice selection of tents in using 10.38 oz. canvas.

BRUCE BOLIND
711 Bolind Building, P.O. Box 9751
Boulder, CO 80301-9751
Telephone: 303-443-9688
Fax No: 303-443-9889
Free Catalog
Return policy: 10-Day Money Back Guarantee

For over 35 years Bruce Bolind has been bringing personalized labels and novelties to thousands of satisfied customers. With the accent on decorative items, as opposed to gadgets, there are hundreds of unique miniatures. Interesting and one-of-a-kind crystal sculptures, like the Cruise Ship, A-1A Tank and Tower Bridge of London, as well as items like lava lites and a life-size Laker Magic Johnson.

HAMMACHER SCHLEMMER
2515 East 43rd St., P.O. Box 182256
Chattanooga, TN 37422-7256
Telephone: 800-233-4800
Fax No: 615-867-5318
Free Catalog
Return policy: Satisfaction Guaranteed

Enjoy the good life with the wonderful products available from Hammacher Schlemmer. Fun, practical and ingenius items are available for every member of the household. An electric jar opener, automatic potato chip maker and cordless grass shears make life a little easier, while antique banks, signed baseballs and restored bicycles from the 50s will excite any collectables enthusiast. There are even electronic cat doors and automatic feed bowls for your pets. All items are the highest quality available or are one-of-a-kind.

INTERNATIONAL STAR REGISTRY
34523 Wilson Road
Ingleside, IL 60041
Telephone: 800-282-3333
Fax No: 708-446-4441
Free Flyers

Return policy: Money Back Guarantee

The International Star Registry offers you the stars. Here's a great gift for the light of your life. There are many stars that have no offical names, so for $40.00 you can have one registered with any name you want. It will be known by that name for as long as the stars shine. Let someone know how much they brighten your days by giving something that brightens your nights. Star maps are also included.

SPACE GEAR/U.S. SPACE & ROCKET CENTER
One Tranquility Base
Huntsville, AL 35807-7015

Telephone: 800-533-7281
Fax No: 205-722-5600

Catalog $2.00

Return policy: Refunds/Exchanges Within 30 Days, $2.50 Return Charge

Space Gear is the ultimate source for gifts that are really out of this world! Part of the U.S. Space & Rocket Center, Space Gear offers NASA hats, insignia, jumpsuits and flight-jackets, as well as unofficial NASA t-shirts, sweats and shorts. Unique gift items include astronaut food, tie tacks and the same type of coke cans that were used in outerspace. Great stuff that you can't get unless you're in orbit, is just a short call away.

THE LIGHTER SIDE COMPANY
4514 19th St. Court E.,Box 25600
Bradenton, FL 34206-5600

Telephone: 813-747-2356
Fax No: 813-746-7896

Catalog $2.00

Return policy: Money Back Guarantee

Satisfaction guaranteed and guaranteed to make you smile, The Lighter Side has been presenting lighthearted gifts and delightful surprises since 1914. Witty T-shirts let you really speak your mind without saying a word. Two-headed quarters, laughing hand mirrors and other novelties make buying the perfect gift easy. Themed merchandise includes things for sports nuts, trekkies and Betty Boopers. Most items are discounted when you buy 2 or more of the same item.

THE SHARPER IMAGE
P.O. Box 7031
San Francisco, CA 94111

Telephone: 800-344-5555

Free Catalog

Return policy: Money Back Guarantee

The Sharper Image is the most widely known mail order house in America, if not the world. Gadgets and toys for big girls and boys. Great ideas like mugs with hollow walls filled with a special liquid; this way you can freeze your mug to chill your drinks instead of getting it watered down with melted ice. The items offered include exercise equipment, executive paddle games and phones in the shape of a slice of pizza.

U
N
I
Q
U
E

&

U
N
U
S
U
A
L

BARR ENTERTAINMENT

12801 Schabarum Avenue
Irwindale, CA 91706-7878

Telephone: 800-331-1387
Fax No: 818-814-2672

Free Catalog

Return policy: 60-Day Money Back Guarantee

Here is a great source of videos, Barr none! Barr Entertainment has a huge selection of video tapes and audio tapes at incredibly low prices, from A Star is Born to Zorro's Fighting Legion. Titles from all genres and subjects, including Of Human Bondage, The Man Who Knew Too Much, The Battleship Potemkin and It's a Wonderful Life. There are self-improvement and education audio tapes, too.

BUTTERFLY VIDEO

Box 184-12CAT
Antrim, NH 03440

Telephone: 603-588-2105
Fax No: 603-588-3205

Free Catalog

Return policy: All Sales Final.

Now you can watch TV to prepare for a night out! Butterfly Video carries instructional tapes on dancing and makeup. Kathy Blake's dance lessons videos cover all major dance styles including Waltz, Tango, Mamba, Charleston, Lambada and Nightclub steps. Renowned make-up artist David Nicholas has been featured on national TV and feature magazines. Now his expertise is available on demand, ranging from Basic Make-up to Pro Photographic Make-up Techniques.

CRITICS CHOICE VIDEO

P.O. Box 549; Dept. 29105
Elk Grove Village, IL 60009

Telephone: 800-544-9852

DISCOUNT

Free Catalog

Return policy: Money-Back Guarantee

Build your video library with the help of Critics Choice, "the complete home video entertainment source." Each catalog lists over 2,000 VHS titles, including new releases, classics, musicals, documentaries and children's videos. They also have 8-millimeter and Laser Disc selections. The Video Search Line service can locate over 35,000 additional movies, including those hard-to-find favorites. There's a large grouping of titles priced under $15. All videos are shipped within 48 hours and Federal Express delivery is available.

MIRAMAR PRODUCTIONS

P.O. Box 15661
Seattle, WA 98115-9963

Telephone: 800-245-6472
Fax No: 206-245-4433

Free Flyers

Return policy: 30-Day Satisfaction Guarantee

What do you get when you mix award-winning photography and music? You get one of Miramar's incredible video albums. Not the kind of videos you'll see on MTV, these lavish productions artistically present wonders of the natural world with such titles as "Dessert Vision," "Canyon Dreams," "Gift of the Whales" and "Natural States." Videos for self-improvment include "Baseball with Ken Griffey, Jr." and "Football with Dan Fouts." Tangerine Dream, Paul Speer and James Reynolds are among the fine audio tapes available.

V
I
D
E
O
T
A
P
E
S

NORTH AMERICAN GATEWAYS, INC.
P.O. Box 1706
Ojai, CA 93024
Telephone: 805-646-8284

Free Catalog
Return policy: 60-Day Satisfaction Guarantee

Supercharge your potential with Gateways self-improvement tapes. Make yourself a better person and upgrade your life by using the sublininal tapes to remove any negative aspects you might have in your personality. Programs cover improving your diet, relieving stress and gaining a positive attitude. Programs are sublinally set to your choice of natural sounds or music styles.

SYBERVISION
One Sansome Street, Suite 1610
San Francisco, CA 94104
Telephone: 800-678-0887
Fax No: 612-479-3751

Catalog $2.50
Return policy: 30-Day Money Back Guarantee

From sports to relationships, SyberVision offers you the power to excel. Titles to advance every facet of your life. Teach your children how to play sports at an early age or increase your own understanding on the fundamentals of human behavior and relationships. Speed reading and verbal advantage videos will improve your communications skills.

TELEGAMES USA
P.O. Box 901
Lancaster, TX 75146
Telephone: 214-227-7694

DISCOUNT

Free Catalog
Return policy: Money-Back Guarantee

If you can't beat 'em, why not join 'em? Video games are here to stay and what's even more obvious is the fact that kids crave them. Once you get a load of the discounted prices on all the hard-to-find video game software available through the Telegames USA catalog, you'll be hooked, too. Sega Genesis, NEC Turbo Grafx, Atari, Gameboy and the legendary Nintendo are just a few of the famous names that head the list of games available. Joysticks, compatible stereo speaker systems and other video accessories round out the list of products offered.

WALDEN BY MAIL
Dept. 011P.O. Box 305188
Nashville, TN 37230-5188
Telephone: 800-322-2000

DISCOUNT

Free Catalog
Return policy: 30-Day Money Back Guaranteed

Walden By Mail offers the same great gift books and videos carried nation wide by their stores. Cinematic classics like The African Queen, The Grapes of Wrath, and Gone With the Wind are available on video tape, as are musicals by Rogers and Hammerstein, and fitness videos by Richard Simmons, Jane Fonda and Kathy Smith. There are also children's videos by Disney. "Who Framed Roger Rabbit", "Pretty Woman" and "Bull Durham" are a few of the terrific comedies waiting for you. Documentaries and Science Fiction are represented, too.

V
I
D
E
O
T
A
P
E
S

YES! BOOKS & VIDEOS
P.O. Box 10726
Arlington, VA 22210

Telephone: 800-YES-0234
Fax No: 202-338-8150

Free Catalog

Return policy: 30-Day Money Back Guarantee

Is there a mail order company that offers insightful, stimulating, reflective and entertaining books, audio cassettes and video tapes? The answer is yes. Yes! Books & Videos makes a myriad of fine tapes and books available to anyone who wishes to develop their inner selves, their leadership & excellence, their creativity, their personal relationships, their health and their vitality. There are also great feature films like Lawrence of Arabia, Out of Africa and Citizen Kane.

AMERICAN BLIND AND WALLPAPER FACTORY   Telephone: 800-735-5300
28237 Orchard Lake Rd.   **Fax No:**   313-553-6262
Farmington Hills, MI 48334   DISCOUNT
Free Brochure and Sample Kit
Return policy: 30% Restocking Charge (Wallpaper), blinds not returnable

Save 35-80% on complete wallpaper selections including Birge, Kinney, Laura Ashley, Ralph Lauren, Sanitas, Thybony, Schumacher, Walltex..plus national brand blinds including Levolor, Delmar, Bali, Hunter Douglas, Louverdrape, Graber, Joanna, Kirsch, Verosol, Duette and more! Free UPS shipping, and there's no sales tax outside Michigan. Special case pricing too! You can defer your payment for 90 days with the American Blind and Wallpaper Factory Credit Card. See coupon in back of book.

AMERICAN DISCOUNT WALLCOVERINGS   Telephone: 800-77-PAPER
1411 Fifth Avenue
Pittsburgh, PA 15219-9803   DISCOUNT
Free Flyers
Return policy: Returns Within 20 Days, 25% Handling Charge

American Discount Wallcoverings carries all major brands of wallcoverings and related fabrics from Academy Handprints to York. Every pattern and color for your walls are available from this low-priced source. Call them with pattern number you are interested in and the book you found it in, and they will quote as low a price as you'll find anyway. They also sell window coverings.

BENINGTON'S WALLPAPER   Telephone: 800-252-5060
1271 Manheim Pike
Lancaster, PA 17601   DISCOUNT
Free Brochure
Return policy: Returns accepted for exchange or store credit only

With a little help from Benington's, you can buy top brand wallpaper and save up to 75% off the retail price. All brands are available, first quality only. Give them a toll-free call pattern number and book name and get instant price quotes. Don't forget to inquire about matching borders, fabrics and accessories. Fast, same-day order processing is available. No sales tax is issued on orders shipped outside Pennsylvania and shipping is free to all states accept Alaska and Hawaii.

DIRECT WALLPAPER EXPRESS   Telephone: 800-336-WALL
374 Hall Street   **Fax No:**   215-933-3930
Phoenixville , PA 19460   DISCOUNT
Free Brochure
Return policy: Money-Back Guarantee

Direct Wallpaper Express offers savings of 40-50% on top brand wallpaper by Laura Ashley, Ralph Lauren, Fashon, Sanitas, Kingfisher, Imperial, Millbrook, Color House, Katzenbach & Warren, Van Luit, Charles Barone and United. Even if your local dealer has changed the pattern number for a specific design, Direct can identify those "scrambled" patterns when an order is placed. Free delivery and a wallpapering kit on orders of $75.00 or more. They also carry window treatments by Bali Kirsch, Del Mar, Levelor, LouverDrape and more.

PEERLESS

Telephone: 412-653-0304

700 Connor Road
Pittsburgh, PA 15228

DISCOUNT

Free Information

Return policy: Money-Back Guarantee on damaged articles within 45 days

In business for over 50 years, Peerless offers first-quality wallcoverings by mail-order from most of America's leading manufacturers. Just give them a call with the pattern number and the name of the book you found it in, and start saving up to 75% off the list price! They'll even give you instant price quotes on the toll-free Customer Service line. Be sure to inquire about matching upholstery fabrics and accessories, too. Merchandise is shipped via UPS in about a week.

POST WALLCOVERING DISTRIBUTORS, INC.

Telephone: 800-521-0650
Fax No: 313-338-7943

2065 Franklin Rd., P.O. Box 7026
Bloomfield Hills, MI 48302

DISCOUNT

No Catalog

Return policy: Exchanges of Damaged Mechandise Only

Discounts up to a full 75% off all wallpaper from any wallpaper book, including borders and murals, as well as window blinds from all manufacturers. They never charge sales tax (except Michigan residents), there are no handling charges, and freight is free. Call for price quotes on any wallpaper or window treatment seen anywhere.

ROBINSONS WALLCOVERINGS

Telephone: 800-458-2426
Fax No: 814-827-1693

225 West Spring Street
Titusville, PA 16354-0427

Free Catalog

Return policy: Satisfaction Guaranteed

Shopping for wallcoverings has always been a chore, until now. Instead of running around to a half dozen stores, dragging those huge pattern books around, the Robinsons Wallcoverings and Coordinates catalog is sent to your home. Full of color photos, it solves the problem of figuring out what a pattern will look like on your walls, since sample rooms are demonstrated for almost every pattern. Shopping for wallcoverings has never been this easy.

SILVER'S WHOLESALE CLUB

Telephone: 800-426-6600
Fax No: 800-821-4000

3001-15 Kensington Avenue
Philadelphia, PA 19134

DISCOUNT

Free Brochure

Return policy: Returns Within 30 Days. 25% Handling Charge

Quality wallcoverings at discounts of up to 81%! With Silver's Wholesale Club (formerly Silver Wallcovering), you pick out the pattern you want from your neighborhood stores and then call Silver's to obtain it at the guaranteed lowest price available. Additional specials have included 4 free rolls with a 20 roll purchase. Also available from Silver's are Levolor blinds, all brands and prescriptions of contact lenses, as well as other merchandise for the home.

SMART WALLCOVERING
P.O. Box 2206
Southfield, MI 48037
Free Information
Return policy: Returns subject to manufacturers acceptance

Telephone: 800-667-0200
Fax No: 202-775-1351
DISCOUNT

Smart Wallcoverings does only one thing - wallcoverings - and they do it exceptionally well. That's why they can discount up to 50% on any wallpaper pattern you take a liking to. What's more, they offer free shipping within 3 days and the lowest prices, guaranteed.

STYLE WALLCOVERING
P.O. Box 865
Southfield, MI 48037
Free Information
Return policy: Returns subject to manufacturers acceptance

Telephone: 800-627-0400

DISCOUNT

Style Wallcoverings offers you every pattern in every book at 50% off depending on the quantity ordered. The more you buy, the more you save. Free shipping is guaranteed to your adress within 3 days. They don't inflate the retail price, they beat it!

YANKEE WALLCOVERINGS INC.
109 Accord Park Drive
Norwell, MA 02061
Free Flyers
Return policy: Returns Within 30 Days. 30% Restocking Charge

Telephone: 800-624-7711
Fax No: 617-871-1650
DISCOUNT

With over 180,00 patterns available, Yankee Wallcoverings Inc. definitely has the pattern you want. Like other mail order houses, Yankee will send you the pattern of your choice no matter what brand it is. What sets them apart is their prompt order fulfillment (same day processing) and free shipping for orders over 6 rolls. They also include a money-saving coupon with every purchase.

ALAN MARCUS & COMPANY
Telephone: 800-654-7184

815 Connecticut Avenue NW, Suite 204
Washington, DC 20006

DISCOUNT

Free Catalog

Return policy: Money-Back Guarantee within 5 days from date of receipt

When only "the real McCoy" will do...save up to 50% on jewelry from one of America's largest fine watch and precious gem discounters. All the famous brands are there in the catalog, including Rolex, Breitling, Patek Philippe, Audemars, Omega, Cartier, Ebel and Chopard. They also offer notable discounts on crystal by Lalique and Baccarat, as well as silverware by Christofle and Buccellati. But even at these great savings, they offer trade-ins, lifetime warranties and service.

ALPHA OMEGA FINE WATCHES
Telephone: 800-447-GEMS

57 JFK Street; Harvard Square
Cambridge, MA 02138

DISCOUNT

Free Information

Return policy: Money-Back Guarantee

Watch hunting? It's time to call the largest authorized dealers in the country for more than 18 brands of prestigious watches and over 1,500 styles to choose from, like Breitling, Tag-Heuer, Raymond Weil, Kreiger, Concord, Lasalle, Rado, Omega, Movado, Seiko, Tissot, Hamilton & many other distinctive brands. Shop around and when you're ready to really save, just call them direct with the brand name and style number. You'll be glad you did. They have a professional and knowledgeable sales staff. All manufacturer's warranties applied.

EMPEROR CLOCK COMPANY
Telephone: 205-928-2316

Dept. 4592; Emperor Industrial Park
Fairhope, AL 36532

DISCOUNT

Catalog $1.00

Return policy: Money-Back Guarantee if returned within 30 days

Do-it-yourself kits are available at factory-direct prices from this the world's largest manufacturer of grandfather clocks. Choose from grandfather, wall and mantel clocks, as well as furniture accent pieces like curios, tables, TV/VCR cabinets and more. All clocks and furniture pieces are crafted in the finest quality, hand-matched solid hardwoods, namely oak, cherry and black walnut.

GRAFSTEIN & COMPANY
Telephone: 714-835-6100

1851 East First Street; Suite #715
Santa Ana, CA 92705

DISCOUNT

Free Brochure

Return policy: Money-Back Guarantee

"The Watch King" is the title that's guided Grafstein & Company as America's oldest and largest non-authorized purveyor of fine watches, jewelry, diamonds, gemstones and pearls. Call their experienced staff and save up to 55% on new Swiss watches, and up to 60% on pre-owned watches, all restored to showroom perfection. They have a huge selection, backed by all major brands, including Rolex, Audemars Piquet, Baume & Mercier, Cartier, Omega, Chopard, & Patek.

YAEGER WATCH CORPORATION

578 Fifth Avenue
New York, NY 10036

No Catalog

Return policy: Satisfaction Guaranteed

Telephone: 212-819-0088
Fax No: 212-719-2481

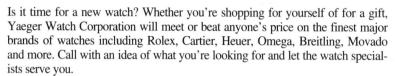

DISCOUNT

Is it time for a new watch? Whether you're shopping for yourself of for a gift, Yaeger Watch Corporation will meet or beat anyone's price on the finest major brands of watches including Rolex, Cartier, Heuer, Omega, Breitling, Movado and more. Call with an idea of what you're looking for and let the watch specialists serve you.

WATCHES & CLOCKS

ALL STATES DECORATING NETWORK

Telephone: 800-334-8590
Fax No: 908-505-9459

1605 Badger, Suite 206
Toms River, NJ 08775

Free Flyers

Return policy: Damaged Merchandise Exchanged

Here's a great place to get first quality, custom made, name brand mini and micro blinds, vertical blinds, duettes, shades, wood blinds and woven wood blinds. The friendy staff of All-States Decorating Network are waiting to assist you and help with your measuring and installation questions, and they're ready to take your orders for low-priced window treatments by almost every manufacturer available.

AROUND THE WINDOW

Telephone: 800-642-9899

326 North Stonestreet Ave., Suite 204
Rockville, MD 20850

DISCOUNT

Free Buyer's Guide

Return policy: 30-Day Satisfaction Guarantee, Custom Orders Not Returnable

Around the Window offers exactly what you want around your window! Top notch blinds in a multitude of colors and fabric styles at discounts of up to 76%. While they offer Levolor brand products as well, Around the Window brand blinds are available as horizontal or vertical blinds, and can be sold with a vinyl backing to help block out light and can save you energy all year long.

COLOREL BLINDS

Telephone: 800-877-4800

8200 E. Park Meadows Dr., Suite 8204
Littleton, CO 80124

DISCOUNT

Free Flyers

Return policy: Only Defective Merchandise Is Returnable

Ordering from Colorel Blinds has certain advantages that sets them apart from other blinds dealers because Colorel Blinds has advantages over other manufacturers. A lifetime guarantee is standard, as is a price of 40% to 81% off other manufacturer's suggested retail prices for similar blinds. Since these are custom-made, there are no returns. For an extra 10% of the purchase cost, you are given 30 days to preview your purchase. If you are not satisfied, send them back, provided they aren't damaged, for a full credit towards the blinds you do want.

HARMONY SUPPLY, INC.

Telephone: 617-395-2600
Fax No: 617-396-8218

P.O. Box 313
Medford , MA 02155

DISCOUNT

No Catalog

Return policy: 30-Day Returns, 25% Restocking Fee, Custom Blinds Not Returnable

Carrying more than 2,500 designs and patterns of wallpaper, grass cloth and string cloth, this is not your run-of-the-mill window treatment supplier. Harmony Supply carries just about everything you'll need for window decor. Brand names like Bali, Flexalum, Duette and more, at discounts of up to 60%! There is no catalog available, just call them or write for price quotes on the items you are interested in.

W
I
N
D
O
W

T
R
E
A
T
M
E
N
T
S

226

HEADQUARTERS WINDOWS & WALLS

Telephone: 800-338-4882

8 Clinton Place
Morristown, NJ 07960

DISCOUNT

Free Information

Return policy: Only authorized returns allowed on small quantities

Known for rock-bottom prices on all major brands of wallcoverings, fabrics, custom blinds and window treatments; Headquarters Windows & Walls also offers personalized customer service for all your decorating needs. Just give their representatives a toll-free call with the pattern number and book name and they'll get you the first-quality decorating materials you're looking for. The more you order, the more you save. Its that simple. What's more, they offer free shipping and no sales tax is issued on purchases shipped outside the state of New Jersey.

KING OF WINDOWS

Telephone: 800-940-2500
Fax No: 305-968-7092

2150 Northwest 33rd Street
Pompano Beach, FL 33069

DISCOUNT

No Catalog

Return policy: Only Damaged Merchandise is returnable

King of Windows' unique concept allows you to work with a personal decorating consultant from order placement through installation, including assistance with color, fabric and style coordination. As the manufacturer, they offer you up to 76% savings on verticals, duettes, micro and mini blinds, pleated shades, wooden blinds and replacement tracks.

NATIONAL BLIND FACTORY

Telephone: 800-388-2400

400 Galleria; #400
Southfield, MI 48034

DISCOUNT

Free Information

Return policy: Returns subject to manufacturer acceptance

National Blind Factory is your number-one resource for mini-blinds direct from the factory at savings of up to 75% off retail prices. They guarantee shipment of your blinds within 5 days or they're FREE! With a policy like that, they must be confident in a superior product/service combination. Call them toll-free for style and price quotes.

PINTCHIK HOMEWORKS

Telephone: 800-847-4199
Fax No: 718-996-1966

2106 Bath Avenue
Brooklyn, NY 11214

DISCOUNT

Free Booklet

Return policy: No Returns Unless Damaged Or Shipping Mistake

Famous in New York since 1912 for service and selection, Pintchik is now offering Shop-by-Mail convenience, and low prices with discounts of up to 79% on famous brands like Levolor, Bali, Graber, Duette, Hunter/Douglas, Verosol, Del Mar and LouverDrape. Free UPS shipping in 48 states. Call Pintchik Homeworks for a completely free blind ordering kit.

WINDOW TREATMENTS

PREMIER BLIND COMPANY

317 East Hempstead
Giddings, TX 78942

Telephone: 800-441-1288
Fax No: 409-542-1382

Free Catalog

Return policy: Exchanges Only

Save up to 81% on Levolor, Del Mar, Hunter, Douglas, Loverdrape, Graber, Verosol, M & B, Joanna Shutters, and Duettes. Call Texas first for the lowest prices guarantee. Free UPS shipping and no sales tax outside the state of Texas. Order you free color samples today. Lifetime service guarantee on all blinds.

SHUTTER SHOP

P.O. Box 11882
Charlotte, NC 28220-1882

Telephone: 704-334-8031

Free Flyers

Return policy: Custom Orders Not Returnable, Except For Defects

We shutter to think of anyone looking into interior wood shutters without contacting the Shutter Shop. They offer shutters of the highest quality, custom fitted to your windows and custom painted in your choice of any Glidden paint or stain. All shutters come with solid brass hinges, but custom are given a choice of a bright brass finish or an antique brass finish. Although orders are not returnable, since your order is customized to your specifications, you won't be dissatisfied!

SHUTTERCRAFT

282 Stepstone Hill Road
Guilford, CT 06437

Telephone: 203-453-1973

Free Brochure

Return policy: No Returns

Shuttercraft offers handsome, sturdy indoor and outdoor shutters at 30% off retail prices. Traditional exterior shutters are available with moveable louvers in white pine or cedar. Sizes run up to 30 inches wide by 144 inches tall. As an attractive alternative to curtains, interior shutters, shutter hinges and holdbacks are also available. All varieties can be primed, painted, or trimmed in the brand and color of your choice at an additional fee. Shipping is free, via daily UPS (hardware), or ground freight in 6-8 weeks (shutters).

WELLS INTERIORS

7171 Amador Plaza Road
Dublin, CA 94568

Telephone: 800-547-8982

Free Catalog

Return policy: Returns For Defective Merchandise Only

Why make Wells Interiors your source of window furnishings? Because they will meet or beat any competitor's price. They offer brand name blinds and shades to fit any and every window. Metal and wood blinds by Levolor, Graber, Kirsch, Del Mar and HunterDouglas are waiting for you. Not to be missed is the list of the top 20 window covering mistakes to avoid. This will help you in the future, and makes their catalog worthwhile.

WINDOW TREATMENTS

1 EAST CUSTOM COLLECTION
P.O. Box 3577
New York, NY 10163-3577
Free Catalog
Return policy: Money Back Guarantee

Telephone: 800-322-2991
Fax No: 212-370-7231

The 1 East Custom Collection offers clothes for every facet of your life. Casual cotton tops for a night at home or a night on the town are available at very reasonable prices. Creating your own outfits is easy since there is a different outfit on every page. You can see how the individual pieces work together, as well as separately. Bright, bold colors and cool pastels are perfect for year-round fashionable comfort. After all, cotton is cool in the summer and warm in the winter, and so will you be, too.

APPLESEED'S JUST RIGHT!
30 Tozer Road, P.O. Box 1020
Beverley, MA 01915-0720
Free Catalog
Return policy: Satisfaction Guaranteed

Telephone: 800-767-6666
Fax No: 508-922-7001

Fashions with a feminine touch for sizes 14 and up. Appleseed's Just Right catalog offers clothing for hard to fit women that are guaranteed to fit just right, as the name says. Comfortable knits to flatter you and lace gowns to entice him. Outfits for career, casual days and formal nights, all with a guaranteed fit or your money back. Designed for larger women, pieces are wardrobe essentials.

ARIELLE
3131 Randall Parkway
Wilmington, NC 28410
Free Catalog
Return policy: Money-Back Guarantee

Telephone: 919-251-8555

Flattering sportswear essentials and confident career clothing can be found in the stylish Arielle catalog for misses and petite sizes. Comfortable basics like patterned tops, unconstructed blazers and easy, flowing dresses exemplify the sportswear selection. The career clothing is a mix of attractive suits, dresses and separates in smart, contemporary styles. The catalog also includes a guide to proper fit to insure your ultimate satisfaction with the look of their wares on you.

BEDFORD FAIR LIFESTYLES
421 Kandmark Drive
Wilmington, NC 28410-0001
DISCOUNT
Free Catalog
Return policy: Satisfaction Guaranteed

Telephone: 919-763-7300
Fax No: 919-343-1971

Fashions for the way you live today, for misses and petites. Bedford Fair Lifestyles will provide you with top quality fashions to fit every life you lead. There are fresh approaches to officewear in the form of bright crepe de chine shells, casual attire with a sultry side, as well as perfect pastels, all at bargain basement prices. Lined linen jackets are only $29.00. Not only will these clothes fit your lifestyle, they will fit your wallet!

CARROLL REED
1777 Sentry Pky W., Dublin Hall, #300
Blue Bell, PA 19422-2203
Free Catalog
Return policy: Satisfaction Guaranteed

Telephone: 800-343-5770
Fax No: 215-540-9443
DISCOUNT

World famous Carroll Reed offers classic feminine styles for all aspects of today's woman. Mock turtlenecks are available in a palette of colors, and will provide you with a sound foundation for your wardrobe, at less than $20.00 each. Perfect for formal or casual occasions, flannel blazers allow you to dress up or down while leather shoes provide the final touch on any outfit. Gift certificates are available and are suitable for anyone, no matter what their taste.

CHADWICKS OF BOSTON, LTD.
One Chadwick Place, Box 1600
Brockton, MA 02403-1600
Free Catalog
Return policy: Satisfaction Guaranteed

Telephone: 508-583-7200
DISCOUNT

For the woman who's made it, knows she's on her way or just want to look like it, Chadwicks of Boston provides name brand fashions for a lot less. Blazers by Bill Blass and Adolfo for only $39.00? That's no misprint. First quality clothes let you dress like a million, while the prices let spend much less. Scoop neck tees in a rainbow of colors for $12.90 each. Black cocktail dresses for only $59.00. This is only a sampling of what will soon be your source of great fashions at great prices.

DEVA LIFEWEAR
Box SBM3
Burkittsville, MD 21718-0483
Catalog $1.00
Return policy: Money-Back Guarantee

Telephone: 800-222-8024
Fax No: 301-663-3560

Deva is a network of friends and neighbors who handcraft natural fiber clothes for women and men. Styles run the gamut - from drawstring pants and shorts to skirts, dresses and sleepwear, all in pure cotton. The collection is highlighted by versatility, elegant simplicity and fantastic prices. Each Deva garment is created by one talented seamster, from start to finish, in a cottage industry setting.

ESPECIALLY FOR PETITES BY J.C. PENNEY
(Phone orders only)
Free Catalog
Return policy: Satisfaction Guaranteed

Telephone: 800-222-6161

For clothes that will work with your petite-size wardrobe and expand it, contact J.C. Penney and request their Just For Petites catalog. Great fashions and colors from cover to cover, this is a smaller woman's dream. It's all here, from brand name casual separates from Chic and ladies Dockers, to lovely formalwear made exclusively for J.C. Penney. Small in size but big in style, great things have always come in small packages.

FRENCH CREEK SHEEP & WOOL CO.
Elverson, PA 19520-0110

Telephone: 215-286-5700

Catalog $ 3.00

Return policy: 14-Day Money Back Guarantee

Nothing feels as good as wool, just ask any sheep! The French Creek Sheep & Wool Company offers the highest quality wool and sheepskin garments made in the U.S. today. Big, comfortable sweaters and coats are all produced with a classic American touch that will never go out of style. Additional items include a sheerling baby bunting, crutch covers, car seat covers and bicycle seat covers. Earmuffs and moccasins allow you to literally cover yourself from head to toe with the comfortable sensation of wool.

J. JILL LTD.
P.O. Box 3006, Winterbrook Way
Meredith, NH 03253-3006

Telephone: 800-448-4988
Fax No: 603-279-6229

Free Catalog

Return policy: Satisfaction Guaranteed

Comfortable natural fibers have never been as beautiful to wear and easy to buy With free overnight shipping J. Jill will become a source you will take advantage of extensively. Skirts and shirts, and better sweaters in bright, fresh colors. Since all clothes are made from natural materials, you know how great they'll feel when you put them on. Most sizes, from petites to XXL. .

JEAN GRAYSON'S
BROWNSTONE STUDIO COLLECTION
P.O. Box 440
Cresskill, NJ 07626-0440

Telephone: 800-322-2991

Free Catalog

Return policy: Satisfaction Guaranteed

The Brownstone Studio Collection catalog is a concentration of the best items from all of Jean Grayson's collections. It's easy to assemble a dynamic, three season wardrobe that will never go out of style. Fashionable doubleknit suits and sensation two-part dresses are ideal for the office or a formal occasion, while terrific cowl neck sweaters add flair and style to your casual wardrobe. You'll find something for every aspect of your professional and social life.

LA COSTA PRODUCTS INTERNATIONAL
2875 Loker Avenue East
Carlsbad, CA 92008-6626

Telephone: 800-LA COSTA
Fax No: 619-438-4701

Free Catalog

Return policy: Money-Back Guarantee

When you're looking for great getaway gear, look to La Costa's extensive line of elegant resort sportswear, sexy swimwear and spa-inspired skin care products. The stylish resort collection echos the excitement of some exotic port-of-call in crisp cotton tees, leggings, relaxed jackets, easy dresses, sizzling swimwear, racy activewear and luxurious loungewear in the hottest colors going. The advanced skin care line features sun-smart tanning products; plus scientifically formulated cleansers, moisturizers and facial packs.

WOMENS CLOTHING

LANE BRYANT
P.O. Box 8301
Indianapolis , IN 46283-8301
Free Catalog
Return policy: Money-Back Guarantee

Telephone: 800-477-7030
Fax No: 800-456-9838

Lane Bryant is America's #1 retail source for flattering women's clothing for the fuller figure. Comfort is the key element here - generously cut clothing with ample, non-binding armholes, bustlines and hiplines. You'll find a wide range colors, patterns, and styles that were once taboo. The casual clothing highlights are easy tops, pants, sweaters, outerwear, and even jeans that fit you perfectly. For work and dressier activities, they have lovely suits, dresses and separates that are tailored to slim and accentuate the figure, not conceal it. There's also a wonderful group of activewear, loungewear, underwear and uniforms.

MARK, FORE & STRIKE
P.O. Box 5056
Boca Raton, FL 33431-0856
Free Catalog
Return policy: Satisfaction Guaranteed

Telephone: 800-327-3627
Fax No: 407-241-1055

These are fun clothes. Forget casual, this is the garb you will want to wear when you just want to go out and enjoy yourself while also looking fabulous. Mark, Fore & Strike offers spectacular prints and versatile colors that will make them your one stop source for all of your sportswear needs. For even lower prices, the clearance merchandise in the catalog is offered at up to 75% off.

MARY ORVIS MARBURY
1711 Blue Hills Drive, Box 12000
Roanoke, VA 24022-8001
Free Catalog
Return policy: Satisfaction Guaranteed

Telephone: 800-653-7635
Fax No: 703-343-7053

Mary Orvis Marbury offers distinctive fashion and accessories for town and country. Great looking and long wearing, these fashions aren't flashy, but they are stylish and comfortable. Designed for life outside the city and the suburbs, the outerwear, blouses, skirts and jackets offered here are casually refined, and is made from only the highest quality materials. See other Orvis catalogs listed under Family Clothes and Sporting Goods.

NICOLE SUMMERS
P.O. Box 3003, Winterbrook Way
Meredith, NH 03253-3003
Free Catalog
Return policy: Satisfaction Guaranteed

Telephone: 800-642-6786
Fax No: 603-279-6229

Call today, wear it tomorrow. All items are delivered overnight at no extra charge from Nicole Summers. All of the latest colors and styles for your days, nights and weekends. Formal daywear, eveningwear and accessories are here. Their unconditional guarantee is the icing on the cake. Get this catalog, order by phone, and have it in time for tomorrow's party. This is a great a deal as there is.

WOMENS CLOTHING

RED ROSE COLLECTION
P.O. Box 280140
San Francisco, CA 94128-0140
Free Catalog
Return policy: Money-Back Guarantee

Telephone: 800-227-3011
Fax No: 415-692-1750

Knowing how challenging it is to find casual, comfortable, stylish and interesting clothes, the folks at The Red Rose Collection have saved you the time and energy it takes to develop a creative and eclectic wardrobe. Enjoy browsing through page after page of casual solid cottons, colorful ethnic rayons and other clothing as well as truly unique jewelry and accessories. You'll find a limited selection of men's fashions that are equally stylish in fabric and design.

REGALIA
Palo Verde at 34th St.P. O. Box 27800
Tucson, AZ 85726-7800
Catalog $2.00
Return policy: 15-Day Satisfaction Guarantee

Telephone: 602-747-5000

Regalia offers full-figured fashions that emphasize the positive.; from dawn to dusk, from the boardroom to the boudoir. Created especially to compliment women of larger sizes, flattery is just around the corner. Now you can find today's styles in the sizes you need for the look you want. You don't have to look elsewhere for all of your clothing needs. Brand names like London Fog, Playtex, Danskin and Keds are available at low prices and larger sizes.

TALBOTS
175 Beal Street
Hingham, MA 02043-1586
Free Catalog
Return policy: Satisfaction Guaranteed

Telephone: 800-992-9010
Fax No: 617-558-6250

Separates and coordinated elements of classic style. Talbots offers designs to flatter you at the office and items to keep you casual, comfortable and colorful during your weekend time. Not flashy, all of the blouses, skirts, shirts and outerwear are superbly tasteful without being upscale in price. Intimate apparel that is comfortable as either sleepwear or daywear. Subtly flattering, these high-quality clothes have a lifetime, unlimited satisfaction guarantee.

THE HORCHOW COLLECTION
P.O. Box 620048
Dallas, TX 75262-0048
Free Catalog
Return policy: Satisfaction Guaranteed

Telephone: 800-395-5397
Fax No: 214-401-6414

Fresh styles, colorful fashions and great values. Horchow offers all this to anyone who requests their free catalog. Casual coordinates and fabulous dresses have you covered for any occasion, be it a ballroom or a ballgame. Designer shoes and outerwear answers "what should I wear?" Satisfaction is guaranteed, so you may order these terrific pants, suits, skirts and tops with complete confidence.

WOMENS CLOTHING

233

THE SILK COLLECTION
P.O. Box 825
Middleton, WI 53562
Free Catalog
Return policy: Money-Back Guarantee

Telephone: 800-248-0804
Fax No: 800-648-0411
[DISCOUNT]

You don't need to be told about the desirable qualities of the world's most luxurious fabric. What you may be interested in, however, is The Silk Collection's fantastic prices on some of your favorite wardrobe essentials - all in sensual, timeless silk. The beautiful blouses, skirts, dresses and pants will inspire a few oohs and aahs. But what might surprise you are the cozy sweaters, baseball jackets, cotton/silk sweats, turtlenecks, underwear and sleepwear. They also have great silk items for the guys, including shirts, boxers and sleepwear.

THE VERY THING
P.O. Box 3005, Winterbrook Way
Meredith, NH 03253-3005
Free Catalog
Return policy: Satisfaction Guarantee

Telephone: 800-448-4988
Fax No: 603-279-6229

Classic and colorful separates, flattering chemise dresses for going out, cotton casuals for staying in and terrific suits for the office. This is a catalog that will help you find The Very Thing! you're looking for. Belts, earrings and accessories will complete your wardrobe. With several exclusives, this catalog is loaded with the clothes you want, and they're offered at prices you can afford.

UNIQUE PETITE
Palo Verde at 34th St. P. O. Box 27800
Tucson, AZ 85726-7800
Catalog $2.00
Return policy: 15-Day Satisfaction Guarantee

Telephone: 602-748-7086

While many women wish they were small sized, those of us who are know just how frustrating it can be to go shopping and find exactly what you're looking for, but in large sizes only. Those days are now just a memory. The items in the Unique Petite catalog are tailor-made for us. Catering to women 5'4" and under, this is a veritable treasure trove of fashions for the petite. Finally, fashion that fits just right.

WILLOW RIDGE
421 Landmark Drive
Wilmington, NC 28410
Free Catalog
Return policy: Money-Back Guarantee

Telephone: 919-763-7500
Fax No: 919-343-1971

Willow Ridge offers excellent values on lots of the indispensible wardrobe pieces you depend on for work, play and after-five. Cool, crisp cotton tees, shorts, pants, sweaters, denims, and fleece separates are available for afternoon lounging or weekend getaways. There are also dressy blouses, shapely skirts and dresses, roomy blazers and confident suits for the office or semi-formal affairs. Sizes range from misses to petites.

WOMENS CLOTHING

235

1 East Custom Collection, 229
1-800-THE ROSE, 76
47th Street Photo, 43
A. B. Lambdin, 200
A Brass Bed Shoppe, 107
A Cook's Wares, 47
A.L.A.S. Accordion-0-Rama, 162
A To Z Luggage, 155
Abbey Press, 118
ABC Vacuum Warehouse, 131
Ace Leather Products, 155
adaptAbility, 129
Adco Jewelry & Accessories, 145
Adele-Bishop, 61
Adirondack Designs, 107
After The Stork, 32
Aidells Sausage Company, 102
Al's Luggage, 155
Alan Marcus & Company, 224
Albert S. Smyth Company, Inc., 36
Alcina Cosmetic Special of Germany, 9
Alessi & Bourgeat, 47
Alethea's Chocolates, 87
All Ears, 145
All States Decorating Network, 226
Allen-Edmonds Shoe Corporation, 180
Almond Plaza, 92
Alpha Omega Fine Watches, 224
America's Hobby Center, Inc., 51
American Blind &Wallpaper Fctry, 221
American Bronzing Company, 7
American Coin & Stamp Brkrg, Inc., 51
American Discount Wallcoverings, 221
American Frame Corporation, 178
American Home Stencils, 61
American Pie, 160
American Stationery Company, 195
American Tourister, Inc., 155
Amerisound Sales, Inc.
Amigos, 118
Anheuser-Busch, Inc., 202
Anticipations, 118
Apple Tree Quilts, 14
Appleseed's Just Right!, 229
Arctic Glass and Window Outlet, 133
Arctic Sheepskin Outlet, 69
Arielle, 229
Arizona Sun, 9
Around the Window, 226
Artgrafix, 51

ASF Enterprises, Inc., 140
Athletes Wear Company, 184
Atlantic Gallery Publications, 1
Austad's, 191
Authentic Designs, 151
Baby Bunz & Company, 32
Baby-Go-To-Sleep, 7
Bailey's, 205
Baker's Wrap by Karen Metz, 47
Bakers & Builders, 83
Ballards Designs, 140
Barnes & Barnes, 107
Barnes & Noble, 22
Barr Entertainment, 218
Barron's, 36
Bart's Watersports Catalog, 19
Bass Pro Shops Outdoor World, 187
Bates Brothers Nut Farm, Inc., 92
Bearden Bros. Carpet & Textile, 29
Beautiful Visions, 9
Beauty Boutique, 9
Bedford Fair Lifestyles, 229
Bedroom Secrets, 14
Belle Tire, Inc., 5
Benington's Carpet & Rugs, 29
Benington's Wallpaper, 221
Berman Leathercraft, Inc., 51
Berry Scuba Company, 192
Beth's Farm Kitchen, 100
Beverly Bremer's Silver Shop, 36
Bike Nashbar, 185
Biobottoms, 32
Birth Writes, 195
Bits and Pieces, 209
Blackwelder's Industries, Inc., 107
Bloomingdale's By Mail, Ltd., 63
Blue Heron, 92
Blue Star Canvas Products, 216
Bluestone Perennials, 76
Bodacious Buns, 83
Boot Town, 180
Bose Express Music, 160
Bosom Buddies, 157
Boston Gem Connection, Inc., 145
Boston & Winthrop, 108
Boudin Gifts, 83
Breck's, 76
Brentwood Manor Furnishings, 108
Bridge City Tool Works, Inc., 205
Brights Creek, 32

Brookstone, 205
Brownies On Tour!, 83
Bruce Bolind, 216
Burger's Ozark Cured Hams, 102
Business Envelope Mnfctrs, Inc., 165
Butterfly Video, 218
Cachet Antique Linens, 14
Cafe Fanny, 92
Calyx & Corolla, 76
Cambridge Camera Exchange, Inc., 27
Camera World of Oregon, 27
Camping World, 187
Candlertown Chairworks, 108
Capriland's Herb Farm, 47
Car Racks Direct, 5
Carolina Interiors, 108
Caroline's Country Ruffles, 59
Carroll Reed, 230
Carrot-Top Industries, Inc., 75
Carvin, 162
Casual Living, 140
Caswell-Massey, Co. Ltd., 10
Caviarteria, 97
Cedar Works, 209
Cellular Phone & Accessory Whse., 43
Chadsworth Incorporated, 174
Chadwicks of Boston, Ltd., 230
Chambers, 14
Charles Keath, Ltd., 118
Charles W. Jacobsen Oriental Rugs, 29
Checks In The Mail, 195
Cheers, 202
Chef's Catalog, 48
Cherry Hill Furniture, Carpet, 109
Cherry Tree Toys, Inc., 52
Chiasso, 119
Chick's, 189
ChildLife Inc., 209
Children's Wear Digest, 33
China Cabinet, Inc., 36
China Chasers, 41
Chiswick Trading Inc., 172
Chock Catalog, 152
Christian Book Distributors, 22
Chukar Cherry Company, 93
Claire's Angels, 87
Co-op Artists' Materials, 52
Collectables On Call, 119
Collector Books, 22
Colorado Cyclist, Inc., 185

Colorado Saddlery Company, 189
Colorel Blinds, 226
Community Kitchens, 90
Concept II, Inc., 190
Consolidated Plastics Company, 172
Constructive Playthings, 209
Cos-Tom Picture Frames, 178
Cotton Clouds, 52
Country Curtains, 59
Coyote Cafe General Store, 97
Crabtree & Evelyn, 10
Craft King, 52
Crate & Barrel, 170
Crawford's Old House Store, 133
Crazy Cat Lady, 175
Creative Beginnings, 22
Critics Choice Video, 218
Crompond Calligraphy, 195
Crutchfield, 3
Cuddledown of Maine, 15
Current, Inc., 195
Custom Wine Cellars By Vinotemp, 106
Cycle Goods, 185
Daedalus Books, 23
DAK Industries, Inc., 43
Dalton Pavillions, Inc., 116
Damark, 117
Damart, 69
Dana's Curtains & Draperies, 59
Daniel Smith Artists' Materials, 53
David Kay, 170
Dayton Computer Supply, 43
Deerskin Leathergoods, 69
Defender Industries, 19
Dennis Kirk, 5
Design Toscano, 174
Deva Lifewear, 230
Dial A Contact Lens, Inc., 168
Dial-A-Mattress, 15
Diamond Essence, 145
Diamond Organics, 105
Diamonds by Rennie Ellen, 146
Dianthus, Ltd., 60
Dick Blick Art Materials, 53
Direct Wallpaper Express, 221
Discount Music Supply, 162
Discount Reed Company, 162
Divine Delights, 84
Domestications, 15
Douglas Associates, Inc., 109

Dover Publications, 23
Driwood Moulding Company, 133
Durey-Libby Nuts, 93
Dutch Gardens, 77
E & B Discount Marine, 19
E.C. Kraus Winemaking Equip., 106
Earth Science, 10
Eastcoast Software, 44
Echo Discount Aquarium Supplies, 175
Eckler's, 5
Eddie Bauer, 69
Edgar B. Fine Furniture, 109
Edmund Scientific, 53
Eldridge House Corporation, 15
Eldridge Textile Company, 65
Elek-Tek, 44
Elkes, 30
Ellenburg's Furniture, 109
Emperor Clock Company, 224
Enfield Stationers, 196
Enterprise Art, 53
Especially for Petites J.C. Penney, 230
Exoto's Coverup, 6
Explorawear, 184
Exposures, 178
Fabrics By Phone, 65
Fabulous Fortune Brownies, 84
Factory Direct Carpet Outlet, 30
Factory Direct Table Pad Co., 201
Famous Smoke Shop, 204
Fax City, 165
Ferrara, 97
Figi's Gifts, 89
Fines Herbes Company, 105
First Class BMX, 186
Fisherman's Finest, 102
Flags Unlimited, 75
Flap Happy, 33
Focus Computers & Electronics, 44
Folk's Folly Prime Steak House, 102
Follansbee Dock Systems, 19
Fordham-Scope, 44
Fortunoff, 119
Foto Electric Supply, 131
Fotocell, Inc., 3
Fragrance International, 11
Frame Fit Company, 179
Frank Eastern Co., 165
Fratrack Factory, 119
Fred Stoker & Sons, Inc., 204

Frederick's of Hollywood, 152
Freeport Marine Supply, 20
Freeport Music, 163
French Creek Sheep & Wool Co., 231
French Meadow, 84
Freund Can Company, 172
Fuller Brush Company, 140
Furniture "At A Discount", 110
G.H. Bass and Co. By Mail, 180
Gail Grisi Stencils, 61
Gander Mountain, Inc., 187
Garden Solutions, 77
Gardener's Eden, 149
Gardens for Growing People, 149
Geary's, 120
Gibbsville Cheese Sales, 89
Gilbert H. Wild and Son, Inc., 77
Goddard Manufacturing Company, 194
Goldbergs' Marine, 20
Golfsmith International, Inc., 191
Good Directions, Inc., 149
Gotham Shoe Company, 180
Gould Trading, 27
Gracewood Fruit Company, 93
Graffam Brothers, 103
Grafstein & Company, 224
Grand Era Reproductions, Inc., 133
Grandma's Spice Shop, 48
Graphik Dimensions, Ltd., 179
Great Scott! Fudge Kitchen, 87
Greater New York Trading, 37
Greatwood Log Homes, Inc., 138
Greenberg's Desserts, 87
Gump's, 120
Gurney's Seed & Nursery Co., 77
H & F Announcements, 196
H2O Plus, Inc., 11
Hale Indian River Groves, 93
Hammacher Schlemmer, 216
Hanover House, 120
Hanover Shoes, 181
Harmony Supply, Inc., 226
Harrington's, 97
Harris Levy, Inc., 16
Harry and David, 94
Harts Enterprises, 120
Harvest House Furniture, 110
Hastings Nature & Garden Catalog, 78
Headquarters Windows & Walls, 227
Heart Thoughts Birth Announmts., 196

Heartland America,   117
Heath Company,   45
Heirloom Editions,   1
Heritage Lanterns,   151
Herrschner's Crafts,   54
Hershey's Gift Catalog,   88
Hickory Farms,   89
Hidden Assets,   152
Hill's Dollhouse Workshop,   210
Historical Replications, Inc.,   138
Hobby Surplus Sales,   54
Holabird Sports Discounters,   193
Holbrook Wholesalers,   11
Hold Everything,   141
Home Planners, Inc.,   138
Home Sales Dial-A-Discount,   131
Home Sew,   65
Home Shopping Values,   117
Homespun Weavers,   16
Horien Wreath Company,   42
Horton Brasses,   134
House Dressing,   110
Huntington Clothiers/Shirtmakers,   158
I. Magnin,   121
Ideals Publishing Corporation,   23
In The Swim Discount Pool Supp.,   192
International Homes of Cedar,   139
International Male,   158
International Star Registry,   216
International Wine Accessories,   106
Interstate Music Supply,   163
Into The Wind,   210
Ivy Imports, Inc.,   54
J.C. Whitney & Co.,   6
J. Crew,   70
J. Jenkins Beds,   110
J. Jill Ltd.,   231
J. Peterman Company,   158
J. Schacter Corp.,   16
J&R Music World,   3
J-B Wholesale Pet Supplies, Inc.,   175
JC Penney Co. Inc.,   63
Jackson & Perkins,   78
Jacquelynn's China Matching Svc.,   41
Jaffe Brothers Natural Foods, Inc.,   105
James River Traders,   70
Jamison Farm,   103
Jan's Small World,   54
Jazzertogs,   184
JDR Microdevices,   45

Jean Grayson's Brownstone Studio,   231
Jeannie Serpa Stencils,   61
Jerry's Artarama,   55
Jessica's Biscuit Cookbook Catalog,   48
John Deere,   170
Johnson's Carpets,   30
Jos. A. Bank Men & Women,   70
Just For Kids,   33
Just Justin,   181
Justin Discount Boots,   181
K-Paul's Louisiana Mail Order,   98
Kaydee Bead & Craft Supply,   55
Ken-Wis, Inc.,   210
Kentucky Art and Craft Gallery,   121
Key West Aloe, Inc.,   11
KidsArt,   55
King of Windows,   227
Kitchen, Etc.,   37
Kitts Industrial Tools,   205
Krup's Kitchens & Bath Ltd.,   134
L & D Press,   197
L.L. Bean,   70
La Costa Products International,   231
Lady Grace Stores,   152
Lanac Sales,   37
Land's End Direct Merchants,   71
Lane Bryant,   232
Laughing Bear,   71
Laura D's Folk Art Furniture, Inc.,   111
Lee's Comfort Shoes,   182
Lefthanded Solutions, Inc.,   121
Lehman's Hardware & Appliances,   206
Leichtung Work Shop,   206
Leisure Woods, Inc.,   116
Lembick,   141
Lenox,   121
Lens Direct,   168
Lensfirst,   168
Leonard's Antiques,   111
Lewis & Roberts,   146
LibertyTree,   23
Libertyville Saddle Shop,   189
Lighting By Gregory, Inc.,   151
Lillian Vernon,   122
Lindal Cedar Homes,   139
Lindam,   146
Linen & Lace,   60
Little Colorado, Inc.,   210
Loftin-Black Furniture,   111
Logee's Greenhouses,   78

London Lace, 16
Lone Star Percussion, 163
Long Island Bath Wholesalers, 134
Louisiana General Store, 122
Lyben Computer Systems, 45
MacConnection, 45
MacWarehouse, 46
Magellan's, 214
Maggie Moore, 34
Manderley, 24
Mandolin Brothers Ltd., 163
Mapleleaf Workshop, 17
Marel, 37
Marion Travis, 112
Mark, Fore & Strike, 232
Marlene's Decorator Fabrics, 65
Mary Maxim, 55
Mary of Puddin Hill, 88
Mary Orvis Marbury, 232
Mason Shoe Manufacturing Co., 182
Masseys, 182
Master Animal Care, 175
Matthew's 1812 House, Inc., 84
Maverick Sugarbush, 100
McCutcheon's Apple Products, 100
Mecklenburg Furniture Shoppe, 112
Medi-Mail Pharmacy, 129
Mellinger's Garden Catalog, 78
Metropolitan Music Company, 164
Michael C. Fina, 38
Michigan Bulb Company, 79
Mid Western Sport Togs, 71
Mid-America Designs, Inc., 6
Midas China & Silver, 38
Mikasa, 38
Miles Kimball of Oshkosh, 141
Miller Nursery, 79
Mills River Industries Inc., 141
Minnetonka By Mail, 182
Miramar Productions, 218
Miss Grace Lemon Cake Co., 85
Missouri Dandy Pantry, 94
Modern Farm, 206
Mom's Apple Pie Company, 85
Monterey Mills Outlet, 66
Mosaic Records, 160
Mother Hart's Natural Products, 17
Mother Nature Cookies, 85
Mothers Work Maternity, 157
Mount Nebo Gallery, 1

Moultrie Manufacturing Co., 134
Museum Collections, 122
Nancy's Notions, 66
Nat Schwartz & Co., 38
National Bag Company, Inc., 172
National Blind Factory, 227
National Business Furniture, 165
National Wholesale Company, Inc., 153
National Wildlife Federation, 122
Nature's Jewelry, 147
NEBS, 197
Neiman Marcus, 63
Never Pay Retail, Inc., 112
New Braunfels Smokehouse, 103
New England Basket Company, 142
New MMI Corporation, 46
New York Cosmetics & Fragrances, 12
Newark Dressmaker Supply, 66
Nichole Summers, 232
Nor'East Miniature Roses, 79
NordicTrack, 190
North American Gateways, Inc., 219
Northern, 206
Northwestern Coffee Mills, 90
Nunes Farms, 94
Nuts D'Vine, 94
Objects By Design, 142
Okun Brothers Shoes, 183
Old Grange Graphics, 2
Ole Henriksen Of Denmark, 12
Olsen's Mill Direct, 71
Omaha Steaks International, 104
One Step Ahead, 7
Optical Outlet, 168
Orvis, 72
Orvis Outdoor, 188
Orvis Travel, 214
Overton's, 20
Palm Beach Int'l. Jewelry Col., 147
PaperDirect, 197
Paris International, Inc., 48
Park Seed, 79
Past & Presents Replacements, 41
Pastimes, 56
Patagonia Mail Order, 34, 72
Patio Pacific, Inc., 176
Patternworks, 56
Patti Music Corporation, 160
Paul Fredrick Shirt Company, 159
Paula Young Fashion Wigs, 12

Peachtree Specialties, Ltd., 98
Pearl Paint Company, Inc., 56
Pedigrees, 176
Peerless, 222
Penzey's Spice House, Ltd., 49
Performance Bicycle Shop, 186
Performance Diver, 192
Perillo Tours, 214
Pet Doors USA, 176
Peter de Jager Bulb Company, 80
Pfaelzer Brothers, 104
Pfaltzgraff, 39
Pharmail, 129
Phelan's Equestrian Catalog, 189
Philip H. Weinkrantz Music Supp., 164
Pieces of Olde, 123
Pinetree Garden Seeds, 80
Pintchik Homeworks, 227
Pioneer Table Pad Company, 201
Pleasant Company, 211
Plexi-craft, 112
Plow & Hearth, 149
Porter's Photo Equipment & Sppls., 27
Posh Papers, 197
Post Wallcovering Distributors, 222
Pottery Barn, 142
Pratt & Austin Company, 198
Premier Blind Company, 228
Priba Furniture, 113
Prism Optical, Inc., 169
Prudent Publishing Company, 198
Queen Anne Furniture Company, 113
R. C. Steele, 176
R.S.V.P., 98
Rainy's, 147
Rand McNally Atlases/Maps, 24
Ranger Kennels, 177
Rapid Forms, 166
Reader's Digest Books, Videos, 24
Ready Made, 166
Red Rose Collection, 233
Regalia, 233
Rejuvenation Lamp & Fixture Co., 151
Reliable Home Office, 166
Rent Mother Nature, 95
Replacements, Ltd., 41
Richard Phillip Designs, 147
Ring My Bell, 143
Ringer Corp., 150
Rizzoli Bookstores, 25

Road Runner Sports, 184
Robin Importers, 39
Robinsons Wallcoverings, 222
Roby's Intimates Bras By Mail, 153
Room & Board, 113
Rosehill Farm, 80
Ross-Simons, 148
Rowe Pottery Works, 143
Rowena's Gourmet Foods, 99
Rubens Baby Wear Factory, 34
Rue de France, 17
S & S Arts & Crafts, 56
S & S Mills Carpet, 30
Saks Fifth Avenue Folio Collections, 63
Samuels Tennisport, 193
San Antonio River Mill, 99
San Francisco Herb Company, 49
Sea Island Mercantile/Provisioning, 104
Sears Outdoors Catalog, 188
Sears, Roebuck & Company, 64
Sears Shop-At-Home Beauty Btq., 12
Selectronics, 4
Selectronics Kitchen Appliances, 131
Sensational Beginnings, 211
Sentry Table Pad Company, 201
Service Merchandise, 117
Seventh Generation, 202
Sewin' In Vermont, 67
Shannon Duty Free Mail Order, 123
Shaw Furniture Galleries, 113
Shepler's Western Wear, 72
Shillcraft Latch Hook Kits, 57
Ship to Shore, Inc., 49
Shoecraft Corporation, 183
Short Sizes Inc., 159
Showcase of Savings, 153
Shutter Shop, 228
Shuttercraft, 228
Sierra Trading Post, 188
Signals, 123
Silver's Wholesale Club, 222
Silverton Victorian Millworks, 135
Simply Whispers Earrings, 148
Sir Maxwell's, 177
Ski Limited, 20
Skin Diver Wet Suits, 192
Skipper Marine Electronics, Inc., 21
Smart Wallcovering, 223

Smith & Hawken, 72, 81, 150, 171
Soundprints, 25
South Bound Millworks, 135
Space Gear/U.S. Space & Rocket, 217
Specialty Seafoods, 104
Spiegel, 64
Sportline of Hilton Head, Ltd., 193
Sporty's Preferred Living Catalog, 143
Springmaid-Wamsutta, 18
Staples, Inc., 166
Star Professional Pharmaceuticals, 129
Stark Brothers, 81
StenArt, 62
Stencil House of New Hampshire, 62
Stonehill Farms, 101
Storybook Heirlooms, 35
Strand Book Store, 25
Stuckey Brothers Furniture, Inc., 114
Style Wallcovering, 223
Suburban Sew 'N Sweep, 67
Sugra Photosystems, 28
Suncoast Discount Arts & Crafts, 57
Sundance General Store, 123
Sunglass America, 169
Sunnyland Farms, Inc., 95
Susan Green's California Cuisine, 99
SyberVision, 219
Talbots, 233
Tartan Book Sales, 26
Taylor Gifts, 143
Telegames USA, 219
Thai Silks, 67
Thanksgiving Coffee-By-Mail, 90
That's a Wrap, Inc., 173
The Antique Hardware Store, 135
The Bartley Collection, Ltd., 114
The Bed Factory, 114
The Body Shop, 13
The Bombay Company, 114
The Business Book, 167
The Button Shop, 67
The Canine Fence Company, 177
The Children's Catalog, 95
The China Warehouse, 39
The Cockpit, 124
The Coffee Connection, 90
The Company Store, 18
The Complete Collegiate, 202
The Cracker Box, 42
The Dancing Dragon, 124

The Enchanted Doll House, 211
The Enchanted Forest, 211
The Engraver's Block, 124
The Fabric Outlet, 68
The Farmer's Daughter, 124
The Faucet Outlet, 136
The Finals, 200
The Frugal Fox, 57
The Gazebo of New York, 18
The Grayarc Greenwoods Cllctn., 198
The Great Valley Mills, 86
The Greatest Scapes
The Harrons of Simpson & Vail, 91
The Hemmeter Collection, 125
The Horchow Home Collection, 115
The Horchow Collection, 233
The House of Tyrol, 125
The Iron Shop, 194
The Johnson Smith Company, 125
The Jompole Company, 40
The King Size Company, 159
The Learning Company, 212
The Lighter Side Company, 217
The Linen Source, 18
The Little Fox Factory, 49
The Livonia Catalog, Inc., 8
The Mac Zone, 46
The Maples Fruit Farm, 96
The Music Stand, 125
The Native Hand, 2
The Old Wagon Factory, 136
The Oreck Corporation, 132
The Ornament Retailer, 42
The Paragon, 126
The Perfect Notion, 68
The Perfect Shirt Company, 73
The Petticoat Express, 153
The Popcorn Factory, 88
The Red Flannel Factory, 73
The Right Start Catalog, 8
The San Francisco Music Box Co., 126
The Sharper Image, 217
The Silk Collection, 234
The Smart Saver, 154
The Sock Shop, 154
The Sock Source, 154
The Source For Everything Jewish., 126
The Squire's Choice, 96
The Stationery House, Inc., 198
The Swiss Colony, 89

The Toy Works, 212
The Ultimate Outlet, 64
The Vermont Wildflower Farm, 81
The Very Thing, 234
The Walt Disney Catalog, Inc., 212
The Warner Brothers Catalog, 203
The Wooden Soldier, 35
The Wooden Spoon, 50
The WoodenBoat Store, 21
The Writewell Company, 199
Think Big!, 126
Thomas H. Kramer, Inc., 115
Thompson & Co., Inc., 204
Thurber's, 40
Todd Uniforms for Business, 215
Tools On Sale, 207
Tortellini, 35
Totline & First Teacher Books, 26
TOVA Corporation, 13
Tower Hobbies, 58
Trend-lines, 207
Trifles, 127
True Blue Music, 161
Trumble Greetings, 199
Tweeds, 73
Ujena International, 200
Undergear, 159
UNICEF Cards & Gifts, 199
Unique Petite, 234
Unique Simplicities, 171
UPCO, 177
Used Rubber, USA, 156
Value-Tique, Inc., 136
Van Bourgondien Brothers, 81
Van Dyke's Restorers, 136
Van Dyke's Taxidermy Supply, 58
Vermont Castings, 137
Victoria British, Ltd., 6
Victoria's Secret Catalog, 154
Viking Office Products, 167
Village Carpet, 31
Villeroy & Boch China, Crystal, 40
Vintage Wood Works, 137
Visible, 199
Vitamin Power Health & Fitness, 130
Vitamin Specialties Company, 130
Vixen Hill Gazebos, 116
Vulcan Binder & Cover, 167
W. Atlee Burpee & Company, 82
Walden By Mail, 219

Wally Frank, Ltd., 204
Walnut Acres, 105
Walt Nicke Company, 150
Walter Drake, 144
Warehouse Carpets, 31
Warner-Crivellaro, Inc., 58
Wasserman Uniforms Company, 215
Wathne Corporation, 73
Wayside Gardens, 82
Wellington's Furniture, 115
Wells Interiors, 228
West Manor Music, 164
West Marine Boating Gear, 21
Westminster Pewter & Gifts, 127
Weston Bowl Mill, 50
Whale Gifts, 127
Whitaker's, 130
Whole Earth Access, 207
Wild Wings, 127
William B. Hugg, Inc. Swimming, 200
Williams-Sonoma, 50
Willow Ridge, 234
Windsor Gift Shop, 40
Wintersilks, 74
Wireless, 128
Wisconsin Wagon Company, 213
Wolferman's Fine Breads, 86
Wood Classics, Inc., 171
Wood's Cider Mill, 101
Woodcraft, 207
Woodplay, Inc., 213
Woodworker's Supplies, Inc., 208
World Book Family Catalog, 26
World Wide Games, 213
World Wildlife Fund Catalog, 128
Worthington Group Ltd., 150
Yaeger Watch Corporation, 225
Yankee Pride Rugs, 31
Yankee Wallcoverings Inc., 223
Yes! Books & Videos, 220
Yield House, 144
York Spiral Stair, 194
Zimmerman Handicrafts, 144
Zone VI Studios, Inc., 28